D0551329

A Good African Story

LIBRARIES NI
WITHDRAWN FROM STOCK

LIBRARIES NI
WITHDRAWN FROM STOCK

A Good African Story

HOW A SMALL COMPANY BUILT
A GLOBAL COFFEE BRAND

Andrew Rugasira

THE BODLEY HEAD
LONDON

Published by The Bodley Head 2013

2 4 6 8 10 9 7 5 3 1

Copyright © Andrew Rugasira 2013

Andrew Rugasira has asserted his right under the Copyright, Designs
and Patents Act 1988 to be identified as the author of this work

This book is sold subject to the condition that it shall not,
by way of trade or otherwise, be lent, resold, hired out,
or otherwise circulated without the publisher's prior
consent in any form of binding or cover other than that
in which it is published and without a similar condition,
including this condition, being imposed on the
subsequent purchaser.

First published in Great Britain in 2013 by
The Bodley Head
Random House, 20 Vauxhall Bridge Road,
London SW1V 2SA

www.bodleyhead.co.uk
www.vintage-books.co.uk

Addresses for companies within The Random House Group Limited can be found at:
www.randomhouse.co.uk/offices.htm

The Random House Group Limited Reg. No. 954009

A CIP catalogue record for this book
is available from the British Library

ISBN 9781847922069 (Hardback)
ISBN 9781847922076 (Trade paperback)

The Random House Group Limited supports the Forest Stewardship
Council® (FSC®), the leading international forest-certification organisation.
Our books carrying the FSC label are printed on FSC®-certified paper.
FSC is the only forest-certification scheme supported by the leading environmental
organisations, including Greenpeace. Our paper procurement policy can be found at
www.randomhouse.co.uk/environment

Map by Darren Bennett

Typeset by Palimpsest Book Production Ltd, Falkirk, Stirlingshire

Printed and bound in Great Britain by
Clays Ltd, St Ives PLC

For Jackie

Contents

Acknowledgements

A story of this nature owes a debt of gratitude to very many people, all of whom I can't mention here due to limited space. I trust, though, that when they read these pages, they will recognise themselves and their important contribution. I am eternally grateful for all their support and I owe it to them to give an account, to document this testimony in honour of their enriching this journey. But it is also to those whose expectations I have not met that I offer an account too; may this book show them that their efforts were not in vain.

My mother sowed much in me and has always encouraged me to write my story. She taught me the importance of staying the course, however difficult the obstacles. As a working mother raising us through the turbulent 1970s and early 80s in Uganda, she showed great courage and perseverance; from her I have drawn much inspiration. My father stirred my entrepreneurial instincts both while alive and in his absence. He was a role model of resilience and tenacity, the two things I have learned to value in my life. My sisters have always been a great source of encouragement, support and advice. To them I owe many thanks.

Words cannot capture the gratitude I have for my founding team and co-labourers. They stayed the course, endured many challenges and have contributed immeasurably to the Good African story. The transformation we have witnessed in the lives of many of our farmers is a result of their dedication and commitment.

The stories in the following pages would not exist without my three other supportive shareholders – Hans Paulsen, Ndema

Rukandema and Peter Chappell. They exhibited great loyalty and commitment in backing me in what was a highly risky business proposition. Over the years I have also greatly benefited from the counsel of the directors of my board, both past and present: Aimable Mpore, Jeff Sebuyira-Mukasa, Rachael Dumba, Charles Byaruhanga, Simon Rutega, Francis Gimara, Phillip Karugaba, David Barry, Kibby Kariithi and Musarait Kashmiri gave their time and advice freely and with much patience. Also, my UK distributor LDH (La Doria) – specifically David Fine, Robert Wiltshire and Barry Fine – were extraordinarily supportive and patient during our difficult entry into the UK market. They went beyond what commercial partners are expected to do and are the key reason we have a presence in the UK today. KEHE Distributors in the USA – and critically Jerry Kehe, Darryl Humphrey, Brandon Barnholt, Ted Beilman, Mark Kroencke and Sheri Yount – took a giant leap of faith to back our US market entry; we are in that market largely thanks to them. The farmers in Kasese always kept the faith, were generous with their time and commitment, and with pride and dignity proved that they could transform their livelihoods through hard work and self-motivation. This is what encourages us to show up at Good African Coffee each working day. My pastor Michael Kyazze and my church community were very supportive and a strong pillar for my faith on this journey.

Professor John Sender encouraged me to write this book during one of his research visits to Uganda, as did my longtime friend from our days at the University of London, Anthony Mosawi. I am thankful to Stephen Barasa, Robert Kibuuka, Joseph Esule, Andrew Lumonya, Tim Adams, David Anderson, Andrew Mwenda, Daniel Bergner and Alex Elliot for making valuable suggestions about my early thoughts surrounding the writing of this book. My agent, Felicity Bryan, brought the book to life through her great enthusiasm, energy and the networks that she generously brought to the project. I am grateful to Professor David Anderson at Oxford University for introducing me to Alex Duncan, who became a good friend of mine during my time at Oxford. Alex then suggested I speak to Felicity about the book and over a lovely dinner at their home the connection was made.

Kay Peddle, my editor, gave me the support and encouragement that first-time authors can only wish for. Her skill, thoughtfulness and wisdom helped me weave a set of stories I had verbalised for years into a narrative worth publishing. I am also grateful for all the editorial support Gemma Wain gave me as she shepherded the final manuscript through to publication. Needless to say, I take responsibility for the shortcomings.

But it is to my wife Jackie, and my children Cezar, Andrea, Karabo, Jonathan and Isaiah, that I reserve my deepest gratitude. My children never fail to energise me with their humour, and are always generous with their patience when I fall short or get tied up in my work and am away from home for long periods. To Jackie – my wife, friend and ally – I dedicate this book. Her love, friendship and encouragement have been strong pillars on which much of this story is built. I have walked this journey with her; and this book is as much about her as it is about me.

Writing a book of this nature poses some real challenges in terms of maintaining accuracy, and avoiding the temptation to embellish the past, putting events in a better light. I have tried to address these concerns through detailed interviews with most of the people involved with this story: my team, our farmers, commercial partners, friends and family. I have also referred to contemporaneous notes I kept along the way. I have endeavoured to remain true to all the characters documented here and in most cases I have written their names. But where I feel that the sensitivity of their work or their preference for anonymity is justified, I have decided to protect their identities. Given the length of the period covered and the breadth of the subjects involved, I have had to compress some of the details both for clarity and flow.

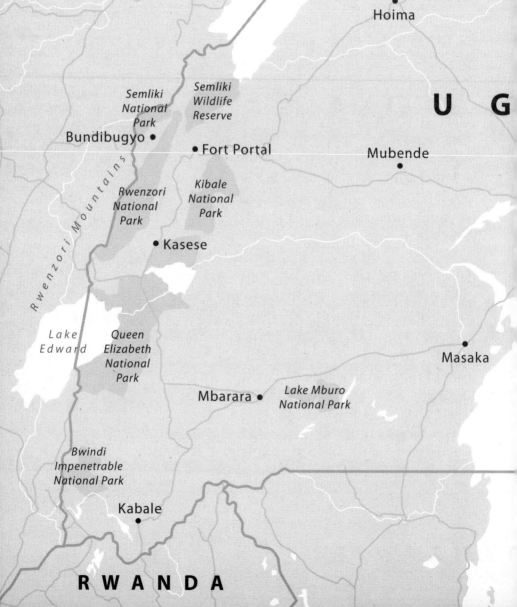

Introduction

Now finish the work, so that your eager willingness to do it may be matched by your completion of it, according to your means.
2 Corinthians 8:11

In 2003, I had an idea: to work with coffee farmers in the Kasese district in western Uganda, and to support them in producing quality coffees, which we would roast, pack and brand for both the local and international markets. Uganda produces over three million bags of coffee a year (approximately 200,000 tonnes) but most of this coffee is exported in its raw form – as green beans for processing in the consuming countries of the developed world. What no Ugandan coffee company had done before was to place a branded coffee product on supermarket shelves in South Africa and the UK. This became my mission and has been my journey for the last eight years. Under the 'trade not aid' banner and a profit-share commitment to our farmers, I developed the building blocks for my social enterprise based in Uganda. I introduced programmes that would invest in the areas of coffee agronomy support that would improve crop quality, post-harvest handling, productivity and environmental stewardship, and institutional capacity building through financial literacy training and the development of Savings and Credit Cooperatives (SACCOs) for the farmers. My challenge, though, was: could an African social enterprise that aspired to empower the rural community develop a profitable, global brand?

Good African Coffee has come a long way since 2003. When I began, I met significant resistance to our business model both at home and abroad. At home, it came not only from the bankers and private equity firms from whom I sought capital, but also from coffee farmers who were cynical after decades of exploitation by the industry. Abroad, the supermarkets I approached about selling our coffees were hesitant about working directly with an African-based brand, simply because they hadn't done it before and the risks looked too great. Underpinning all this were the many tough questions being asked: could we consistently deliver a product of high quality? Did we have the managerial competencies to drive the business forward? Were we actually credible? Despite this resistance, farmer by farmer, village by village, foreign trip after foreign trip, banker's meeting after banker's meeting, we gained credibility, acceptance and momentum.

When we started buying coffee from farmers in the Kasese district in 2004, the average market price was $0.43 per kilogram (unless otherwise specified, prices in $ throughout this book refer to US dollars). We paid three times this price in that same year – $1.25 per kilogram for quality arabica coffees – and we purchased around 7 tonnes. Seven years later, in 2011, the average price that we paid was $4.25 per kilogram, almost 25 per cent above the average market price, and we bought over 400 tonnes. Today, Good African Coffee has a network of more than 14,000 coffee farmers, organised in 280 producer groups, and we have partnered with these farmers to set up seventeen SACCOs.

The majority of the farmers we met in 2003 lived in mud-and-wattle huts with few assets and could be described as very economically insecure. Today, many have built more permanent structures; they own bicycles or motor bikes, are rearing goats or chickens as a business, and grow a variety of crops in addition to coffee. In a modest way, Good African Coffee spurred their entrepreneurial talents. This story is a testimony to the potential impact social entrepreneurs can have on Africa's agricultural economy. But it is also a story that speaks of the challenges that constrain many entrepreneurs on the continent, in the areas of logistics, market access and access to capital, as well as the pressure to surrender that constantly confronts many entrepreneurs. What is important to keep in mind is that, just as small businesses are critical to the growth of western economies, smallholder farmers can become a powerful engine for rapid economic growth in Africa. They just need to be encouraged, equipped and empowered.

I decided to write this book because very few African entrepreneurs document their experiences. Like many other subjects on the continent, African enterprise remains largely unpublished. The result is that non-Africans continue to dominate the production and articulation of knowledge on Africa. By default they are given privileged status, called 'experts', 'analysts' or even 'specialists on Africa'; they are perceived as credible and institutional voices, who understand the continent even better than its inhabitants. Feeding into this architecture is the constant flow of negative narratives that define most of the news coverage and analysis of Africa. These narratives have been cemented into a widely accepted construct of a desperate, violent and hopeless continent. While this is a partial portrait of the continent, admittedly, Africa's leaders have generously fed this perspective through prodigious misrule, greed and brutality, many more complex and dynamic factors are simply ignored or purposely overlooked in the analysis.

Now, because most knowledge published on Africa comes from the West, intellectual capital and power invariably have been transferred to the West's institutions. This has led to a debilitating asymmetry that can clearly be seen in the area of research. Africa's contribution to independent research is pitiful:

only 0.5 per cent of the world's scientific publications are produced by Africans.[1] Worse still, women constitute only 6 per cent of the professoriate of African universities.[2] The *Forbes* list of 'African Billionaires' in 2012 celebrates sixteen of the continent's business titans – not one of them has published a memoir about their incredible success. The result is that future generations of African entrepreneurs are denied the pride and inspiration that would come from these highly motivating stories. We must change this.

According to the African Development Bank (in their 2012 African Economic Outlook report), by 2015 Africa's young population (those between fifteen and twenty-five) will represent 75 per cent of the continent's total population. With over one in five of those in this age bracket at present out of work, both the public and private sectors must intensify efforts to stimulate them – not just to seek jobs, but to become tomorrow's entrepreneurs and job creators in their communities. This requires inspiring them to engage and participate. I found much of my inspiration in books by business leaders and innovators such as Jack Welch, Warren Bennis, Richard Branson, Muhammad Yunus, Jim Collins, Steve Covey, John Maxwell, Leonard Sweet, Peter Drucker, Patrick Lencioni, Tom Peters and Lee Iacocca. And while many business principles can be globally applied, some experiences are unique, and even geographically specific, meaning that future African business leaders should not only read about western experiences but also their home-grown business stories.

Over the years, I have received numerous requests to carry out research on our coffee operations. These requests tended to focus on the impact of our business model on the communities in which we work and our general experience in the rural economy of Uganda. For a while, I accommodated many of these requests, and in fact appreciated the interest. But I have now reached a point where I have done enough to empower other people's knowledge; I need to write this story myself.

In September 1992, after graduating from the University of London with a bachelor's degree in law and economics, I immediately returned home and took up a research position at the Centre for Basic Research in Kampala, with specific focus on the impact of World Bank policies on the industrial sector in Uganda. Less than a year later, my father, who ran a school chalk manufacturing plant, died; he was fifty-one. Overnight, I started running the family business and went from researcher to entrepreneur, from theory to practice. I began to live many experiences I had only read about in books. In 1994, I started my first business, VR Promotions Ltd, a promotions, logistics and events management company. VR designed and managed an array of events, ranging from large international concerts to public awareness initiatives, from small rural health promotion campaigns to large World Bank and UN project launches to logistical and transport support for public sector clients. VR also provided extensive event support for the White House during President Bill Clinton's 1998 visit to Uganda. In 2000, I expanded the company to a full communications agency offering a wide range of services that included advertising and communication support before later divesting my interests to focus on the coffee project.

But even after my shift from research to business, I remained interested in the debates around models for transformation of the African rural economy. I can trace this interest back to my undergraduate years, when my economics professors and the course reading material lit a spark in me. However, as much as I wanted to write about these issues then, I really didn't have anything new to add. But now, after close to a decade spent building a social enterprise that has developed into a prototype for community transformation from the bottom up, and gained valuable experience navigating the perilous corridors of capital and the difficult-to-access export markets, I can confidently put pen to paper.

Agriculture has long been neglected by many governments in sub-Saharan Africa through underinvestment and lack of policy focus. A recent study by the Harvard economist Calestous Juma shows that over 64 per cent of Africans are employed in the agricultural sector, which contributes about 34 per cent of Africa's GDP.[3] The study further notes that agriculture is two to four times more effective than other sectors in reducing poverty and is also powerful in stimulating growth in non-agricultural sectors, as can be seen in industrialised countries. The neglect has led to a worsening hunger situation, with over 239 million Africans going hungry in 2010, up from 150 million in 1990.[4] The problem is compounded by the very small crop area (4 per cent) that is irrigated in rural Africa.[5] Professor Juma also shows that fertiliser usage is less than 10 per cent of the world's average of 100 kilograms per hectare, in addition to very low mechanisation (tractor use) on the continent.[6]

However, the case of Malawi's efforts illustrates the tremendous opportunities for transformation that exist in the agricultural sector. In 2005, having just come out of the worst harvest in a decade, the Malawian government implemented an ambitious programme to tackle hunger and food insecurity in the country.[7] The president, the late Bingu wa Mutharika, personally took responsibility for the agricultural portfolio and implemented an aggressive and effective set of initiatives against hunger. Through an ambitious input subsidies programme and farmer training, combined with better rainfall conditions, maize production doubled in 2006 and then tripled in 2007.[8] In 2005, Malawi experienced a food deficit of 43 per cent; by 2007 the country was producing a 53 per cent surplus, some of which was exported to neighbouring countries.[9] Malawi's experience gives us tremendous hope in the possibility of achieving food security through smallholder farming in Africa.

As my knowledge of the coffee industry in Uganda grew, we began to develop a field operations strategy for the company. In mid 2004, we drew up plans to organise farmers into producer groups, train them and provide extension support and inputs.

This was followed by guidelines for an environmental management system that we developed with NOGAMU, a local non-governmental organisation that focuses on environmental standards training and certification support. We then opened our field office in Kasese and retained a small team there on a full-time basis, which freed me to begin looking for markets in South Africa and the UK.

This book chronicles the past seven years of our business operations: the triumphs and the trials, the discoveries and the lessons. I once asked an American friend what his business mission was. In jest, he said it was to make mistakes and help others avoid them. In essence, my friend was right. One's journey can encourage, mentor and even caution others. And as pointed out earlier, business experiences represent a form of intellectual capital. This capital can be documented, disseminated and exchanged; it can catalyse new and innovative ideas, and spur challenger brands and entrepreneurs. But because very little of this intellectual capital is created by Africans, the next generation of entrepreneurs lose the opportunity to appropriate and build on it.

Good African has been a journey of intellectual discovery. Because I come from a country that has been dependent on foreign aid for a long time, I have had the opportunity to witness, at first hand, the frequently impoverished rhetoric of aid proponents, who often argue that it can transform countries. What is seldom highlighted is how in reality aid and its policy prescriptions don't address the structural constraints facing most African producers and entrepreneurs who are trying to do business in the global market. Aid generates three critical distortions. First, foreign aid is not really aid. Most aid programmes are poorly structured, fungible, insincere and conditional. While important for infrastructure and some other sector support, aid to government treasuries obscures the reality of who actually creates wealth in an economy. It is the private sector that creates wealth and employment and generates government revenues through taxes. In my view, the private sector should therefore be the target of a large portion of this capital. Western economies know this and have always aggressively supported their private sectors, yet the design of their aid programmes does not reflect this practice. This hypocrisy in the way donor policy packages rarely resemble the policies that they themselves adopted in the early stages of their development has been well documented by eminent economists like Ha-Joon Chang,[10] Robert Wade and Hernando De Soto.

Secondly, despite all the talk about accountability and transparency, providing aid through government agencies in poor countries actually makes accountability worse. Governments tend to become more accountable to donors than to their own people. According to a Brookings Institution study, the government of Tanzania, for example, prepared over 2,400 reports for donors and attended close to 1,000 meetings annually in the 1990s.[11] In many instances this accountability deficit is reinforced by the small size of the private sector, which has limited leverage over the state and direction of its policies.

The third distortion is that aid leads to a chronic dependency. This is primarily because of the failure of recipient governments to mobilise adequate domestic resources from tax collections to fund their budgets. When this is compounded by low domestic savings, poor countries continue to depend on aid inflows. Such dependency stifles creativity and innovation, and invariably undermines dignity. Dependency leads to compromise, which undermines sovereignty. This can be witnessed in the way that recipient countries are unable to resist donors' insistence on ideologically driven aid packages (liberalisation, privatisation, among other prescriptions) that are fundamentally committed to western neoliberal thought. While the recent global financial crisis in the developed nations has led to a lot of debate between 'free market' proponents and those in favour of greater regulation, with a huge volume of stimulus capital injected directly into private businesses, the overarching ideological bent of most aid programmes remains firmly market driven and neoliberal.

Jeffrey Sachs is a celebrated economist and well-known aid champion. His central thesis regarding the problem of under-development is the 'poverty trap'. Sachs defines this as 'any self-reinforcing mechanism that causes poverty to persist', which many poor countries find themselves in and it is his biggest justi-fication for pumping more money to kick-start their economies.[12] What is needed, he argues, is a commitment to inject large sums of money in order to fill the capital gaps that poor countries face. This extreme lack of capital leads to poor countries remaining poor because they are poor, unable to make critical investments in healthcare, education, infrastructure, and many other areas of the public sector. It is an inextricable and self-reinforcing trap. But is lack of capital the real problem? New York University econo-mist William Easterly and author and economist Dambisa Moyo both point out that, empirically, the issue isn't about less money – over two trillion United States dollars (at today's prices) in aid has been dished out over the last half century – it is that there isn't much accountability for what this money has done.[13]

Obviously, in this discussion I make the distinction between foreign aid that goes to government coffers and the humanitarian assistance that targets disasters and emergencies. There are exam-ples of successful aid interventions, such as the provision of vaccines for infants and retroviral treatment for people suffering with HIV and Aids in sub-Saharan Africa. These programmes have succeeded because they are accountable, measurable and inclusive of recipient views and participation. However, Sachs' book lacks examples of countries that have been lifted out of poverty by foreign aid, and this challenges his aid thesis.

More than 200 years of economic experience in developed countries shows that these nations prospered by developing the manufacturing and processing base of their economies. From Adam Smith to Milton Friedman, it has long been established that trade is welfare enhancing. It is also well accepted that in the early stages of development in industrialised countries, the state had a very interventionist role. Today's western policy experts harp on about market forces while cynically ignoring the powerful role of the state in the development of their own economies. In most aid-dependent African countries, state intervention is discouraged as it will distort the proper workings of the market. This has been the ideological framework of the Bretton Woods agencies of the IMF and World Bank that coordinate and oversee economic policies on behalf of the donor countries and exercise enormous influence over economic and social policy in Africa. Ironically, neither institution is accountable in any meaningful way to the citizens of those countries on which it imposes its worldview. Part of the problem is that the Bretton Woods institutions are governed through a system based on weighted voting, where each member country has a number of votes which depends on its allocation according to that country's financial stake in the institution. This tends to enhance the power of the United States, at the expense of all other member states. Developing countries account for more than three-quarters of the IMF membership, but only have one-third of the voting share. Such structures give the northern governments an undue influence and have created what Samuel Huntington has termed the 'democratic deficit'.[14]

The importance of an interventionist state in Asia's rapidly developing economies has been well documented by numerous scholars.[15] Professor Chalmers Johnson, an expert on Japan's rapid development after the Second World War, has written extensively on this, and his groundbreaking book, *MITI and the Japanese Miracle* examined the role played by Japan's Ministry of International Trade and Industry (MITI) in fostering the country's industrial policy. He points to the Japanese government's commitment to value-addition manufacturing as the foundation for the country's extraordinary economic take-off and transformation.[16] Like Johnson, economist Peter Evans has researched how interventionist states in many Newly Industrialising Countries (NICs) in South East Asia created strong institutional incentives for industrial growth, especially within the technology and light industries. Affordable long-term capital was made available to businesses in strategic sectors and an aggressive incentive regime was established, which all led to an accelerated social and economic transformation in many of these countries. What has worked for the Asian countries is precisely what Africa's foreign aid donors have argued against. If the African private sector is to be fully unlocked as the engine for the continent's economic growth, then we need to expose the policy contradictions that end up constraining many of the continent's entrepreneurs. This has been a key motivator for me in writing this book.

Good African has also been a faith journey. When I started the business it coincided with a season of self-evaluation in which I was searching for a deeper meaning in my life. I recognised a lack of fulfilment and inner peace and I was increasingly dissatisfied with a hectic work life that often took me away from my family, creating tension in my relationship with my wife Jackie. To her, putting business before family was inconsiderate. Work was firmly subordinate to family and she insisted that I embrace that reality. To me, she was being unfair and unappreciative, not fully recognising what it took to build a comfortable life for our family. But in all this, something in me just didn't seem right. The pursuit of prosperity was not equating to inner happiness and peace. Making money wasn't living up to the promise of contentment; and as much as I didn't want to admit it, I was feeling restless and unfulfilled.

I grew up in a Christian home and went to missionary boarding school when I was eight but I abandoned my faith at university. Nevertheless, I couldn't ignore the nagging within, and as it grew more intense, I could no longer rationalise it away. People have different reasons for their faith – or lack of faith. I believe that the most important day of one's life isn't just the day you were born, but also the day you discover why you were born. In my heart, I began to sense that I wasn't put on this earth just for the pursuit of my personal, selfish needs but for a bigger and meaningful purpose that included contributing to the lives of others in my community. This self-evaluation led to my reconnection with my Christian faith and community. I discovered that after all those years my renewed faith was not only refreshing but also experientially fulfilling. And so I developed a firm anchor for my commitment to community transformation through the biblical teachings and the person of Jesus Christ. I found the principles of love, sacrifice, respect, humility and generosity to be a radical counterbalance to what was manifestly a cold, selfish, damaged and disjointed world. I truly believe that if we conduct our business according to these principles, we can create genuine and sustainable community transformation. If we sow kindness, love and respect, we shall reap the rewards: a kinder, more gentle and respectful world.

Over the years many people have asked me why we named the company 'Good African'. The comments I encounter have ranged from sheer curiosity at applying the value 'Good' to 'African' and to a coffee product, to questioning whether such a combination could ever resonate with the wider public, especially in the export markets of the West. Very little information that is presented in the media about Africa is positive or attests to good things happening in the continent. Part of the reason, which I explore further in Chapter 7, is that there is a whole industry that benefits from this desperate and apocalyptic imagery of Africa.

Take the example of the periodic outbreaks of the Ebola virus in Uganda. The recent outbreak of mid 2012 is a good example of how imagery and approach betray bias and perception. Again, the headlines lacked subtlety: 'Uganda races to stop spread of Ebola virus', 'Ebola prisoner escapes . . .', 'Outbreak of Ebola in Uganda kills 13'. CNN, BBC and Al Jazeera – all transmitted stark images of medical personnel, wearing white protective outfits and hunting down victims of the virus, in-between their coverage of the London Olympics.

A palpable sense of anxiety hung over Kampala and throughout the month of August the country received a large dose of unwanted publicity. This might be understandable if people were breaking out in haemorrhagic fevers all over the city. But the numbers and the attention just didn't add up. The intense media focus was for a disease which resulted in 859 deaths across Africa between 1976 and 2003. No comparable alarm is raised when we are confronted by more shocking public health realities. According to the World Health Organisation (WHO), one-third of the world's population has tuberculosis, and twenty-five million people are living with HIV or Aids in sub-Saharan Africa. The United Nations predicts that there will be fifty million deaths from HIV and Aids in Africa by 2025. Today, cancer kills more people globally than HIV, Aids, tuberculosis and malaria combined, which according to the WHO's 2010 figures, is over eight million people per year. Still, over one million people die per year from malaria in Africa alone – one million per year! These are not just depressing statistics but should generate outrage in a world that has the resources and capability to do something about it.

Yet we seldom exhibit the same level of alarm and urgency as for Ebola. The 859 deaths I mentioned earlier are obviously 859 deaths too many. But are they comparable to, say, the 141 children per 1,000 that die annually before their fifth birthday in Uganda? Or the 435 in every 100,000 mothers who die in labour every year? Or the 16 per cent of under-five year olds in Uganda who are moderately to severely underweight?

There is a medieval approach to public health responses to Ebola and other epidemics in Africa. The cataclysmic edge to the language and the graphic imagery employed by the media and public health agencies reinforces an asymmetry of power and resources between the advanced countries seeking to combat the disease and the poor countries infected with it.

Images of scientists from the advanced world travelling to Africa to contain the disease appear with disturbing frequency. This reduces the affected people to the level of transmitters or vectors instead of drawing attention to the underlying social and economic aspects of the disease. It is clear that epidemics are about susceptibility and it is critical that the social, economic, political and gender factors are examined.

Books like *The Hot Zone*, by Robert Preston, that document the history and incidents of haemorrhagic fevers from Africa have been published widely and Hollywood films have been made on the subject. In most cases, highly ethnocentric language is used to describe the people in danger (Africans) and the virologists hunting down the disease (western scientists). The psychological import is one of the 'coming plague' with its 'nightmare scenario'; the rest is left to your imagination.

Language is important because once you call something an epidemic, you have to put money into it. Most money is then likely to be invested in vaccine research and emergency responses than, say, in water and sanitation infrastructure, or in improvements to healthcare delivery systems that will change the public health consequences for the people in affected areas. Ebola is a virus with horrific manifestations; but to privilege the attention we give to it over other more pernicious and systemic healthcare challenges is hypocritical, myopic and self-serving.

The manifest failure to address the underlying conditions that give rise to epidemics, exacerbates them and makes combating them difficult. Weak healthcare infrastructures – poor supply-chain systems, human resource weaknesses, corruption and the theft of public resources – all need to be vigorously monitored and improved. We shouldn't only raise the alarm for dangerous viral outbreaks, but also for any death that could have been avoided if we offered more efficient healthcare. There needs to be as much outrage when a mother dies during childbirth for lack of adequate medical attention, or when our children die from preventable and treatable diseases.

Fear alone cannot be the driving metric; equality and justice should be our overarching values. Africa's children constantly see images of outsiders coming to our rescue. This doesn't build confidence in the idea that we can be the masters of our fate and the solution to our problems.

The continent has many legitimate gripes of its own; many African leaders, through their brutal, undemocratic and klepto-cratic rule, have contributed to its negative image. Nevertheless, this doesn't obliterate the many positive attributes of the continent. The persistence of the 'bad African' story derives from deep-seated prejudices, which underpinned and informed much of the colonial experience and linger today, making doing business in the West without being stereotyped very difficult.

Early on, I began to appreciate that the largest barrier facing African exporters is limited access to high-value markets in the advanced economies; and this is rooted in the nature of those markets. For most African exports, free and open markets are not the norm. Most markets are controlled, distorted or even closed. They are dominated by large firms with huge financial resources, advanced technologies and complex supply chains and capital structures. Reinforcing these market distortions are the subsidies that western governments give their firms, espe-cially those in the agricultural sector. In many instances they maintain uncompetitive and inefficient companies and keep the price of commodities artificially high. There is also very limited processing taking place in Africa, meaning that a significant portion of the value of African commodities is surrendered to economies in the West. As has often been recognised, for decades Africans have produced what they do not consume and consumed what they do not produce. With few exceptions, processing and value addition has historically taken place outside the continent. Only 18.6 per cent of Africa's exports are manufactured or value-added products, yet 65 per cent of the continent's imports are manufactured products.[17] In 2010, Africa's share of world manufactured exports was just 0.9 per cent, while East Asia's share was over 25 per cent.[18]

One of my key aspirations was to set up a roasting and packaging facility in Kampala, and this became a reality in July 2009. Processing the coffee in Uganda allowed us to retain a greater proportion of the value added in the country and to better support the farmers and empower our communities. Domestic value addition would reverse the historical model of exporting raw materials and importing finished products. Western economies have tried to address these constraints through initiatives like the European Union's Economic Partnership Agreements (EPAs) with African, Caribbean and Pacific countries (ACP) and the US African Growth Opportunities Act (AGOA). When we talk of constraints to market access, many observers think that reduction of tariff barriers or the provision of market incentives in the West is sufficient mitigation; however, this is false.

The critical issue is one of power; the negotiating parties are grossly unequal. In 2005, the ACP economies represented 3.2 per cent of the EU GDP.[19] The combined GDP of EU countries was $13,300 billion whilst that of the total ACP was $425 billion.[20] The ACP countries are made up of thirty-nine of the world's fifty poorest countries (in fact, the smallest group, the Pacific Islands, has a combined GDP 1,400 times smaller than that of the EU).[21] While EU negotiators might recognise the import of this calculus, they don't fully embrace its implications on the outcome of the negotiations because such a disparity can only produce a distorted and unfair result. The EU frequently states that EPAs stand to benefit ACP countries more than the EU. If this were the case, then why doesn't the EU just acquiesce to the fair and well-documented objections raised by the ACP countries? The truth is that most ACP countries are former colonies negotiating from very weak psychological, economic and political positions. They are dependent on EU funding not only for their domestic budgets but also to enable them to participate in these negotiations.

All the talk of market-access incentives is largely rhetoric. Duty-free access to western markets is really not free because ACP exporters still face many other obstacles, such as stringent rules-of-origin and the ever-increasing product standards and regulations that make market access very difficult. The World Bank has itself recognised this problem in a paper which estimates that the EU's new aflatoxin requirements will cut African exports to the EU of nuts, cereals and dried fruit by 64 per cent of what they would be under normal international standards.[22] Non-tariff barriers make a mockery of the market-access provisions. The reality is that ACP countries will remain where they are today – as producers of primary commodities that they do not consume and consumers of finished goods they did not produce. These non-tariff barriers are much more pernicious because they are hidden, difficult to quantify and unpick. Also, trade agreements do not necessarily translate into increased competitiveness. For example, I export my coffees to the UK and USA duty free. But does this market access make me competitive? No. In the majority of cases, my brand will compete with other coffee brands that already have significant advantages: access to cheaper and longer term capital, access to technologies and skilled labour for the processing of their products, and better logistics and supply chain infrastructures. The signing of a trade pact will not necessarily reverse decades of unequal and unjust trade between Africa and the Northern Atlantic countries. More has to be done.

This book is structured in three parts. The first provides the context to the story. I have assumed that I am writing for many readers who may not be familiar with Uganda or Africa's general political and economic history. For this reason, the first two chapters of the book provide this context. I have narrowed my scope in these two chapters to two themes: the causes of state institutional failure in many sub-Saharan African countries and the possible reasons for the preponderance of expatriate or non-indigenous capital in the Ugandan economy from which I operate. The second theme I appreciate is sensitive because it tackles a racialised economic structure with roots established in the country's colonial history. Nevertheless, it is crucial that we discuss it if we are to understand the country's economic environment and the opportunities for sustainable and equitable growth for its people.

My outlook has undeniably been shaped by the political and economic history of my country and continent; it is for this reason that I begin the story there. I then go on to relate the Good African story through the critical themes: logistics, markets, access to capital and perseverance. This is the heart and substance of the story. In the third part of the book, I draw lessons from the journey, and reflect on our business model, with the aim of sharing my experience and encouraging the entrepreneurs of my generation and the next.

PART ONE
Context

1 What's Wrong with Africa?

Dictators ride to and fro upon tigers which they dare not dismount.
And the tigers are getting hungry.
Winston Churchill

My first encounter with soldiers carrying machine guns was one morning in May 1979, a month after Idi Amin, the Ugandan dictator, had been overthrown. I was eleven. That morning in our home in Kampala, I heard loud, strange, voices in the courtyard; they sounded agitated. I could also hear the pleading voices of my mother and father. I rushed outside to find my parents and a group of about a dozen soldiers with guns. They had come to forcefully claim our household property. This was common in the aftermath of the Amin regime, when an atmosphere of lawlessness pervaded the country. Drunk and violent soldiers roamed the city and its suburbs, taking people's property at will, looting and ransacking shops and homes. They raped women, and on many occasions, carried out summary executions. The abduction of innocent civilians was a tragic continuation of the brutality that these soldiers, the so-called 'liberators', had fought to overthrow. There was virtually no effective law-enforcement agency and various armed factions in the country were rife with divisions along ethnic and tribal lines.

The soldiers accused my father of being an Amin agent on the pretext of not having escaped into exile during the war. My parents pleaded, explaining that they had nothing to do with politics and were only in business. They even brought out samples of the chalk my father produced for Ugandan schools in his factory. The soldiers wouldn't budge. Outside, other soldiers were guiding a truck as it manoeuvred into our driveway. Those in the house were busy surveying the bedrooms, living room and kitchen to see what could be carried off. At this point my mother told us to go to our rooms. Together with my two younger sisters, who were seven and five, I went into my room, knelt by the bedside and began to pray.

A soldier opened the door to my room, looked around and asked what we were doing. We just stared at him and didn't utter a word, and he left. They then began loading our living-room furniture, electronics and kitchenware into their truck, and demanded money and the keys to the two cars in our garage. The only things they didn't take were our beds, mattresses and cooker. By late morning, when the madness had subsided, we had lost almost everything and we were left shaken and insecure. However, we were comforted by the thought that things could have been far worse. My parents could have been abducted or killed on the spot. Context is important: many successful businessmen, professionals and academics were targeted, abducted and killed at the time. On this day, therefore, we felt lucky.

Three days later, another contingent of soldiers climbed over the gate, came into the house and threatened to blow up the place with what I later learned was a bazooka. I had never seen this green-painted tube-like weapon before. The soldier holding the thing spoke with slurred speech, obviously drunk, and his posse was rowdier than the first lot. When they found out that most of our property had already been taken they became agitated, cocking their weapons and threatening to shoot us. Suddenly, we heard a commotion from outside on the street, which distracted the soldiers. The noise was coming from the attempted arrest of an alleged Amin soldier. He and his family were pleading their innocence and resisting being put on a truck. The soldiers in our house became engaged in the fracas outside and lost interest in us; we had survived again. But a few months later, matters became worse.

On Monday 13 August 1979, my father went to work at 7.30 a.m. as usual. At about 11.30 a.m., three plain-clothes security men came to our home saying they wanted to talk to him. They said that they had been to his office but hadn't found him there. When they realised that he wasn't at home, they began threatening us in the hope that we would reveal his whereabouts. One man even pulled out his pistol and began brandishing it, pointing it at my youngest sister, Cathy, saying she should tell them where her father was hiding or they would hurt her; she was only five years old. Finally, frustrated, they left.

My father didn't return home that evening and it took another two days before we found out that he had in fact been picked up as he returned to his office from a doctor's appointment. He was then sent to Luzira prison, without any charge being brought against him. No reason was ever given and no one ever took responsibility, although we later discovered that one of the politicians in the government had wanted to acquire the chalk factory and thought that by keeping my father behind bars he could achieve this. Many businessmen were imprisoned at that time; as it turned out prison was safer than being on the outside and having to live with the constant danger of abduction and murder, a fate many other Ugandans faced. When my father was released a little over a year later, he and my mother fled to Nairobi, where they lay low for eight months. But exile wasn't easy for them, especially my father, and they returned to Uganda. A few months later he was arrested again and locked up for another seven months. Again, no charges were ever brought against him. During his imprisonment my mother ran the chalk factory, took care of us and also fought the legal battle to secure my father's release. She exhibited great courage and tenacity throughout this ordeal.

Upon his release, my father was a changed man. Prison had stolen his enthusiasm and focus. Once a driven and pioneering industrialist – gregarious, generous and outgoing – he withdrew, becoming more circumspect, a loner. In his isolation, he would have a drink on his own, most days, quietly on the porch at home. Finally, diabetes and high blood pressure claimed his life on the morning of 15 August 1993; he was fifty-one years old.

Witnessing state failure and its ramifications on my family led me to question, at an early age, why an African regime would become the worst enemy of its people. Growing up, I saw state failure and warlordism in Somalia, Liberia and Sierra Leone in the 1990s, an almost permanent state of war in parts of east and central Africa, and the lethality of the civil wars of the 1970s and 80s in the southern African states of Mozambique, Angola, Zimbabwe (formerly Rhodesia) and Namibia (formerly South West Africa). A narrative of a continent in permanent conflict, economic crisis and widespread disorder became well established. As a businessman, it is clear that the private sector cannot become the engine for economic growth when it is being constrained by dysfunctional, corrupt, extractive and repressive regimes.

Few would dispute the importance of strong states and political institutions in delivering the necessary environment and incentives for a peaceful and prosperous society. Political institutions represent the body of rules, procedures and norms that shape behaviours and attitudes of ordinary citizens.[1] That many African states have been weak is not in dispute; what is are the causes for this weakness. There has been much progress since the mid 1990s, when many African governments began to democratise, hold elections and pass from single-party dictatorships to multiparty politics. They posted impressive economic growth rates and made great strides in tackling systemic problems like HIV and Aids, conflict-related internal displacement of their populations, low literacy and poor provision of healthcare. Nevertheless, many states on the continent remain blighted by structural weaknesses and complex problems that are not only rooted in their history but also in how they have evolved since independence. The coups in Mali and Guinea Bissau in 2012 remind us of how the fragility of these states is not only a historical issue – it is very much a contemporary one.

So why is there so much state failure on the continent? What factors can help us understand this situation? Is it pre-colonial factors, the colonial experience, or factors rooted in the post-independence state and its mode of rule? These are big questions, and they demand in-depth and detailed analysis. I cannot pretend that I can do this in the following pages. However, I believe that I can legitimately share my observations and analysis of things, and my reading of the literature. Africa is a diverse continent, and no set of generalised observations can be made of its fifty-four countries, but many sub-Saharan countries share similar historical, political and economic experiences, and it is on these shared experiences that I build my analysis. I will begin with a case that I believe captures the many hopes, and failed promises, of post-independence Africa. It is a sad story that began in hope and has ended in tragedy.

On 24 June 1960, Patrice Lumumba became the first post-independence prime minister of the Democratic Republic of Congo, then known as Leopoldville. His tenure as prime minister was short-lived – just three months later he was brutally killed in Katanga by a coterie of conspirators that included the country's future president, Marshall Joseph Mobutu Sese Seko.[2] Lumumba epitomised both the promise and the tragedy of post-colonial Africa. For Congo, independence was a hollow victory compromised by deep and structural constraints on effective self-rule. Very little human capital and physical infrastructure existed. There were no experienced Congolese civil servants and, at the time, the entire nation of approximately fourteen million people had only sixteen university graduates and 136 high-school graduates.[3] There were no indigenous doctors, teachers or army officers, nor a significant class of indigenous entrepreneurs. Managing an independent Congo would have been difficult enough with sufficient human resources, but to gain independence without strong governing capabilities was a recipe for disaster. In the end, the autonomy of the young republic was quashed by the realities of weak state capacity and the direct meddling of foreign powers, including the USA, the Soviet Union and Belgium, Congo's brutal former colonial master. Belgium retained significant influence after independence over Congo's strategic sectors of the economy, such as the mining industry and the army.

Lumumba's nationalist voice, as well as those of many others like him on the continent, was extinguished by the contradiction of independence without freedom and the protection of colonial interests even after independence. There was a handover of power, but without the instruments for effective self-rule, an inheritance for which the new leaders were unfamiliar and largely unprepared. Independence in many former colonies ushered in what Kwame Nkrumah, the Pan Africanist who led Ghana to independence in 1957, termed neocolonialism: the continued colonial control of former colonies through the economy, cultural forces and other means, in lieu of direct political and military control. After independence, a pattern of dependency and extractive linkages in the newly independent states became increasingly apparent. Whether it was to their former colonial powers or the Cold War protagonists – the US and Soviet Union – the clearest expression of this linkage was in the case of the Francophone states in West and Central Africa, many of who belonged to the *Communauté française d'Afrique* (French Community of Africa).

They had their currency pegged to the French franc and received significant foreign aid. For these countries, like Benin, Burkina Faso, Côte d'Ivoire, Guinea Bissau, Mali, Niger, Senegal and many others, France continued to be a key source of economic aid and military assistance. In many cases, France maintained military bases in these countries, and intervened to protect dictators in the Central African Republic, Rwanda, Côte d'Ivoire and Chad.

The Cold War enabled African ruling elites to shape their political agendas and ideological allegiances in line with the main contenders. Newly independent African states were fertile ground for superpower contestations and these superpowers greatly influenced the decolonisation process.[4] As the anti-colonial struggles gained momentum, they were increasingly inspired by either the Soviet Union or the American worldview of modernism. Post-colonial rulers also played a key role in courting and abetting superpower interventions in their local situation, leaving many African countries in a state of constant civil conflict. The Ogaden War of 1977–8 between Somalia and Ethiopia; the civil wars in Angola between the National Union for the Total Independence of Angola (UNITA) and the People's Movement for the Liberation of Angola (MPLA), and in Mozambique between the Liberation Front of Mozambique (FRELIMO) and Mozambican National Resistance (RENAMO); and conflicts in Algeria, Guinea Bissau, Congo Brazzaville and Congo – all destroyed infrastructure and left these countries with badly brutalised and traumatised populations. These seismic disruptions greatly undermined the post-colonial states' capacity to consolidate political gains at independence, rendering many states weak and ineffective. The Cold War was a repeat of colonialism by different means. Although it was in certain respects anti-colonial, it fell into the trap of old forms of domination experienced by the colonies and left a legacy of lethal and destructive local and regional conflicts that greatly scarred the countries involved. The Cold War made the military elite dominant and ushered in a militarisation of politics;

by 1974, there was not a single democracy in mainland Africa.[5]

Daron Acemoglu, an economics professor at the Massachusetts Institute of Technology (MIT), and James A. Robinson, a Harvard professor of economics, have written an important, well-researched and intellectually ambitious book entitled *Why Nations Fail: The Origins of Power, Prosperity and Poverty*.[6] What these authors have accomplished in this elegantly titled book is a scale of research and depth of analysis that is truly extraordinary. They wrestle with the question of what makes some nations prosper and others remain poor. Their central thesis is that there are two kinds of states: those that are extractive and those that are inclusive. In their words: 'economic growth and prosperity are associated with inclusive economic and political institutions while extractive institutions typically lead to stagnation and poverty'.[7] Extractive states suppress economic and personal freedoms, extinguishing incentives for innovation and wealth-creating activities. A small, elite group tends to control the pipeline of extraction, through predatory behaviours such as theft of state resources, corruption, forceful appropriation of contracts and state assets, clientelism and coercion. All this keeps the bulk of the population insecure, suppressed, poor, and without protection for their human and property rights.

The authors illustrate their point with many examples but for me, their historical analysis of the fourteenth-century Kongo Kingdom (Democratic Republic of Congo), is a good example of a state built on extraction. What is illuminating is the similarity between the extractive institutions of pre-colonial Kongo and post-independence Congo under President Mobutu. Through slavery, patronage and the payment of exploitative taxes and tributes, the fourteenth-century Kongolese lacked any incentives to engage in wealth-creating activities, since any wealth made would be carefully appropriated. They had neither hoe nor engaged in any writing; not because it was their want but rather there were no incentives to do so. By independence in 1960, Congo was characterised by entrenched backwardness and an extractive model that was in many ways a modern version of fourteenth-century Kongo. Predation became the preferred and more lucrative aspiration for Congo's post-independence kleptocrats, or *les grosses legumes* ('big vegetables'), as they were popularly known.

On the other hand, with inclusive institutions, the ruling elite's vested interests are constantly challenged in a bid to improve society-wide conditions and do things better. These institutions motivate people to be productive through the protection of property rights. There is a clear and predictable framework for the enforcement of contracts and the protection of wealth because investments and money will not be arbitrarily confiscated. Britain and France are examples of the inclusive state model; this motivated the rest of western Europe to become more inclusive and also spawned inclusive states in North America and Australia.[8]

Acemoglu and Robinson dismiss in quick fashion other contending hypotheses for inequality and poverty among nations, such as geography, culture and ignorance. The authors put in stark terms what they believe is the real cause of poverty: 'Poor countries are poor because those in power make choices that create poverty. They get it wrong not by mistake or ignorance but on purpose.'[9]

Unlike Acemoglu and Robinson's dismissal of the geography hypothesis, in his book *Guns, Germs and Steel: The Fates of Human Societies*, their forerunner and 'bold intellectual synthesiser' Jared Diamond gives geography far more importance in how it contributes to poverty. Jared's thesis is that there are other non-institutional factors that contribute greatly to the economic disparity between nations; and geography is one of them. For example, there are far more diseases in tropical countries than temperate climates because in the latter, the winters kill parasite stages outside our bodies. Yet in the tropics, the parasites can survive. This contributes to the health condition of its inhabitants, and so impacts on worker efficiency and productivity. Also, differing plant biology and the characteristics of microbes and soil fertility have all contributed to the differences in agricultural productivity between temperate and tropical regions. Diamond argues that these factors act independently of institutions and have huge implications on power, poverty and prosperity.[10] However, Diamond pays scant attention to the inequality of land distribution, the unequal distribution and dissemination of technologies and capital, and the politics of disease that result from African governments' poor service delivery, management and lack of political will to undertake aggressive public health measures that can combat diseases.[11]

The journey from extractive states to inclusive ones is defined by the struggle between ruling elites and those they govern. Charles Tilly, the American sociologist and political scientist, has extensively researched state formation in Europe from the Middle Ages. Tilly postulates that high population densities, combined with land scarcity and the cost of warfare, led to the development of state institutions to collect taxes in order to pay for the prosecution of wars or the defence of territory. This led European rulers to develop efficient bureaucracies, gather information, map and document their territories, and carry out a census of their people. To collect more taxes, the ruling elite made political concessions resulting in regular parliaments and a growing citizen voice. This contributed to the institutional infrastructures that led to the modern European state.

Jeffrey Herbst, the respected American political scientist who has written extensively on politics and international affairs in Africa, follows a similar trajectory to Tilly but makes his observation specific to Africa and argues that a similar process of state formation hasn't taken place on the continent. Unlike Europe, Africa is land rich and sparsely populated.[12] This has led to the weak capacity of many African nations to control their territories, especially their border regions. The Democratic Republic of Congo, Sudan and Mauritania are good examples of the challenges of maintaining territorial integrity. This failure to extend power effectively has led to weak national bureaucracies, vague and poorly monitored borders, poor population and census data, and low tax collection. European colonialism compounded this problem by focusing on plundering and exploiting Africa's natural resources rather than the building of institutional capacity. Low population densities led to property rights in people – like slavery – being well defined as opposed to land rights, which tended to be communally held.

Let's go back to our example of the Democratic Republic of Congo (DRC) and the problems it faces on its eastern border region, which neighbours Rwanda and Uganda. The eastern DRC region has a complex history moulded by pre-colonial cross-regional migration, and colonially established ethnic identities and groupings who have assumed different rights and privileges. This situation was engendered by the genocide in Rwanda in 1959 and 1994 and the subsequent mass exodus to eastern parts of the DRC. This has led to the deep social and political fissures, and the spawning of a myriad militias, warlords and armed groups seeking their fortune from a resource-rich area. In my view, however, it is the capital Kinshasa's inability to broadcast its power to the eastern part of the country, to control and administer the entire geography of its territory, that is the fundamental challenge here. When sovereignty is exercised only partially this leads to a political no man's land, a vacuum where numerous state and non-state actors compete for influence, resources and power. It is in this theatre that the population bears the brunt of the conflict, entrepreneurs are discouraged and prosperity fails to take root.

By extension, this lack of political reach means that states are not able to build competent and efficient tax-collecting bureaucracies. This leads to a narrow tax base, poor institutional checks and balances, corruption and impunity, poor governance and poor delivery of services, and personalised and clientelistic relationships. Today in many African countries, tax collection as a

percentage of GDP is quite low. In Uganda, tax collection represents only 13 per cent of GDP whilst in the UK and South Africa
the figure is 26 per cent.[13] Robert Bates, the Harvard University
academic who specialises in the science of government, has made
an interesting observation regarding tax collections and the implications of the size of the tax base on state behaviour towards its
citizens. The lower the tax base, the greater the incentive is for
predation and coercion by the ruling elites. The higher the tax
base, the greater the motivation for the provision of welfare and
protection.[14] Both options are predicated on the ruler's measure
of potential threats to his regime. Such rulers, or 'specialists in
violence' as Bates calls them, continuously deploy a calculus of
choices in determining whether to support predation and coercion or protective and welfare-enhancing behaviours. In my view,
the smaller the private sector contribution to GDP, the less
capacity the private sector has to hold its government accountable. When you add large amounts of foreign aid, the problem of
poor accountability is exacerbated rather than ameliorated.

But surely, one cannot privilege geography over other critical
factors that determine why nations fail. Neither can exclusive
attention be given to institutional factors, because in reality there
are other factors at play that have shaped how African institutions
have developed, such as the impact of military conquests and
domination of African societies by colonial powers. Much of
nineteenth-century Africa was militarised and many of the great
kingdoms and powerful warlords on the continent rose and fell
on account of the fluctuations in the slave trade.[15] he Atlantic slave
trade had a very significant and sustained impact on the political
and social institutions in Africa and as such, African states organised themselves around slave raiding and predation of their own
citizens, instead of providing protection and welfare for them.
This point is highlighted by the demands African kingdoms made
to exploring Europeans, for guns and other weapon technology.
That was where the incentives were and the key determinant of

the political outcomes of the day. In Uganda, for example, in the mid nineteenth century, coastal traders from the Kenyan coast brought guns among other products which they sold in exchange for ivory, salt and slaves. Trading in ivory became the monopoly of kings and rulers in the area and a major cause of inter-state wars. As Kenyan historian and chancellor of Moi University B. A. Ogot confirms: 'The important social effect of the coming of the coastal traders on the peoples of south-western Uganda was arms trade. Weaker societies were raided for slaves while inter-state warfare became rampant'.[16]

While Britain might have spawned inclusive states in Australia and North America, this certainly was not its brand of rule in its colonies. The colonial order was a brutal, oppressive and extractive mode of rule, with indelible features that have endured to this day. Colonialism served particular interests and negated others. It promoted extraction and exploitation of labour through the export of primary commodities, such as cotton and coffee, that would be processed in factories in the UK. The next chapter will explore the impact of the colonial economy in more detail. Even in the face of the administrative constraints and wide geographical territories to govern, the colonial state invented new strategies for control of its possessions. Mahmood Mamdani, the renowned Ugandan scholar and professor of government at Columbia, has written extensively on this. For Mamdani, weak and extractive political institutions today are a direct colonial legacy. Through indirect-rule, especially in British-ruled Africa, the state established a different set of rules for the natives and non-natives; this 'bifurcation' was the prototype of the apartheid regime in South Africa.[17] He notes that everything 'customary' (i.e., African) was rendered under native jurisdiction – overseen by the chiefs, who themselves were a colonial invention – while non-natives were administered under civil law. The distinction between the two was a legal one. For the non-native, there was a clear separation of powers. For the native, power – administrative, judicial and legislative – was in the hands of one man, the native chief. It is this fusion of considerable powers in the hands of one man that led to the syndrome of the African 'big man': an unaccountable, personalised and patrimonial ruler. Mamdani terms this process 'decentralized despotism', a colonial construct whose legacy didn't die at independence but instead found expression in the management style of many post-colonial African leaders. The post-colonial political system carried with it the infrastructures of a particular type of rule and control from the colonial period: authoritarianism, elitism and paternal-istic concepts of democracy.[18]

This promoted personalised rule and negated institutional autonomy in political and economic affairs. The one relationship that has endured to this day is the one between the chief and the peasant. In Uganda, for example, the colonial chief–peasant nexus has found modern expression in the executive–local government relationship. The local government ministry is a decentralised structure that is concerned with services such as schools, hospitals and roads, at the local or district level. It is, in effect, a micro-state bureaucracy within the broad state structure of government. The office of the president is also structured, with many functional roles parallel to the official bureaucracy. The president presides over a massive civil service, alongside which he appoints resident district commissioners (formerly known as district commissioners in the colonial period) and internal security officers in every district, over 110 presidential advisors, and many other auxiliary security and political organs. They play a functional role in how power is administered and distributed not only in Uganda but also in many other African states.

The post-colonial state and its extractive institutions mirrored the colonial project, and what the American historian (and specialist in African history) Frederick Cooper has termed the 'gatekeeper state'. Cooper observes that 'Africa was systemati-cally conquered but not so systematically ruled'. Colonial states had trouble extending their power across the geography of the countries they ruled due to the limited transformational aspirations of a pernicious agenda of extraction. They had a very poor record of investing in the colonies; Britain, in particular, administered its colonies on the cheap in a deliberate policy of neglect. In 1888, the United Kingdom placed Uganda under the charter of the British East Africa Company, owned by William Mackinnon. However, they did not rule it as a protectorate until 1894. Northern Rhodesia (Zambia) was initially administered under charter by the British South Africa Company, but it was only in 1924 that it was administered by the British government as an official British protectorate. Lord Lugard, the first Governor General of Nigeria, who introduced indirect rule in Africa, put it clearly when he said: 'European brains, capital and energy have not been and never will be expended in developing the resources of Africa, from motives of pure philanthropy.'[19] This external orientation of the colony focused attention on the 'gate': the interface between the local and imperial economies. This was a place of extraction, where collection of taxes, import–export licences, foreign currency movements, foreign aid and many other economic activities intersected between the local economy and those who guarded it. In the 'gatekeeper state', power and control are maintained and reproduced at the gate; whoever controls the gate, controls access to resources and power.[20]

For the imperial state, the logic of the 'gatekeeper state' was greater efficiency in controlling the colonies at a low cost; all they had to do was control the gate. It is the hallmark of post-colonial Africa that the stakes of controlling the gate became high. The African elites who took over at independence used patronage, corruption, coercion and scapegoating of opponents to reinforce their control of the resources that flowed through the gate. This narrowed the channels of access for others and energised the extent to which those locked out of the gate sought to fight for it and control it. It undermined political institutions and caused the gate to be a constant source of struggle and political ambition because the gate enabled resources to be extracted for political gain. Predatory elites became the new face of the post-colonial political actors in Africa.

Weak state capacity has also been attributed to the timing of decolonisation; from a long-term project, where the colonial state thought handover would take decades, it actually ended up happening in a matter of years. This affected the capacity of the post-colonial state to manage the transition to effective self-rule. Ghana was the first Black African state to gain independence in 1957. The quick transition of power there and in other African countries forced nationalist organisations to mobilise huge new electorates in a very short time. Most of the new African rulers were urban-based intellectuals or from the trade union movement, and they did not have broad national constituencies. This lead to political alignments being based on ethnicity, religion and other social factors. It also meant that the state failed to 'penetrate society, regulate social relationships, extract resources, and appropriate or use resources in a determined way.'[21]

The challenge of building electoral constituencies immediately after independence meant that the state institutions became a source of patronage and clientelism. All energies and critical resources were deployed in the pursuit of power; once high office was attained, the focus shifted to regime maintenance. To be accepted as the legitimate ruler by the population became a key preoccupation for many post-independence rulers. While the colonial state had ruled by fear rather than affection, it became a major challenge, in the context of a multi-ethnic and multi-religious society, for the post-colonial ruler to exact the same compliance without using similar coercive and repressive interventions. Governing the newly independent states presented an unprecedented challenge, as the state was not modelled on pre-colonial forms of statehood but on the modern western nation state that itself had developed over centuries. In western democratic models, the people own the state, in effect seeing the ruler as their servant, and demand greater accountability and performance. However, in most African nations the ruler owns the state and devises methodologies for the ruled to serve him by rewarding loyalty and compliance directly.

Nevertheless, the shift to authoritarianism in the post-colonial era failed to mitigate the insecurities of the independent regimes, instead ushering in an era of political coups and attempted coups that became the hallmark of the post-colonial Africa. The coup against President Kwame Nkrumah of Ghana in 1966 was a classic response to an increasingly dictatorial leadership that was receiving dwindling popular support. Patrick J. McGowan, Arizona University political scientist, has produced a comprehensive data set on African military *coups d état* in forty-eight sub-Saharan African countries between 1956 and 2001. This quantitative analysis shows that there were a total of 80 coups, 108 coup attempts and 139 reported coup plots over the period. Such figures remain high to this day, with coups in Mali and Guinea Bissau taking place in 2012. Coups and coup plots became a symptom of military-led political instability because once a successful coup has occurred it incentivises others. When one compares this to the relatively low level of nation-to-nation conflicts, we quickly find that the internal context in many African countries as opposed to the external threat remains the primary theatre of conflict. Therefore, the choices African leaders make can impact the shift from extraction to institution building. This requires sacrificing their personal ambitions for the collective good, and determines the level at which peaceful transitions of power can be attained.

Other observers consider the state failure, political disorder and chaos that we witness in many African countries to be part of a durable and culturally rooted system of rule and state craft. Political scientists Patrick Chabal and Jean-Pascal Daloz are strong advocates of this perspective, having written a provocative book titled *Africa Works: Disorder as Political Instrument*.[22] They argue that most of the perceived features of the African state are, in fact, natural aspects of the African political order and something that dates back to the pre-colonial period. Power in Africa has always been distributed in ways that may not be immediately obvious, and certainly not in the clear and transparent way of the western model. They say that the interaction between power, war, capital accumulation and various illicit activities 'constitutes a specific political trajectory' and has become a process in how Africa works. The extreme of this process is the 'criminalisation of politics' that reflects the increasing normalisation of criminal practices, war and disorder as the dominant mode of state formation in contemporary Africa.

Many sub-Saharan African countries are characterised by an 'informalisation of politics', where governments operate in an informal, personal and non-institutional manner. This informality is a hallmark of the patrimonial state and is characterised by intensely personal and localised political contestations. Interests are 'particular' and the ruling elites are motivated by narrow personal interests. Corruption is endemic in Africa; in fact, they argue, it is society-wide and represents 'vertical relations of inequality'. Chabal and Daloz argue that this is a peculiarly pathological African condition and defines Africa's unique development path. Political actors see opportunities to maximise their returns during state confusion and chaos, and this undermines the capacity of the state to 'emancipate' itself in any meaningful sense.[23]

The use of state resources by rulers in order to secure the loyalty of their subjects has become a central feature of the African state. This has made the state weak and has resulted in elites engaging in what French scholar and political scientist Jean-François Bayart has termed the 'politics of the belly', which sustains appropriation of state resources for private benefit.[24] According to this perspective, predatory elites weaken and compromise the bureaucracy for their private gain and the line between private and public sector is no longer there. Few days go by without a corruption scandal being reported in the newspapers of many African cities, scandals involving business elites and politicians. This has distorted the marketplace, disadvantaged those seeking to do business outside the complex web of informal and illicit private/public interactions. Poverty has become the defining feature of African politics and the key motivation for leaders to capture, accumulate and then partially redistribute wealth. Due to the personalised rule of the president in these countries, political elites will take advantage of this by hiding behind the 'big man' in an attempt to claim immunity for the crimes they have committed.

In extension to this line of argument, there is also the need to draw particular attention to the role of presidentialism in the undermining of state institutions in Africa, especially in its informal guises. Professor of political science Nicolas van de Walle has stated that: 'Regardless of constitutional arrangements . . . power is intensely personalised around the figure of the president . . . He is literally above the law, controls in many cases a large proportion of state finances without accountability, and delegates remarkably little of his authority on important matters . . . Only the apex of the executive really matters.'[25]

Corruption, clientelism, and 'Big Man' presidentialism – these are all dimensions of neo-patrimonial rule and they tend to come as a package. They are recurring patterns of behaviour to which all political actors are acutely attuned. Indeed, these practices are so ingrained in the post-independence African political life as to constitute veritable political institutions.

Several challenges, however, have been mounted against this perspective and the principal limitation seems to lie in its failure to appreciate that neo-patrimonialism can be a response to, and not just the cause of, weak post-colonial institutions. Fragile bureaucratic networks, narrow political constituencies and limited state resources from poor tax collections give rise to frequent, informal and particular interventions by the ruler. Also, bureaucratic inefficiencies victimise the ruled as well as the ruler. Over time, factionalism builds up in the bureaucracy to the point where it can become a 'sphere of resistance'. Contestation between the bureaucratic factions and political elites leads to failure to deliver services and public goods, thus eroding the ruler's legitimacy and popularity.

The outcome may be one of greater informalisation of the state, but this can also speak of the state's response to its inherent limited capacity as opposed to a strategic option of rule. To state that war and illicit activities are a dominant mode of state formation is an over-generalisation and ignores the evidence of countries like Benin, Botswana, Ghana, Mauritius, Niger and Zambia, who have all made significant progress in democratisation. The arguments advanced by Chabal and Daloz also are unconvincing in showing how disruptive and dysfunctional factors such as war, crime, corruption and economic dependency in African politics can have a functional role.

This type of analysis of state failure in Africa also fails to appreciate the historical influences – specifically the impact of colonialism – on the modern African state. Whilst Chabal and Daloz concede that 'without a doubt, imperial rulers did divide the continent . . . certainly did disturb, or even destroy, the existing socio-political communities', they nonetheless reject the notion that colonialism was decisive in shaping these societies.[26] The authors are unapologetic about this: 'The time has long passed when we, Westerners, had to expiate the colonial crime of our forefathers'.[27] Instead, they argue that the essential feature 'most important to emphasise is the significance of continuities in political practice from the pre to the post-colonial period'.[28] The impact on the social and political structures of colonial Africa was deep, and it had tremendous ramifications. As noted earlier, 'European colonialism wrought profound changes in Africa and many of the pathologies of modern Africa can be traced to the particularities of colonialism in Africa.'[29] A failure to appreciate the role of colonialism denies the authors a broader perspective that highlights the role of history in Africa's current crisis. It is also important to appreciate the impact of the process of decolonisation on the nationalist struggles of many African countries – the strategic choices the leaders made, and the constraints they inherited. The relatively quick process significantly affected the nature of the post-colonial state by effecting the transition to independence via the agency of limited representative elections. The haste with which the elections were introduced required nationalist organisations to mobilise huge new electorates in a very short time, leading to use of patronage as a system of constructing large electoral constituencies.

Uganda's nationalist leaders made their transition to power in only a few years; they did not have the timeframe required to build sustainable national constituencies. Opportunistic alliances were cobbled together in order to achieve power. These alliances of convenience didn't last and became major cleavages in the post-independence politics of the country. The swiftness of the ascension of Milton Obote, Uganda's first independence leader, is a clear example. In 1956, Obote joined the Uganda National Congress (UNC) political party, and was elected to the colonial Legislative Council in 1957. Two years later, the UNC split into two factions. One, under Obote, merged with the Uganda People's Union to form the Uganda People's Congress (UPC) and became the dominant party. Over the next two years, in the run-up to independence elections, Obote formed a coalition with the Buganda royalist party, Kabaka Yekka, which enabled him to garner a majority in Parliamentary elections and become the prime minister on 25 April 1962. The whole process – from his return from Kenya, where he had been involved in Kenyan nationalist politics, to becoming executive prime minister – took place within a period of six years. The subsequent political crisis of 1966, which led to the abrogation of the constitution, the abolishment of the monarchy and the sowing of the seeds of Idi Amin's coup of 25 January 1971 can be traced back to the struggle to maintain viable political constituencies across the national spectrum.

The same struggle can be seen in the cases of both Ghana and Sierra Leone's transition leaders at the turn to independence. In both situations, there was an over-reliance on individuals with considerable local followings, and the use of clientelist politics to bind local notables to the party and local voters to the candidates. In essence, voters were offered material benefits in the form of public goods like roads, schools and clinics for their votes, while candidates and notables were offered individual benefits (cash, access to licences, credit or land, etc.) as well as being portrayed as responsible for the arrival of the collective benefits. Chris Allen, one of the founding editors of the *Review of African Political Economy*, states that 'this combination produced a set of locally based Members of Parliament and deputies, responsive to local demands, and loosely organised into parties whose leaders had access to private or public resources'.[30]

Also, the use of the European concept of the state as the ideal, against which African institutions should be measured, leads to a Eurocentric premise of analysis, which posits that Africans are bound to follow the developmental path of western states. The over-emphasis of the 'peculiarity of African political pathologies' contributes to the privileging of western state models, as in Tilly's approach, and fails to take into account the unique and diverse political experiences of the African continent. The argument that western states are the ideal archetype of the modern state remains unconvincing. Modern states in Europe and North America have developed modern order, education, healthcare and welfare services, but they have also spent vast sums on the military and weaponry. This militarisation has led to two catastrophic world wars, the use of atomic bombs, and the pursuit of a dangerous arms race that can only lead to the annihilation of humanity if unleashed.

AFRICAN AGENCY

I tend to be persuaded by the argument that political and economic outcomes in most African countries are framed by the political choices African leaders make, and the quality of their decisions. An African leader, like any other, is constantly faced with myriad difficult decisions and sacrifices that must be made. Such decisions have at various times had the capacity to mitigate some of the problems and contradictions we have discussed, but they can also undermine political stability in a given country. The right decisions can reap huge long-term pay-offs. Peaceful handovers of power can reduce the intensity of the struggle at the 'gate'. The case of Julius Nyerere's exit from power in Tanzania in 1987 is apposite. Cape Verde's former president Aristides Pereira's peaceful handover to António Mascarenhas Monteiro, after a resounding defeat in the 1991 election, is another example of setting positive precedents, as is Jerry Rawlings in 2001 in Ghana. Even Nelson Mandela's handover after just one term set a powerful precedent that undermined Thabo Mbeki's attempt at a third term in office in South Africa. Peaceful transitions are established when incumbents act in the national interest.

Ultimately, though, even in the face of considerable political challenges and contradictions, what remains available to African leaders is the power of their decision-making and their capacity to do well by their people. If we take the geo-political meddling in African affairs as a given and the inheritance of weak states at independence as undeniable, it is clear that some institutional weaknesses result from the misguided and damaging leadership choices made by many African leaders. On the other hand, despite their shortcomings, some leaders – such as Leopold Senghor, Julius Nyerere, Nelson Mandela, Jerry Rawlings and Aristides Pereira – created opportunities for their countries to build, aspire and remain vested in their political institutions. They took the responsibility of laying down the framework of peaceful political transitions. Other promising leaders shirked this responsibility, subverting their own institutional reforms in favour of their selfish interests. However popular an incumbent may be, a failure to build a platform for the next generation is a poor leadership choice; and in fact failed leadership in itself. The old cliché captures this point well: success requires a succession which requires a successor. Failure to build this platform under the next generation results in increasing the stakes for those seeking to capture the spoils of the 'gate'. The costs of the contest for the gate become much higher and more intense. It is this particular issue that has greatly undermined African state institutions and their autonomy.

Predictable and institutionalised transitions of power can be an important element in fostering peaceful handovers of power and building inclusive institutional capacity. The spectre of an incumbent's entrenchment can only escalate the resistance to his rule, creating deeper insecurities among the elites and the wider society. When a leader's grip on power begins to weaken in the face of institutional failure, widespread corruption and the manifest failure of the state to deliver public services, the logic and efficacy of regular and predictable transitions of power must be considered. However, incumbents tend to become more insecure, assailed by the increasingly critical and loud voices of civil society leaders, opposition politicians and some elites demanding greater accountability, efficiency and political participation. The state then begins to follow a well-trodden trajectory: huge deployments of resources in the areas of security and control of opposition, the quashing of media freedoms, and assaults on freedoms of association and assembly. This becomes an increasingly desperate bid to maintain a hold on power and it diverts attention from critical challenges such as an economy that is made increasingly fragile by insecurity, economic uncertainty and social dislocation. Such economies really require broad-based national focus and attention.

Incumbents set precedents for the next generation. Their actions either discourage or promote self-interest, and increase or reduce the premium on trying to dislodge the incumbent from power. Therefore, the decision by a leader to depart from office peacefully and in a predictable and systematic way, rather than to hold on and entrench themselves, strengthens opportunities for institutionalised peaceful transitions of power.[31]

In 2005, Uganda's constitution was amended to remove presidential term limits that had initially been limited to two five-year terms. In his 2001 manifesto, President Museveni had expressly committed not to seek a third term, having recognised that part of Africa's problem were leaders who stayed too long in power. However, he stood for a 'third term' in the elections of 2006 and also in 2011, winning both. Several members of his party, the ruling National Resistance Movement (NRM), opposition politicians and civic and church leaders have all voiced concerns about the lack of clarity surrounding the president's retirement plans after more than two and a half decades in office. Despite the president's considerable personal popularity across the country and a feeble and uninspiring opposition, many observers nevertheless fear that failure to manage a peaceful transition of power by the incumbent, something that Uganda has never experienced since independence in 1962, threatens the hard-fought peace and stability the country has enjoyed over the last two decades.

In my view, there is also a deeper and more complex dynamic when it comes to transitions within post-armed-struggle regimes. Most of the regimes that have captured power through guerrilla wars exhibit particular ways in which power is distributed and maintained. The regimes assume power with the same traits, outlook and mindset that they had as guerrilla movements. They are secretive, and concentrate decision-making among very few people. They are protective of their fellow comrades and place a huge premium on loyalty, sometimes over efficiency. They also often use informal and hidden infrastructures of rule outside the official bureaucracy and system of government. It is evident that what were assets in the 'bush' can quickly become liabilities once formal authority has been attained. For example, a 'need to know' information system during the armed struggle is understandable because of the huge risks of information leakage and infiltration. However, this becomes a liability, leading to uncoordinated policy direction and communication, insecurity and a lack of predictability by those who work in government. It tends to breed sycophancy and compliance rather than independent-mindedness and efficiency. Social networks among the ruling elites have a premium in this situation but they also breed resentment and disharmony among those who cannot capitalise on these networks. I believe that the several post-armed-struggle regimes in Africa, such as those of Uganda, Ethiopia, Eritrea, South Sudan, Angola, Rwanda, Burundi and Zimbabwe, face transitional challenges rooted in their historical experiences as well as the choices their rulers make to try to mitigate these constraints and pathologies. Others like Namibia and Mozambique have managed to establish transitional frameworks that have largely broken the trends of their fellow post-armed-struggle regimes.

Weak political institutions in many African countries frustrate and undermine the innovations and creativity of their entrepreneurs. Poor institutional capacity leads to poor delivery of services, poor infrastructure, poor governance and poor law and order, which means that governments are not creating the enabling environment for private sector growth. The private sector then ends up having to mitigate these dysfunctionalities at a cost. When the paying of bribes is systemic, the cost of doing business is both high and unpredictable. The lack of adequate distribution of electricity means that businesses have to acquire generators, raising their energy costs and making manufactured goods uncompetitive. When piped water cannot reach homes or business premises then boreholes have to be drilled, again raising capital costs of projects. Roads that are full of potholes cause the cost of transporting goods to shoot up: the majority of people cannot afford to buy four-wheel-drive vehicles, and so take longer to get to and from work. All this discourages investment and makes doing business costly and unpredictable, yet huge potential exists on the continent. If an ambitious, focused and committed leadership can create the necessary institutional incentives that will foster socio-economic transformation, this potential will be realised.

2 In Search of an African Capitalist Class

No sun sets without its histories.
Zulu Proverb

History is past politics, and politics present history.
Sir John Seeley

In 1973, my father started a manufacturing plant to produce chalk for Ugandan schools. The factory marked an important milestone for Uganda's emerging indigenous capitalist class. At the time, there were very few entrepreneurs in the country. Africans mainly engaged in petty trading, subsistence farming and export commodity trading of cotton, coffee, tea and other produce through various cooperative unions. I have always tried to understand why the majority of capital in Uganda is concentrated in the hands of a few expatriate companies, and mainly in the Asian business community. The ranks of the African entrepreneurs only grew significantly after the expulsion of the Asians by Idi Amin in 1972. My other concern was why the expulsion of Asians galvanised many in the country behind Idi Amin who justified his actions on the premise that he was Africanising an economy that was owned by foreigners. These concerns raise important issues.

On 5 August 1972, Idi Amin, the president of Uganda, announced that he was giving Asians living in the country ninety days to leave.[1] Amin outlined a range of accusations, from economic exploitation and discriminatory practices of Asian businesses, to a failure of the Asians to integrate with the indigenous population. In the end, he argued that the Ugandan economy needed to return to the Africans. Amin couched his message in nationalist terms by making the expulsion part of an 'economic war' against Asian commercial dominance.[2] The expulsion announcement came in the wake of a long line of statements that had been issued over the preceding months, since his coup of January 1971. This time, though, Amin would give his incendiary attack on the Asian community legal sanction. Political posturing evolved quickly into political resolve, and by the end of 1972, more than 50,000 Asians had been violently expelled from Uganda.[3]

Thirty-five years later, on 12 April 2007, Kampala experienced a day of riots in response to President Museveni's proposed donation of a portion of the Mabira forest, 54 kilometres to the east of Kampala, to an Indian sugar baron.[4] The controversy surrounding this allocation had been building up for some time and many observers, environmentalists, members of parliament and civil society organisations all vehemently opposed the give-away. However, the president stubbornly insisted on pushing it through and this provoked a public demonstration, with thousands gathering in the central business district in Kampala to voice their objections. Hundreds of people carried placards with slogans like: 'Asians go home' and 'For one tree, cut five Indians dead'.[5] With emotions running high, and a large police presence seeking to control the crowd, what started as a peaceful demonstration turned violent and led to the unfortunate death of an innocent Indian passer-by. By the time the riots had been quelled, several Indian bystanders had been attacked and a number of their properties targeted and damaged. Eventually, police tear gas, water cannons and batons brought order to what had become a volatile and tense morning.

Many Ugandans were shocked that such sentiments existed, almost four decades after the Amin expulsion. What had become known as 'the Asian question' definitely still existed but, as one observer commented, this time the question meant different things to different people.[6] There was the question of the Asian investors, perceived as arrogant and insensitive, and that of the immigrant petty traders who appear to acquire work permits with ease and have come to be seen as the modern-day indentured labourer. The events of 12 April 2007 illustrate the fact that the Asian question is still very much alive and will continue to define the business landscape of Uganda's future.

Uganda's Asian question has frequently been framed in terms of the expulsion of 1972 and the result of its negative impact on the economy. Few observers have acknowledged the expulsion within the context of the country's colonial past. In my view, the Asian expulsion must be placed in a historical context if we are to understand why we still have a small African capitalist class today, and if we are to learn any lessons that can point to the future economic landscape of the country.

Undertaking an enquiry of this nature is fraught with challenges. Firstly, however careful I am, I am bound to offend and anger my Asian friends or embolden my fellow Africans. I seek to do neither. I am not an apologist for the expulsion; it was a brutal and tragic moment in Uganda's history. Nevertheless, it is important that we revisit even those uncomfortable aspects of our history to recognise their importance in shaping our future. For this we must avoid caricature and conjecture. I seek to address two key questions: why has the Ugandan economy always been characterised by a predominance of non-indigenous capital? What dynamics were at play that led to this condition?

In this chapter, I review the factors leading up to the Asian expulsion of 1972 and the attempts to 'Africanise' the Ugandan economy;

in the process, I establish three main findings. The first is that the expulsion was a consequence of major socio-economic cleavages created by the distorted capitalism established in colonial Uganda, which privileged the Asian minority and disadvantaged the majority Africans. A racialised division of labour was established, with Africans consigned to the production of cash crops like cotton and coffee for export, while Asians were given a path to 'middlemen' status in an economic system where they dominated the processing and export sector, and the majority of import trade.[7]

My second finding is that the hardening of African attitudes towards Asians was a result of increased Asian dominance of the trading and commercial sectors. Riots and boycotts after the Second World War gave rise to the colonial policies aimed at Africanising economic activity but this too remained within the logic of colonial rule and control. Attempts at Africanisation followed a very haphazard path even after independence, with President Milton Obote's government embarking on various nationalisation initiatives that were poorly articulated and implemented. Crucially, the agency for change was the cooperatives and not private enterprises. These ill-conceived economic policies became the primary cause of significant socio-economic insecurities that led to increased fragility of the economy demonstrated by an extensive capital flight. By the time of the expulsion in 1972, the economy was already suffering from significant balance-of-payment problems, inflationary pressures, and high costs of living; the expulsion was merely the death knell to an already crippled economy.[8]

The third finding is that the post-expulsion deterioration of the economy cannot be wholly attributed to the absence of the Asian entrepreneurial class, as has frequently been argued. In my view, the economy deteriorated more on account of gross fiscal mismanagement, poor governance and institutionalised terror by the Amin regime. It is true that the forced exodus of 1972 destroyed Asian trading networks, production capacity and the loss of key skill sets in the economy. But the gap created by the expulsion also ushered in several pioneer African entrepreneurs like James Mulwana, Gordon Wavamunno, Leonard Basudde, Stanley Bemba, Thomas Kato and a few others. This nascent business class managed to navigate the political insecurity of the day to become Uganda's indigenous capitalist class.

The post-expulsion economic decline cannot just be seen as proof of the failure of the Africanisation programme or the loss of the critical Asian business acumen; rather, it is the Africans who were supposed to become central actors in the new economic dispensation who became victims of the Amin regime's gross violation of human rights and oppression. Asian dominance in the marketplace was replaced by regime oppression of Africans in the wider society. 'Africanisation' therefore became a psychological balm applied to the wounds of the economic disadvantage suffered by Africans. Africanisation was, in essence, an ideal, a worthy aspiration, of what could become but in fact never did.

THE BURDEN OF HISTORY

On 15 November 1884, German Chancellor Otto von Bismarck organised a meeting of the leaders of thirteen European countries to formalise and regulate European colonisation of Africa. This meeting, known as the Congress of Berlin, established the 'Scramble for Africa' territories and by 1902, 90 per cent of all the land that makes up Africa was under European control. Countries were partitioned, borders arbitrarily drawn; communities and families were separated. In 1888, Uganda was assigned by royal charter to William Mackinnon's Imperial British East Africa Company (IBEAC), an arrangement strengthened in 1890 by an Anglo-German agreement confirming British dominance over East Africa.[9] However, the high cost of occupying the territory caused the company to withdraw in 1893, and its administrative functions were taken over by the British commissioner, Sir Harry H. Johnston.

Uganda formally became a British protectorate in 1894. It was Johnston who later signed the 1900 Buganda Agreement, which essentially parcelled out one half of the land in Buganda (the largest of the traditional kingdoms in present-day Uganda, comprising all of the country's Central Region, including the Ugandan capital Kampala) to the 'Crown' and the other half to the Bugandan chiefs, imposed a tax on huts and guns, and designated chiefs as tax collectors. British rule remained in place until 9 October 1962, when the Union Jack was lowered and the newly designed Ugandan flag with the Crested Crane emblem was raised and power officially transferred to Ugandans, with Milton Apollo Obote as executive prime minister and Sir Edward Mutesa as president.

What was the impact of the colonial project in Uganda? There are two lines of argument here. The first, which we shall call the imperial argument, assumes that colonialism had a modernising impact on the country by fostering the capitalist development in a backward and traditional society. The impact here is transformational: installing new values, monetising and developing markets, and creating new avenues for capital accumulation. The second, and opposing, argument says that colonialism introduced a distorted form of capitalism into the colonies with long-lasting implications. This distorted capitalism was deliberate and aimed at supporting colonial interests in metropolitan Europe. It was a system that privileged expatriate capital and discriminated against the indigenous Africans. This type of racialised division of labour created an economy with both modern and traditional sectors. The modern sector was served by the merchant capital of Europeans and Asians while the traditional sector was served by Asian inputs, technical skills and the supply of goods and services; Africans were consigned to cash crop production. The colonial state extracted surpluses when the modern sector was grafted onto the traditional economy.

The flow of Indian immigrants into the region began with the construction of the Uganda railway from Mombasa to Uganda in

1896. Those that emigrated were mainly commercial workers and indentured labourers. Many were poor and desperate and came seeking greener pastures. As construction of the railway advanced, demand rose for artisans, clerks, carpenters, brick-layers and blacksmiths, all from India. This flow was reinforced, as more Asians returning to India encouraged their relatives and friends to seek work in the East African colony.

This pattern of development was completely unlike that of early capitalist Europe. In Britain, for example, the evolution of capitalism produced an indigenous class that was firmly anchored in the country's social structure and culture. It relied upon internal sources of support to legitimate and defend its claims to social predominance.[10] In Uganda, external dominance meant that the commanding heights of the new economy were occupied and controlled by expatriate groups – the Europeans at the top followed by the Indians. Among the Indians, there was stratifica-tion into two classes – the commercial workers (those engaged in wholesale trade and processing) and the petty retailers or *duka-wallahs*.[11] These dominant expatriate groups derived their ability to exploit Ugandan resources from the power of the colonial state on the one hand, and lack of opportunity for Africans to compete with them on the other. Where the indigenous Africans attempted to acquire skills and some capital, the power of the colonial state could be used to destroy this and allow expatriate interests full play. The Indian class operated under the protective umbrella of the colonial state. Furthermore, because it was a class that was of external origin, it shared no common cultural heritage with the masses, and there was no motivation to do so.

Colonialism in Uganda was characterised by the state's exten-sive use of the law to prescribe and entrench economic privilege for the expatriate interests. The state created monopoly markets and supporting interests that were largely foreign to those of the indigenous inhabitants of the colony. This left tremendous distor-tions that remain to this day. In fact, this economic structure meant that an indigenous economic class never fully replaced the colonially facilitated expatriate capital. The colonial state was primarily concerned with connecting Uganda's primary export production to British metropolitan interests. Colonialism did not, therefore, facilitate the degree of structural change required for more sophisticated levels of economic activity in the country. The colonial strategy was to extract the surplus from the agricultural sector and keep, to a basic level, indigenous forms of production and exchange. Africans were tied to the production of cash crops and were taxed significantly higher to ensure that they met the volume targets.[12] Together with Asian capital, British merchant interests engaged in primary processing of these export commodities. It is noteworthy that the available processing and marketing infrastructure for commodity cash crops was determined by the requirements of the export economy. This became a pattern of the economic structures of most tropical African colonies and helps explain the almost total absence of industrialisation, and an effective indigenous entrepreneurial class at independence.

To appreciate the importance of moving to higher levels of production and value addition in the agricultural economy, it is crucial to understand the impact on outlook and lifestyle when producers shift from subsistence farming to activities associated with marketing, processing and exporting. As outlooks broaden so do life choices. Exposure to higher forms of production and economic activity means that both individuals and groups acquire the attitudes, skills and capital that kick-start the move into processing. Some observers have rightly pointed out that in the case of cotton processing in Uganda, 'inhibiting this freedom to move into this sector and appropriate some part of the surplus which it generated would be likely to destroy the only avenue likely open to Africans to move out of an environment bounded by almost exclusively "traditional" values and modes of operation into one which provided open-ended opportunities for upward mobility'.[13]

When Good African set up the coffee roasting and packing facility in Kampala in 2009, we were immediately exposed to production systems, operational etiquette and global packaging standards that we wouldn't have come across had we remained exporters of raw coffees. Moving up the value chain facilitates growth in intellectual equity and creates opportunities for greater competitiveness. So, limits upon entrepreneurial opportunities constrained the potential for advancement among the African population and denied Africans a share of the agricultural surplus in the economy. Their costs also increased through licence fees, which negatively impacted the largest sector of economically active agents. The colonial state also created barriers of entry, which limited the number of players in the field and artificially inflated the value of the cash crop processing assets. This process was repeated across every significant crop and most colonies in tropical Africa.[14]

COTTON AND COFFEE: EXAMPLES OF PLANTATION ECONOMICS

The impact of this distorted capitalism began with the formation of the British Cotton Growing Association (BCGA) in 1902, as Britain grew increasingly concerned with its dependency on US cotton supplies.[15] It was cotton that ostensibly linked Ugandan production to British manufacturing industries and effectively stratified the relationship between the African cash crop producer and expatriate capital. The colonial state used a number of legal instruments to manage both cotton and coffee production and processing in Uganda in a pattern of development akin to a plantation economy as experienced in the European colonies of the West Indies, where sugarcane production was first carried out by African enslaved labour and later by indentured Indian labour.[16] Asian inability to own land in Uganda drove them into the commercial sectors and here they began as middlemen between the African cotton farmers and the European ginners. Gradually they moved up into ginning.

All this had a lasting and damaging effect on the development of entrepreneurship in Uganda. Colonial arguments that African communities were backward and caught up in 'traditional beliefs' and lacking in 'achievement orientation' were among the myths circulated to justify the structure. Theories were purported about the supposedly irrational peasant responses to economic incentives. Josiah Wedgwood, a member of the British parliament, was emblematic of this perspective and had this to say:

I think that the Government might even now see what can be done, with the help of Lancashire, to stop this drift towards using the black man as labourer. That is at the bottom of the whole business. Ultimately it may be that to pursue this policy will mean that you kill out the black race . . . It is a frightful responsibility to try to impose a form of civilisation which suits us best upon a savage people. Leave them alone, give them freedom, cease to try to press them into the labour market, whether by driving them off the land or by taxation.[17]

Eliminating Africans as middlemen ended the possibility of them penetrating the higher levels of the industry as independent operators. This left them with no options for capital accumulation, and most began to operate as touts, a role that tied them to the ginner and the new Indian middleman.[18] Africans would be unable to free themselves from this inferior relationship and certainly unable to set up enterprises in opposition to expatriate ginners and exporters. The colonial system did not even pretend to make a commitment to competitive markets. It was a controlled system, one designed to safeguard those who had invested their capital and to exclude new entrants who might interfere with their profits. In the end, even when the Africanisation initiatives began in the early 1950s, Africans were never able to operate on a private enterprise basis; instead, the change was spearheaded by cooperatives that were opened up to African ownership.[19]

The rapid growth in ginning facilities in Uganda and expansion in the scale of Asian participation in both ginning and buying of cotton followed the shift in external markets from Britain to India and the increase in production of the crop. According to Mahmood Mamdani, a leading scholar on Ugandan political economy, in 1916 there were only nineteen ginneries. By 1925, this number had expanded to 155, more than 100 of which were owned by Asians.[20] A high number of these ginneries belonged to large Indian firms with considerable capital back in India. Narandas Rajaram & Co. was the biggest, while others belonged to small operators who had begun as middlemen themselves.[21] The thirty-two British ginneries were now being openly challenged by small Indian operators with their low-cost operations. British costs and efficiency standards were determined at colonial headquarters and could not out-compete the Indian operators. Asian traders thus grew in numbers through strong links to Indian capital back home, and also the heavy reliance on family relations. As the late Indian industrial magnate in Uganda Manubhai Madhvani observes in his autobiography *Tide of Fortune,* early Indian economic émigrés to Uganda developed a pattern of inviting their poor relatives or friends to join them as assistants or partners. When these assistants had saved enough they would open a shop and act as an agent of the supplier where they had worked.[22] This process would then be repeated.

Vithaldas Haridas Madhvani, for example, came to Uganda as a trader and was instrumental in bringing over Manubhai's father, Muljibhai Madhvani – they became business partners. Vithaldas also invited his brother Kalidas Haridas Madhvani to join him.[23] Another example is Nasser Virjee who came to East Africa as an assistant to Allidina Visram, the legendary pioneer of East African traders in the 1890s. By 1910, he had his own shop and was setting up branches and importing assistants himself. Karmali Alibhai who was brought as an assistant by Nasser Virjee in the 1910s, had, by the 1920s, set himself up as a *dukawallah*.[24] These patterns of emigration and commercial consolidation meant that the vast majority of traders came from a small number of castes and this tightly knit unit remained largely non-inclusive. As Madhvani observes, 'there was in those days little social contact between Indians and Africans. This fact, and some cases of outright prejudice of our own, gave rise to further mistrust and resentment on the part of Africans.'[25]

THE SEEDS OF BITTERNESS

This economic privileging of Asian capital and the economic disenfranchisement of the indigenous Ugandans brought about a racialised division into economic spheres creating a traditional and a modern sector of the economy.[26] The traditional economy had very little impact on trade in the economy and was characterised by a peasant, non-monetised class working with traditional and rudimentary inputs such as hoes to produce a small array of food crops and crafts, with the rest of their time allocated to growing cotton and coffee. Demands for new skills in this sector were satisfied by the Indian artisans. The import and export business was controlled by the Indian *dukawallahs*, while supervision of the economy and government was carried out by European civil servants. The modern economy comprised of commerce, industry and government, used imported factors of production and combined with labour to produce new goods and services.[27]

The Indians and Europeans between them provided the skills required by the modern economy, and received a disproportionately high return. Although they never made up more than 2 per cent of the population, they received several times their per capita share of the national product. Economist Ram Ramchandani, who has written extensively on Indian-African relations, observes that: 'while the taxable number of Asians was thirty-four times that of the Africans, their actual income compared to that of the African incomes was ninety-three times higher'.[28] He further shows that by 1926, the colonial government was spending on average 24 Uganda shillings per Asian schoolchild compared to 1.70 shillings per African schoolchild. This neglect of the indigenous human capital early on in the colonial period contributed significantly to the small number of entrepreneurs and commercial enterprises at independence. It also translated into a grossly inequitable per capita income situation by 1962, with Europeans at £990 per capita income, Asians at £288 and Africans at £12.[29] This economic structure has remained largely in place to this day with close to 80 per cent of the population surviving on the land that controls the smallest portion of the value chain.

Although Asian commercial dominance was a source of significant tension with Africans, another area that generated hostility was the civil service. As Mamdani correctly observes, the commercial sphere created several points of contact between Asians and Africans: Asian shopkeeper and African customer, Asian housewife and African domestic servant, Asian commercial employer and African shop employee; all shaped each other's attitudes and fuelled racial stereotyping. The colonial civil service, like the rest of the economy, was a three-tiered structure: European, Asian and African. While some observers have argued that the Africans being at the bottom of the scale was an inevitable result of a lack of skill to fill middle-tier jobs, this was more of a deliberate strategy of colonial control, it had logic and a purpose.[30]

The colonial justification was always that Africans were unable to familiarise themselves with new ideas or with occupations pertaining to an industrial society. As early as 1896, protectorate government officials travelled to India to recruit staff and returned with six clerks, plus eighteen artisans, hospital assistants and compounders. This was the start of a process of 'Indianisation' of certain lower echelons of the Uganda civil service.[31] Availability

of Asians with experience and training kept Africans in the background doing menial, clerical work and as spectators watching
the British and their Asian collaborators carry out a wide range of
exotic and seemingly complicated activities. Institutionalised
unequal pay led to the wage scales being challenged in March 1918
by eighteen African clerks who petitioned the government for
stabilised terms of employment. The Young Baganda Association
(YBA), founded in 1919, wrote many public letters to the Indian
Association calling for a change in attitude of the Indian community upon the African.[32]

Madhvani captures the constant tensions caused by the colonial system of economic segregation: 'The colonial government
had strictly regulated trade in cash crops throughout the 1930s
and 1940s, and African resentment grew as indigenous Ugandans
continued to be excluded from cotton ginning.'[33] When the
nationalist struggle began after the Second World War, starting
with the riots of 1949, Asian privilege was at the heart of the
native Ugandans' grievances. Madhvani recalls the 1949 worker
strikes as follows: 'They had three main demands: first, the
removal of what had effectively become an Asian monopoly over
cotton ginning; second, the right to bypass price controls on
export sales of cotton; and third, the right to local government
representation . . . like it or not, we were perceived as benefi-
ciaries of the colonial system.'[34]

On 9 October 1962, Uganda gained its independence from
Britain. Milton Obote became the country's first executive prime
minister, and Kabaka Muteesa II the ceremonial head of state.
This proved to be a tense relationship, with Buganda federal aspirations pulling against Obote's republican stand. In 1966, following
a power struggle between the Obote-led government and King
Muteesa, the UPC-dominated parliament abrogated the constitution and removed the president and vice-president, abolished the
traditional kingdoms and passed a new constitution proclaiming
Uganda a republic – doing all this without calling for elections or

a referendum. Obote was then declared the executive president. After this, Obote attempted to create an economic road map to redress the imbalances in the economy through a number of initiatives aimed at increasing the number of Africans engaged in higher levels of economic activity in wholesale trading, manufacturing and the service sectors. However, because the initiatives were ill-defined and poorly planned they gave rise to significant economic uncertainties, especially after the constitutional crisis of 1966. The 1965–70 period was marked by significant fragility in the economy with extensive capital flight from an insecure Asian community, foreign exchange constraints, a high cost of living and an increasingly inflationary environment.

By 1972, the economy was under serious strain. Large government projects like the construction of the International Conference Centre in Kampala and the renovation of Entebbe airport needed huge amounts of foreign exchange. Also, the lack of confidence in the economy by the Asian business community was evident in the extensive capital flight and this increased the running of business operations on bank overdrafts rather than on company revenues. All this added pressure to a deteriorating economic situation. It is this uncertain business environment that crippled the Ugandan economy. When analysts look at the post-expulsion economy they tend to make the case that the expulsion was a disaster for the economy and that the Africanisation programme was an outright failure. They do not point out that by the time the Asians were expelled, the economy was already in trouble and Africanisation had no economic base from which to be launched.

Obote's 'Move to the Left' in the form of a document entitled 'The Common Man's Charter' was published in October 1969.[35] This document gave a hint as to the nationalisation strategy of his government but didn't build a coherent actionable programme. Up to 1969, most government Africanisation initiatives were concerned with commerce, industry and agricultural marketing and processing.[36] Nevertheless, the widespread feeling among African businessmen and petty traders was that apart from agriculture, which had achieved a reasonable degree of African participation through the cooperative ordinances of 1946 and the subsequent creation of Marketing boards, Obote's government was not aggressively committed to pursuing Africanisation.[37] On 1 May 1970, Obote made the 'Nakivubo Pronouncement', which set out a programme that would address the Africanisation aspirations of the business community. All import and export business (except oil) would be transacted by a public corporation, and 60 per cent of shares of a large number of industries, banks and financial institutions would be acquired by government and run by state corporations, trade unions, municipal councils and cooperative unions.[38] However, the programme of nationalisation had not spelled out certain issues sufficiently clearly, for example, which firms would be added to the list that was initially announced, and whether compensation would be paid out of future profits. Also, once again the drive for economic transformation was being channelled through the public sector and not through private enterprise.

Obote also did not clarify whether the pronouncement would be a complement to the more effective policy of Africanising commerce or whether Africanisation just had a purely 'socialist dimension'. Despite Obote's assurances, the 'Nakivubo Pronouncement' was widely anticipated and there was a substantial increase in the level of repatriation of assets and profits prior to the announcement. A major criticism of the Nationalisation Plan was that the government failed to manage the administrative challenges following the announcement. Private foreign capital began to dry up and reinvestment was discouraged, restrictions on the convertibility of the Uganda shilling and the repatriation of profits created a money black market, and there were extensive shortages of goods and increases in the consumer price index.[39]

By 1969, there was strong evidence of a deteriorating balance-of-payments position.[40] According to Michael Tribe, a development economist who has written on Uganda: 'Had it not been for the "windfall" gain through a favourable cotton crop and favourable world prices in 1970, a serious payment crisis would have arisen at the end of the year'.[41] Asian capital flight was also a result of the immigration and trade licence legislations in 1968 to 1969 added to the 'Nakivubo Pronouncement'. All these combined to increase the anxiety of the Asian business community and provided a strong incentive to export funds to neighbouring Kenya. Obote's government tried to counter this with the introduction of the East African exchange control. While this move had the desired balance-of-payment effect, it created considerable challenges for Kenyan workers seeking to repatriate funds.[42]

Another initiative introduced during this period was the Trade Licensing Act of January 1970, which excluded non-citizens from certain items of trade and from trading points in the rural areas. This dampened the investment enthusiasm in the economy and led to a reduction in imports of capital goods such as machinery and transport equipment. In addition, the Immigration Act of 1969 required non-citizens to obtain work permits by 1 May 1970. This caused further anxiety and panic among Asian businessmen, exacerbating the already considerable capital flight.[43] They also started reducing their stock levels in order to retain as much non-liquid commitment to Uganda as possible.[44] At the same time, legitimate transfers by Asian emigrants increased the money drain. There was a growing feeling among Asians that the attack on non-citizens was only the beginning of what would later develop into a policy excluding them entirely from certain lines of business and professional activity. One indication of panic and disillusionment was the eagerness on the part of Asian businessmen to obtain convertible currencies at black market prices.[45] On

25 January 1971, Milton Obote was ousted in a military coup and many in the city, Asians included, celebrated Amin's entry.

Amin's coup emerged from an attempt to manage serious factional interests within the Ugandan army. Upon taking office, Amin immediately targeted Obote's northern-based army constituency of Acholi and Langi through brutal arrests and murders. He brought in an essentially mercenary force comprising of 4,000 Sudanese ex-Anyanya forces and members of his Kakwa tribesmen from West Nile.[46] Particular groups like the Nubian trading community who formed his support base in Kampala sought to extract trade concessions and redressing of the serious income inequalities. The expulsion was preceded by a series of meetings with the Asian community leaders, beginning in 1971 and ending with the announcement in Tororo in August 1972 that they would have ninety days to leave the country. The expulsion announcement was met with a popular response, which by itself revealed the different class expectations from the expulsion. William Kalema, a leading businessman and consultant, makes an interesting observation that the expulsion's populist appeal lay in its being targeted to the person on the streets of Kampala. It represented 'an action the common man on the street could relate to and delivered in a timeframe (ninety days) that was tangible.'[47] It gave the impression that huge benefits would trickle down. Eyewitness accounts also report an element of 'psychological liberation' that came with the expulsion. Kalema said further that: 'It opened people's minds to what could be possible, that commerce was not the preserve of the Asians. But while it unlocked the mind to the potential for indigenous Africans, the state repression that quickly followed undermined any such hope.'[48]

The expulsion was followed by the transfer of Asian assets left behind into Ugandan hands as part of the so-called 'Africanisation' effort. These included 5,655 firms, factories, ranches and agricultural estates, as well as personal property such as cars, and household goods that had been left behind.[49] The transfer of this wealth was placed in the hands of the Business Allocation Committees of the Ministry of Industries and Commerce, and the somewhat chaotic process was characterised by the setting up of financial and occupational qualifications, which largely favoured the African middle class, bureaucrats and soldiers. Adverts would be placed in the Uganda *Argus* and those interested in being allocated assets would then report to the particular shop or factory on the day of the disposal. The interested parties would wait outside the shop with their documentation – bank statements, business letters or some evidence of trading. Soldiers would set up a desk, review the documentation for several minutes then announce the winner to much cheering. Thereafter, the padlock on the shop would be broken and the shop given away.[50] Most buildings were nationalised and placed under the Custodian Board. Industries that were too big or operationally complex to run were handed over to parastatals and the Uganda Development Corporation (UDC) to operate.[51]

Amin also distributed some of the businesses to supporters and cronies – it is estimated that more than 500 businesses were personally distributed by him to army officers and his friends.[52] The UDC soon became overwhelmed by the speed with which the state transferred assets to them. The lack of Asian technicians who were conversant with the particular technologies of some of the factories, and the general administrative burdens of managing subsidiaries that exceeded $100 million by 1973 proved challenging.[53] What's more, these subsidiaries did not assume repayment obligations for the loans taken out on their behalf by the UDC, which meant that the UDC had to assume responsibility for those debts and soon got into serious financial trouble itself.[54]

The economy in the post-expulsion period deteriorated fast. GDP contracted by 20 per cent by 1980 and there was a significant shift towards the subsistence sector.[55] Production contracted by 40 per cent due to reduced state-marketed coffee, and foreign exchange earnings fell as the tourism and mining sectors perished.[56] Agricultural production also shifted to the supply of food crops for urban populations. The smuggling of coffee and consumer goods out of Uganda further eroded the tax base of the economy. Huge scarcities led to the growth of a vast black market *(magendo)*, which soon accounted for more than two-thirds of the monetary GDP and became the dominant mode of production.[57] Transport, which was foreign exchange dependent, deteriorated, leading to scarcity of goods and, in turn, sharply rising food prices.[58] The cost of living in the capital city Kampala in 1980 was thirty-three times what it had been in 1972. Public sector employees had to find alternative sources of income just to make ends meet. They resold government-allocated goods on the local market and pocketed the difference. The result was an unfocused civil service paying little attention to state affairs.

The *magendo* economy was the defining economic phenomenon in the 1970s and early 1980s, a profit-oriented response to scarcity in the legal sector of the economy. The sharp fall in foreign investment produced a decline in Uganda's dependence on the outside world and an increased reliance on its neighbouring countries, particularly Kenya. Goods were bought at retail from Kenya, smuggled into Uganda, sold at the going rate and the process repeated. Coffee smuggling increased at this time, especially after 1975 when the world market prices soared because the Uganda government was paying its growers far lower prices than its neighbours. *Magendo* created its own class structure, with a few exceptionally wealthy '*mafuta mingi*' (so wealthy they were dripping with oil).[59] In addition to the *magendo* economy came the pernicious business attitude of accumulation via acquisition rather than investment. The distributive nature of Amin's 'economic war' left a damaging legacy on business attitudes amongst Ugandans, promoting short-term approaches and operations over long-term planning and concepts.

Several analysts have treated the Asian expulsion as an isolated event, presenting a straightforward cause-and-effect interpretation of the pre- and post-expulsion realities.[60] The arguments tend to go like this: scarcity and the *magendo* economy were the result of the collapse of the supply side of the Ugandan economy, which was itself a direct consequence of the expulsion of the Asians. The expulsion did, of course, destroy trading networks and so too did the nationalisation of enterprises. Many appropriated businesses allocated to Ugandans were plundered and distributed within Amin's patronage system, reaching very few Africans. Also, few of the new owners had adequate capital or the business expertise to run them. Poor access to capital and lack of foreign exchange meant that spares, machinery and other goods could not be imported.[61]

Racialised tensions emanating from distortions in the structure of the economy can lead to violent responses. In Uganda, what was left after independence and the Obote regime was an explosive situation waiting for a demagogue. The economic conditions during the Amin regime were dire, but attributing them exclusively to the expulsion overlooks the other contemporary political dynamics: a collapse in governance and institutionalisation of state terror under Amin. These two factors drove the economy into a tailspin.

Advocates of the perspective that the expulsion led directly to economic decline tend to wander into uncritical celebration of the supposedly unique role of Asians in the Uganda economy.[62] They outline what is essentially a case for Asian exceptionalism: intrinsic and particular attributes to this community that drove their commercial success. Attributes like the propensity to work long hours, the ability to live frugally and a willingness to operate on a small scale and plough back profits and, according to Ugandan Asian economist Vali Jamal, an ability to just be 'simple people, using local foods in their diets and locally fabricated goods in their households' characterises this ethic.[63]

All this raises an uncomfortable problem. Whilst it is acceptable to celebrate discernible attributes of a community of people, it can come dangerously close to ethnic posturing and chauvinism, particularly within the context of a repressive colonial order that offers one race of people a path to capital accumulation and consigns another to economic subservience. If the economic environment had been equitable, the same entrepreneurial qualities would have been evident in the Africans themselves.[64] It almost implies that the Ugandan economy's only entrepreneurial engine was the Asian community. That Africans lacked the skill, talent and compulsion to take advantage of the commercial and retail opportunities is a self-serving and impoverished argument propagated by the colonial state. Constraints to accumulation are seldom due to the lack of entrepreneurial talent; they are more often due to a lack of peace, security, good governance, markets, technology and capital. Where these factors are available, entrepreneurship will flourish. The argument of Asian exceptionalism remains unconvincing.

Put in this context, one can see how the colonial history of Uganda, combined with the country's post-colonial leaders, created an environment where entrepreneurship was severely constrained and with it productive capacity, ability to accumulate capital, industrial output and a vibrant export sector. These structural constraints, unless firmly appreciated by policy experts and politicians, will not be corrected.

Malaysia is a good example of a country with similar economic distortions at the time of independence. They inherited a multi-racial society by independence from Britain in 1957. Like Uganda, the post-independence period was marked by serious income inequalities between Malays and non-Malays, resulting in riots in May 1969. And, as with the British occupation of Uganda from the second half of the nineteenth century until the 1930s, the British had encouraged large-scale Chinese and Indian immigration to what was then Malaya to supply their manpower needs for the tin mines and rubber plantations. The Malays, like the Africans in Uganda, remained in the traditional subsistence agriculture and were left out of the modern sector of the economy. After independence, each ethnic group was separated by their economic functions. Malays were largely engaged in subsistence agriculture and fishing, the Chinese were involved in commerce and modern sectors of the economy and the Indians were labourers in the rubber plantations. There was little interaction between the ethnic groups. One of the reasons was that the Chinese and Indians, like the Ugandan Asians, saw Malaysia as a transition land rather than their homeland, hence they saw no need to integrate with Malays because they would be returning home after accumulating enough savings.

In response, the government introduced the New Economic Policy (NEP) in 1970, which accorded the Malay preferential treatment to correct the significant economic imbalances. The programme was succeeded in 1990 by the New Development Policy (NDP). During the NEP/NDP Malaysia achieved a very rapid economic growth, saw significant reduction in poverty and brought Malays into the mainstream of economic activities. Ethnicity dominated all aspects of Malaysian life. 'These groups were divided by coinciding cleavages of race, language, religion, customs, area of residence and to a large extent, by type of occupation,' notes political analyst D. K. Mauzy. 'Predictably, they lined up on the same opposing sides on every politically relevant issue.'[65] Apart from aiming to overcome the perceived socio-economic imbalances within Malaysian society, the ultimate goal was to achieve national unity and to foster nation building through active government intervention. In other words, inter-ethnic equality was depicted as a prerequisite to social peace and stability. The results were remarkable: economic growth and development, transformation from dependence on agriculture to a more broad-based economy and exceptional success in poverty eradication. All this was made possible through effective governance and macroeconomic management.

The current economic situation in Uganda reflects a continuation of the historical economic distortions. According to the Uganda Revenue Authority (URA), of the twenty-five top tax-paying companies in 2010, fourteen are foreign multinationals, five are Asian or Ugandan Asian-owned enterprises, five are government parastatals and one is a Ugandan franchise of Pepsi International.[66] Yet the number of African small business operators has increased considerably, with more than 89,000 businesses registered by 2009, according to the World Bank: nevertheless, this has not altered the structure of capital possession.[67] Another example is in the banking sector: of the twenty-four licensed commercial banks in Uganda, two are indigenous Ugandan, five are Asian owned, and sixteen are registered as foreign banks.[68]

Idi Amin was overthrown in 1979 by a coalition between the Tanzanian army and Ugandan forces. The economy continued to deteriorate throughout the political turbulence of the mid 1980s and by the time Yoweri Museveni's National Resistance Army marched into Kampala and captured power on 26 January 1986, the economy was in deep crisis. Inflation had risen relentlessly to 150 per cent per annum, export earnings had collapsed and there was a cumulative drop in Gross National Product (GNP) creating an economy of underutilisation, scarcity of consumer goods and low real wages. The new liberators marched into an empty treasury and an economy in near collapse. In 1987, Uganda signed its first Structural Adjustment Program with the IMF, and under much better stewardship began its economic recovery.

Post-independence politics not only failed fully to reverse the colonially established distortions; it cemented them with a brutal dictatorship, corruption, impunity and the systemic abuse of human rights. The dashing of the hopes and aspirations at independence was spectacular and has contributed to the state of Africa today. The issues underpinning the contemporary political economy of the continent are deep and complex, nevertheless we must explore them for they hold the key to unlocking the future potential of Africa's entrepreneurs and innovators.

PART TWO
The Good African Story

3 Logistics

Faith is taking the first step, even when you don't see the whole staircase.
Martin Luther King Jr.

One of the major challenges in doing business in many African countries is the poor state of the physical infrastructure and the high logistical costs of getting goods and services around the continent and overseas. This book's first two chapters reflected on some of the political and economic aspects of the state and its management that could have led to the dismal delivery of public goods. I am often amused when I hear policy experts talking about Africa's need for more entrepreneurs to develop a strong private sector that can boost economic growth. The problem is definitely not a lack of entrepreneurs – not if you have ever driven through the bustling streets of Lagos or downtown Nairobi or witnessed the thousands of entrepreneurs in Kampala's suburbs who bring their wares to you whether you are in your vehicle, home or office. Africans are one of the most resilient, innovative and creative business people in the world. To navigate poor and decaying road networks, maddeningly corrupt and inefficient bureaucrats, government regulations that frustrate and hinder business operations, a lack of reliable electricity or water, all demand ingenuity,

agility and determination. I doubt western entrepreneurs operating in such an environment could last long. Such extraordinary
competencies to adapt and navigate very challenging environ-
ments must be recognised, appreciated and motivated instead of
being trampled on by the arrogant rhetoric of 'experts' who harp
on about the need to unlock Africa's private sector. The African
private sector is already unlocked; it is just waiting for the delivery
of the promises of an 'enabling environment'. And what they
receive for their patience is constant failure by Africa's leaders to
deliver on what are legitimate demands.

According to the African Development Bank, 40 per cent of
the population lacks access to safe water, 60 per cent lacks basic
sanitation and only 30 per cent of the rural population in sub-
Saharan Africa has access to all-season roads.[1] Only 30 per cent of
the African population have access to electricity and Africa has
the lowest telephone and Internet penetration – 14 per cent (the
world average is 52 per cent) and 3 per cent (the world average is
14 per cent) respectively.[2] Transport costs in Africa are among the
highest in the world and estimated to be more than 60 per cent
higher than the average in developed countries, especially for
landlocked countries like Uganda. For instance, while it costs
between $1,400 and $1,700 to ship a 40-foot container from Dubai
to Mombasa, the average transportation and clearing cost for the
same container between Mombasa and Kampala is $3,800–
$4,500.[3]

I was confronted with these infrastructure and logistical challenges the moment I stepped into the rural economy to establish
our supply network of farmers, first in the eastern part of the
country in the Mount Elgon coffee-growing region of Mbale and
then in the western part of the country in Kasese district. These
logistical issues, whilst a frustration and a constraint to pursuing
my business goals, nevertheless revealed how transformation in
the rural economy is actually possible in spite of them.

But, first, let us explore this thing called coffee.

A NOTE ON COFFEE

It is believed that coffee was first discovered in Ethiopia as far back as the thirteenth century. A story is told of an Ethiopian goat herder named Kaldi who noticed his flock nibbling on some bright red berries after which they started jumping up and down in apparent excitement. Kaldi then chewed on the fruit himself, finding them to be mildly stimulating, and in his excitement took the berries to a holy man in a nearby monastery. The cherries were then thrown into a fire, releasing a distinct and exciting aroma. After grinding the coffee and dissolving it in hot water, the world's first cup of coffee was consumed. Many historians have observed that this story is probably apocryphal but nevertheless most historical accounts point to Ethiopia as the country from where coffee originated. Coffee was then said to have spread to Egypt and Yemen, with strong evidence of coffee drinking and planting during the thirteenth century, in the Sufi monasteries of Yemen. By the sixteenth century, it had reached other parts of the Middle East, Persia, Turkey and northern Africa. From there it spread to Italy, the Netherlands and to the rest of Europe, and then on to Indonesia, Sumatra and the Americas.

After Ethiopia, Uganda is the second home of coffee. Whilst the variety of coffee originating from Ethiopia is the milder arabica (*Coffea arabica*), in Uganda, like many parts of Africa's equatorial rain forests, the robusta variety (*Coffea canephora*) is indigenous. The Uganda Coffee Development Authority (UCDA), the regulatory authority for the coffee industry, estimates that the robusta coffee constitutes about 90 per cent of the total coffee production that is exported from Uganda. Robusta coffee is a low-altitude crop and is grown around the north and west plains of Lake Victoria. Coffee in Uganda is essentially grown by small-scale farmers on smallholdings and estimates by the UCDA point to between 500,000 and 1,000,000 farmer households engaged in coffee production. Many more Ugandans, in fact almost 5,000,000, depend in some way or another on coffee earnings. Coffee has historically driven the Ugandan economy, providing at times over 90 per cent of the country's export earnings. This is a classic example of the primary commodity and mono-crop dependency of many sub-Saharan African countries and makes countries very susceptible to a number of exogenous factors like global price fluctuations and environmental conditions.

Here is a good illustration. In 1994 to 1995 Uganda exported approximately 2.7 million bags of coffee and earned over $430 million, yet in 2001 the country exported a larger volume of three million bags but earnings dropped to $108 million, less than a quarter of the 1994–1995 value. Today, although the Ugandan economy depends less on coffee than in the past – given a more diversified export base that produces other non-traditional crops like tea, vanilla and other horticultural, aquaculture and floriculture – coffee still makes up a significant contribution to the economy. For many years, Uganda, which is the world's twelfth largest exporter of coffee, didn't process any of its coffee beans but instead imported finished products like Nescafe and other processed coffee brands. This lack of processing and value addition at source has even led to the curious phenomena of prefixing products with countries where the product is not indigenous. Terms like 'Italian coffee', 'English tea' or 'Swiss chocolate' come to mind, yet none of these countries grows a single coffee bean, tea leaf or cocoa bean. But because they have added value to these African agricultural products for decades, they have become known as 'origin' countries. Over 2.25 billion cups of coffee are consumed around the world every day, and over 90 per cent of that coffee is produced in developing countries, yet most of the consumption takes place in industrialised countries. This is a sad testimony to being producers of what we do not consume and consumers of what we do not produce.

Most robusta coffees are 'dry processed', which means that the ripe (red) cherries are sundried by the farmer immediately after picking off the coffee trees. Once dried, the cherries are stored and added to further sundried cherries as the season progresses. The dried robusta coffee is known in Uganda as '*kiboko*', which comes from the stick pounding that the farmers subject the coffee to after it is sundried. This coffee is then usually milled at small factories where the dried berry covering is hulled; what's left is the 'green' bean. Different grades are then sorted out by the exporter before being sold.

Arabica coffee was introduced in Uganda and other parts of Eastern Africa in the early 1900s from Malawi. Unlike the lowland robusta coffees, arabica coffee requires higher altitudes with cooler climates and that's why we see it grown on the mountain ranges of both the east and western parts of Uganda. They also grow it in the west Nile region of north-western Uganda, an area bordering the Democratic Republic of Congo, and in the south-western district of Kisoro. Arabica coffees are either 'dry processed' or 'wet processed' (frequently termed 'washed' coffee). The washing process involves removing the outer covering of the red cherry immediately after picking using a hand-pulping machine, which tends to be owned and operated by a group of farmers or an individual farmer. The outer covering is removed leaving the coffee bean covered by mucilage, which is a sticky covering that essentially contains sugars and enzymes. This mucilage is removed by a process of fermentation over a twenty-four to thirty-six-hour period and then the beans are drip dried. This process leaves a clean, thin, shell covering of the bean (endocarp) known as 'parchment'. The parchment is removed by a milling process to produce green coffee beans, which are sold ready for roasting.

MOUNT ELGON

Early Saturday morning on 18 June 2004 my logistics officer at Good African Coffee, Mathias Nabutele, and I jumped into a borrowed four-wheel-drive vehicle and headed out to Mount Elgon in the Mbale district. The idea was to visit the coffee-growing region of eastern Uganda and establish whether we could launch our Good African model there. That March, we had successfully launched our products in South Africa, but we were still buying coffee from Ugandan traders and not the farmers directly. We wanted to work only with local farmers, and believed that we could do this in Mbale.

Mbale lies approximately 245 kilometres from Kampala, and for those who watch James Bond films, they might have spotted Mbale in an early scene in *Casino Royale*, in which it is depicted as a town in eastern Uganda where an international money launderer and gunrunner goes to do business with a rebel leader with a penchant for chopping off the limbs of his victims. So much for Mbale in the movies.

The trip to Mbale is a four-hour car drive on a congested two-lane tarmac road that goes straight to the border with Kenya. Large trucks bringing in imports from the port of Mombasa in Kenya ply this route. As you head out of Kampala, you pass the Namugongo Martyrs Shrine. The shrine, a Catholic cathedral, was built to commemorate the lives of thirty-two young men who were in the court of the Kabaka (King) of Buganda, Mwanga II, and who were burned to death by orders of the kabaka at Namugongo for refusing to renounce their Christian faith. Mwanga, a Muslim, intended to make an example of them to discourage the growth of the Church and the work of the missionaries in his kingdom. Every year, thousands of Christians from all over Uganda make a pilgrimage to Namugongo to commemorate their deaths. In 1964, Pope Paul VI canonised twenty-two of the martyrs.

When we arrived in Mbale we drove straight to the district council office where we had agreed to meet with John Namisi, a local coffee farmer. I had met John earlier, in March, when he visited my office in Kampala – together with the local district council chairman, Bernard Mujaasi. John is about six feet tall, with a large build and a round, jovial face. In Mbale he was accompanied by a funny and ribald fellow called Wafula, who I had also met in Kampala. Wafula cuts a much smaller figure with idiosyncratic mannerisms, and he constantly interrupted discussions with odd bits of information. Wafula seemed like John's sidekick and they made an unusual team. We were given a warm welcome by Chairman Mujaasi who didn't hide his wish that we would set up our coffee-buying operation there. He assured me that we would get the full support of the district if we decided to establish a coffee procurement business there. I thanked him and requested that we proceed up the mountain as planned while it was still early afternoon.

The Elgon mountain is an extinct volcano rising about 4,300 metres above sea level and straddles the Uganda–Kenya border, and arabica coffee is grown on both the Ugandan and Kenyan sides. We set off for John's coffee *shamba* (small farm) on the south-western slope of the Elgon in a place called Bushibuya, a forty-minute drive from Mbale. En route we passed several homesteads, kiosks and other homes built out of mud and wattle. We reached John's home but the car wouldn't climb up the steep hill and we walked the remaining two hundred or so metres up the hill to his house.

John and his family live in a modest house at the bottom of one of the steep slopes of the mountain. His coffee farm is about five acres in size and is on a slope right behind the house. When we entered his house we found about fifteen people waiting for us. Some were clearly community elders and others were farmers. He invited us to sit down and introduced us to the group. We shook hands and beyond the few words I knew in Lumasaba, the indigenous language, I let Mathias translate. John explained the purpose of our visit: 'These friends are here to look at our coffee, to see the quality and how they can buy our coffee. Mr Rugasira is selling his coffee in South Africa and is the first Ugandan to sell there'. At that point he referred to a newspaper article that covered the launch we had in South Africa and said: 'We need a good market for our coffee, so he is here to discuss his project with us.' The group seemed to defer to John, listening intently as he spoke and when he was finished, they nodded. He then invited me to speak.

I thanked John for hosting us and said that Mathias and I were there to listen, learn and ask questions. I spoke briefly about our vision to build a coffee company that worked with the farmers to produce quality coffees and that would pay them a good price that enabled them to make a profitable return on their harvest. I explained that, as a company, we were committed to empowering Africans. We can solve our own problems, I argued, if we work together. Our commitment could be seen with our recent South African launch. They listened to me quietly, at times nodding, but I didn't know whether what I was saying made sense to them or not. John interjected several times to emphasise a point I was making and to give further assurance that he had visited our offices and found us to be a serious company.

John then invited them to ask questions. One by one, they began to open up and talk about their history of exploitation by unscrupulous buyers who paid the lowest prices and cared little for the quality of their coffee. They complained about the delayed payments by the Bugisu Cooperative Union (BCU) and the failure of the government to support them in a meaningful way by providing new coffee plants and other inputs that would help them improve the quality of the crop. BCU had been formed in 1954 to take control of the procurement and sale of the entire coffee crop in the Elgon area. The initiative was motivated by the then Governor of Uganda, Andrew Cohen. It was an attempt to pacify the cooperatives and turn them from an anti-colonial protest movement to a collaborative organisation. BCU controlled a coffee curing facility and was the main agency for coffee development in the east of the country. The farmers claimed that the

BCU had betrayed them and that they had lost confidence due to the BCU's failure to meet financial obligations with the farmers. Delayed payments, the purchase of poor quality coffees and neglect of the farmers' agronomy issues were their principal complaints. The BCU was a farmer-based union so it was strange that they were the apparent genesis of the problem. They complained that the leadership and management of the union had diverted and squandered farmer finances and coffee and almost brought down the cooperative. Underlying this criticism was a palpable cynicism and a sense that their dignity had been undermined. All eyes then fell on me as I responded to some of their questions. After about half an hour of back and forth, John interrupted us: 'Let us go see the *shamba*.'

John's coffee farm lies on a steep slope about 300 metres up and at an angle of almost 45 degrees; it was a test to our city legs. As we climbed, a couple of the young farmers walking behind us started to chuckle and point at me. Mathias told me they were betting on whether I would make the journey back down without slipping and sliding on my backside. We spent some time among the coffee trees, with John showing us the different varieties, the farm practices he used and some of the environmental challenges the farm was facing, like soil erosion and mudslides. John then explained the difference between the natural dried coffee method used by farmers in the Rwenzori Mountains of western Uganda and the washed method preferred by the farmers on Mount Elgon.

As we chatted, one of the elders, Mzee Watiha, made a suggestion that seemed to bring the discussion to a halt and momentarily left me speechless. Leaning on his walking cane, he suggested that culturally it was in order for me to undergo a local initiation called *Shikuka*, where I would be given a local name, *Mafabi*, to welcome me into the local Bushibuya community. This process apparently involved draping me with a piece of backcloth once the community had established that I was circumcised. I quickly assured Watihi that I appreciated the gesture very much and would be honoured to receive the name *Mafabi* if we stayed away from any talk of circumcision. Watiha responded that he didn't want the matter to scare 'our new friend'. A stick was then placed in my hand and a large piece of backcloth was draped over my shoulders and the group broke out in applause and singing. It was a touching moment for me, and revealed more about the spirit of generosity of these farmers.

We spent the rest of the afternoon and evening travelling to other coffee-growing areas in the region. We visited farmers in Bugigayi and Bubulo and held discussions with larger groups of farmers in local classrooms and shaded outdoor spaces. We heard the same litany of complaints: exploitative middlemen mortgaged coffee farms at usury interest rates, and the effect of depressed prices. These farmers, because there was not much of a personal connection with us, were less open than John's group about what they felt was wrong with the coffee sector. I tried to engage with them on areas of opportunity like improving the quality as a means of trying to get a better price for their coffee.

Mbale seemed to have major coffee buyers located in the area; several of them were subsidiaries of large multinational companies with significant operations. These companies were well funded, with access to finance capital from their group treasuries. Their financial muscle was no small thing when it came to competing for coffee purchases. The BCU, too, had a large hulling and processing plant for green coffee exports, which gave them an infrastructure advantage. I just couldn't see the space for a small company like ours to establish a presence in Mbale.

It was clear that to change the farmers' mindset about new partnership possibilities would require a lot of energy, money, people and logistics. My initial concerns were that I couldn't see how we would make a dent in this environment given our lack of financial resources and the muscle to compete.

Over the next couple of weeks, I processed my findings and reached three conclusions. First, we would not be able to establish a foothold in Mbale given our limited financial resources and staff. Second, there seemed to be a lot of cynicism among the farmers that I encountered, other than those at John's house. We would need to do a lot more community advocacy work to generate the farmers' interest in our programme. Again, when I looked at our finances, we just didn't have sufficient capital to generate a real impact in the short term. By impact, I mean being able to carry out agronomy best-practice training, provide agro-inputs to improve quality and yields of the coffee and financial literacy training to protect the farmers from rural loan sharks. My third conclusion was an aggregate of the first two: accept the reality of the two points and go to another part of the country that grows high-altitude arabica coffees and establish the model there where it would have a better chance of surviving and flourishing.

At the end of July 2004, I sent Mathias to Kasese district and specifically to the Rwenzori Mountains, another major arabica coffee-growing region in Uganda. His brief was to explore the possibilities of establishing a farmer supply network there. He boarded a Kasese-bound bus in Kampala and made our first visit to the region. This would become the place where our Good African model found a community and a home, was tested and, with time, generated the transformation of the farmers and their communities we had hoped for.

THE MOUNTAINS OF THE MOON

Kasese district borders Kabarole and Bundibugyo to the north, Lake George and Kamwenge to the east, Bushenyi and Lake Edward to the south and the Democratic Republic of Congo in the west. It is home to the Rwenzori Mountains, also known as the Mountains of the Moon, which rise up to over 5,109 metres above sea level and have a range of about 120 kilometres and a width of about 65 kilometres. The most well-known peaks of the range are: Mount Stanley, which is 5,109 metres, Mount Speke at 4,890 metres and Mount Baker at 4,843 metres. Mount Stanley is named after the Welsh explorer Henry Morton Stanley who was the first non-indigenous explorer to set eyes on the mountains in 1889. Stanley named them 'Ruwenzori' by apparently combining 'Rwenzururu' and 'Rwenjura'. The mountains were known locally as Rwenzururu by the mountain dwellers and Rwenjura by some of those staying on the lowlands, and is home to the Bakonzo and Bamba people and the Basongora, a nomadic pastoral community. Kasese is also known for its big copper mines at Kilembe and at one point in the 1970s and 1980s accounted for most of Uganda's copper exports. Mining operations have since ceased. The district is now known for its production of cotton, food crops and coffee. It is estimated that Kasese produces over 10,000 tonnes of coffee per annum. This arabica coffee is mainly dry processed, and is known as DRUGARS (dry Uganda arabicas).

Mathias arrived in Kasese and spent a couple of days trying to find a guide with local knowledge and community connections to take him around a few of the coffee-growing areas of the mountain. Given the number of tourists that visit the mountain and the adjacent Queen Elizabeth National Park, trekking experts are in plentiful supply. Once Mathias located one, the community guide took him up the mountains to a parish called Kibandama in Kilembe sub-county. There he was introduced to several coffee farmers and began to gather information about conditions for the farmers and the socio-economic situation they were in. He then moved north-east to the Katabukene village, Maliba sub-county, where he carried out further field work and this time engaged several farmers in a focus group discussion. Katabukene would become one of our early success stories and a strong catalyst for progress in other locations.

A few days later, I decided to travel the 343 kilometres to Kasese to visit Mathias. I spent two days with him, going through some of his research findings and then took a day trip up the mountain to the places he had visited earlier to get a sense of the terrain, the crop and the community. Mathias had expanded his network to include members of the local community. We also connected with the coffee authority representative and got a detailed understanding of the coffee industry in Kasese. Mathias had good instincts, was quick-witted and took initiative. But I decided that I still needed the advice of someone who knew the agronomy sector, someone I could trust. That person was James 'Sunday' Mutabazi , the district agricultural officer in Kabale district, which is 220 kilometres from Kasese and on the south-western border with Rwanda.

Kabale is a hilly, border town, with a scenic and rugged terrain and is home to the Bakiga people. The cool evenings and meandering hills have led it to being nicknamed the Switzerland of Uganda and it is also the place where I trace my ancestral roots. James is a jovial, unassuming and well-liked person who is always on hand to help. I needed his advice and I also had a request: would he agree to travel up to Kasese and give us an independent assessment of the coffee situation and evaluate the chances of setting up our concept of farmer groups there. We met at the White Horse Inn in Kabale and after a couple of hours' talking, he agreed that he would take a couple of days off and drive to Kasese, link up with Mathias and make some preliminary observations.

A week later, Mathias called me in Kampala with interesting news. He had met a young lady from Kasese named Janet Matte who might be able to help us in the field. As Janet explained when we met, any new faces in the area were greeted with suspicion, given the recent insurgency in the Rwenzori Mountains by the anti-government Allied Democratic Forces (ADF). The ADF had been formed by a radical sect of the Muslim community in

Uganda known as the Tabliqs and was headed by a former Catholic, Jamil Mukulu. Between 1996 and 2000 the ADF carried out several attacks on villages and ambushed unsuspecting Ugandan army soldiers on patrol. In 1998, they carried out a number of abductions but it was the burning of over eighty students, who had barricaded themselves in a school dormitory, that shocked many Ugandans and the international community. After this, the Ugandan forces intensified their counterinsurgency efforts, creating a new Alpine unit and placing it under the command of a senior officer from the area. The ADF were routed from their bases in the Rwenzori Mountains and they moved into the Ituri district in the eastern part of the Democratic Republic of Congo where they continued to harass local communities, until a concerted military effort between the United Nations and the Congolese army greatly weakened them and destroyed much of their fighting capabilities. Janet later told me that the insurgents had discouraged coffee growing in the area by spreading stories that coffee beans went into the production of gun powder. They did this to undermine economic activities in the area as part of their insurgency activities.

Mathias and his team embarked on a field visit of six sub-counties in Kyarumba, Kyondo, Kisinga, Munkunyu, Nyakiyumbu and Bwera (where Janet comes from). When James came to Kampala he was hopeful about the prospects for our model in Kasese and he believed that the environment was right for a model that strengthened the farmer supply chain in a sustainable way. With the information from our first in-depth field work, I called on the UCDA, meeting with Henry Ngabirano, the managing director, and shared our findings from Kasese. I wanted to get his support, especially on our concept of introducing the washed cherry processing method we had seen in Mbale.

He was supportive, but cautious in his encouragement, concerned about the costs of establishing an alternative method of processing the coffee cherries: the technology and the training needed would be expensive. He had a point. Whilst the washed method produced an arguably better coffee-cup quality, to introduce it would require a huge mobilising effort and significant resources; resources, he felt, government was better placed to expend. My push-back was that it was precisely because the government had failed effectively to manage agronomy initiatives, that a small private company was now forced to address the issue. To build a sustainable coffee brand, we needed sustainable good quality coffee. Sustainable good quality coffee depends on how the raw coffee cherries are processed and on the whole crop-management system in the area. We didn't have a hope of building a brand if we didn't tackle the issue of quality first. Henry was talking about industry dynamics and constraints; I was thinking about the opportunities for change and transformation.

On 29 July 2004, we opened our field office in Kasese town and appointed Janet Matte as our community liaison officer with the responsibility for organising the farmers into producer organisations. Without a car or an office desk to work from, Janet spent most of her time in the field and also acted as our translator and community guide. She quickly became a very effective voice for the company up in the mountains. Using the ubiquitous motor-bike taxis better known as 'boda-boda' – a popular mode of transport that started as cross-border transportation between Uganda and Kenya in the late 1960s – she also participated in several radio talk shows in Kasese in which she encouraged coffee farmers to join our training programme. She was persistent, confident, dependable and wise.

When I first met Janet I thought she was a young man. She is diminutive in size, cuts her hair very short, and wears baggy T-shirts over an equally baggy pair of denim jeans and trainers. I could see from her shy smile that she was used to having her gender mistaken. We sat down for a chat and I quickly became impressed with her background and experience. She told me that after high school, she got a job as a trainee assistant warden at the

Queen Elizabeth National Park, which neighbours the lowland areas of Kasese district. The park, in similar tradition to the naming of other lakes and landmarks in the country during the colonial era, was named after Queen Elizabeth II and is the most visited game park in the country. Well known for its wildlife, it currently boasts over ninety-five species of mammal and 500 species of birds and more recently has become famous for its species of tree-climbing lions. When I asked Janet to tell me something interesting about her past, without missing a breath she said: 'Maybe I can tell you about the time when a colleague and I almost got killed by three lions.'

'Excuse me?' I exclaimed, disbelief in my voice. 'Almost killed by three lions? Now, you already have the job, there is no need to tell stories, you hear!'

She smiled and insisted, 'It is a true story, sir. I was coming home one evening on the back of my workmate's *boda-boda*. As we were about to reach a bridge, we saw three lions lying on the side of the road. The gentleman I was with immediately panicked, stalled the bike and tried to jump off and run towards a tree.

'I fell next to the bike and just froze. One of the lions approached me and I just sat still. I thought that it was my day to die and I wondered why God had chosen for me to die like this,' she continued.

'I prayed that I would not show fear. The lion roared as it came closer and I could feel its warm breath over my head. At that point, I couldn't think clearly and I felt as though I was going to faint, but I kept very still as the lion circled the bike. I thought that if I remained still it would think that I was dead and not try to eat me. After a few minutes, and with all my muscles aching from the tension, the lion walked away and went and lay by the bridge with the other two lions.'

Her face had now grown serious, as though she was recounting an incident that had just happened a day earlier. 'I eventually found out that my colleague had fallen in a ditch and injured himself.'

They were saved by an armed park ranger who happened to be patrolling the area on his motorbike. He cocked his weapon, thinking that Janet was a poacher. When the lions heard the gun being cocked, they ran off. He came to where she was and pointed the weapon at her, at which point she protested loudly that she was not a poacher and he recognised her as one of the community conservation officers. The park ranger then agreed to escort them back to the nearest village. Her injured colleague couldn't ride the *boda-boda* back so Janet drove it while he travelled on the back of the park ranger's bike. When they got to the nearest village they hired a vehicle and Janet took her colleague to the hospital to have his leg looked at.

I sat in our dimly lit office as dusk was approaching trying to figure out whether or not to believe this incredible story. It sounded fantastic, an amazing survival story and immediately gave me the sense that this was a person I wanted to work with – courageous, motivated and innovative.

In the middle of October 2004, we expanded our field office with the arrival of Edirisa Sendagire, our new extension services manager. He was by far the oldest member of our team and had the most experience in the coffee sector, having worked at the Coffee Marketing Board (CMB) – the predecessor to the UCDA. Sendagire brought extensive knowledge of coffee quality management systems and immediately helped us develop the agronomy training manuals; he also oversaw the establishment of farmer groups. Shortly after, John Namisi agreed to join us from Mbale to help train the farmers in the wet processing system, and to spend the harvest seasons with us in Kasese. This was a big commitment for John, leaving his coffee farm and family to help us set up the new programme in Kasese. His sacrifice was also personal, as I later learned of his diabetic condition that required constant medication and a less stressful environment. But John insisted that he wanted to be there to get the training done.

Together, we began to make inroads in a number of sub-counties across the district. In November 2004, with the help of Sunday Mutabazi, we designed a farmer questionnaire that covered farmer information, marketing and aspects of coffee production and processing. This allowed us to get a sense of the scope of interventions needed in the area. We then carried out a random sampling across the coffee-growing region of the mountain.

Visiting the communities up in the mountains was a major logistical challenge as the road networks in the area are very poor. Access is generally by four-wheel-drive vehicle, although sometimes even then the roads are impassable. The steepness of the terrain and the gravel and dirt roads make certain parts of the mountain impassable during the rainy season. By the time we carried out the field assessments and data collection, we didn't yet have a company vehicle and carried out most of our field work on *boda-bodas*. These bikes are notorious for being involved in road accidents as they tend to be ridden by young, over-eager men trying to show off their riding skills with little regard for safety. My fears for the team's safety became very real when Janet was involved in a terrible accident in which she sustained injuries to her face and skin lacerations and was hospitalised for over a week in Kilembe.

By December, I had made several trips to Kasese to assess our field efforts on the ground and essentially to encourage, get feedback and energise the team. We began to organise the farmers into groups, by reaching out to the communities directly and inviting them to attend meetings which we held at local trading centres in each sub-county. In the beginning, our efforts seemed to elicit only a tepid response. Before our initial meetings, we would post announcements on the local radio stations encouraging farmers to come to what we called 'coffee farmer sensitisation and training' meetings. But those who showed up tended to be elderly women with their grandchildren. With this kind of response, I thought we would not make much headway. We called more meetings and made more radio announcements but the response remained the same – unenthusiastic. Eventually, we identified some local community leaders before whom we presented our model, established a dialogue and line of communication and then appealed to them to help us promote the model to the community. This broke the suspicions and cynicism. Without the early endorsement of several community leaders we would never have gained traction. Mzee Mukirane of Ibanda parish in Bugoye sub-county helped us mobilise our first successful farmer training sessions at the Ibanda Catholic playgrounds. Others, like Charles Kahitson from Rukoki sub-county, Deo Mugaya from Kyabarungira, Xavier Bwanandeke (Maliba sub-county) and the late Mugoha Julius from Kilembe were all instrumental in acting not just as community endorsers of the project but in many instances helping us with local coordination.

One farmer in particular stood out early on. I first met Charles Kahitson at the end of 2004, when we held a lunch for a dozen community leaders from Rukoki, Kilembe and Bugoye at the Margherita Hotel in Kasese. I wanted to use the meeting to speak with a smaller group who would then become active in transmitting the information to their communities and I also wanted to get feedback on where we were in the field. Over lunch, I laboured to explain the vision of the company and why we needed the community leaders' help in communicating this. As they sat quietly, I spoke about my own journey as a student in the UK where, over the years, I never saw products, let alone coffee, manufactured in Africa on supermarket shelves. I explained how this had bothered me for a long time because I believed that we were one of the most blessed continents in the world, with great wealth, people with enormous creativity, innovation and resilience and with the capacity to actually produce great coffees instead of just exporting the raw beans. I shared my frustration at Africans always being seen as nothing more than beggars, and the fact that this defined not only how Europeans in the West saw us but also how we saw each other sometimes: incapable, deprived, poor and hopeless. We could change this view. But it would require us to produce quality coffees consistently. And this was why the farmer training was critical. With their help, I told them, I was determined to make a change, however small, to alter this outlook. The project would only work if we did this together.

A young man who had been sitting quietly at the back put his hand up and asked to speak.

'My name is Charles Kahitson and I am from Nyakabingo in Rukoki sub-county. I want to tell you, Mr Andrew, that I am in fact a model farmer. If you have come to Kasese to work with model farmers then I am one and I am willing to work with you.'

'Thank you, Charles, and pleased to meet you. Can you help us get to know other model farmers like you with whom we can work with on this project?' I asked.

'Of course,' he responded instantly. 'If you people are serious, Mr Andrew, you will find the farmers here in Kasese district.'

With that exchange, a relationship was forged. Charles became a critical support member of our field operations. He helped us organise and strengthen our farmer groups in and around Nyakabingo and across other parts of Kasese. I visited Charles at his home several times and was struck by his self-assured manner and his confidence in his capacity to bring about transformation for himself and his community. He was a far cry from the frequently pandered image of a helpless African peasant farmer waiting for an outsider to come to his rescue and free him from the bondage of poverty. Here was Charles talking about partner-ship, about a relationship of empowerment. He helped us win the confidence of many other farmers. Charles lived in a mud-and-wattle house with a grass thatched roof. When we first met, he introduced me to his wife and children, one of whom was called Macmillan, apparently named after the publisher. When I asked Charles why he had chosen that particular name, he said that he thought that one day Macmillan would publish a book about him as a model farmer. Over the years, Charles became an example of the kind of transformation that could be realised by the farmers in our programmes. Two years later, he managed to construct a more permanent home and also get his children into good schools in Kasese town.

In January 2005, I hired two young students from Kasese, Obed Muhindo and Christine Birungi, to help with our data collection. The data included information on location, acreage under coffee planting and the number of trees per smallholder farm. By mid February, we had registered and trained forty-four producer organisations, and helped them organise elections for their leadership. The farmer groups elected a chairperson, vice chairperson, treasurer and a male and female trainer. John Namisi then assembled the hand pulpers for removing the pulp on the ripe coffee cherries and we distributed them to the established producer organisations.

Our first coffee-buying season, in March 2005, came with palpable excitement and some degree of anxiety. I had many questions: had we done enough preparation? Would we get a reasonable amount of quality coffee? I travelled to several group training locations across the mountain in Mahango, Kyarumba and Rukoki and Kilembe sub-counties. I remember in Mahango, I was approached by a stern-looking lady who challenged me to confirm that the premium price we had offered was actually what they would receive at the buying stores in Kasese town. The buying stores are where farmers deliver their coffee and we purchase it. Our field officers, procurement team, quality team and farmer liaison staff are there for the buying season.

As the stern lady quizzed me, she kept wagging her finger at me. I was not sure whether we were having an altercation or a discussion. She said that she had suffered at the hands of many unscrupulous middlemen who promised one thing at the beginning of the season but never delivered on their promises. Was I one of them? The more she raised her voice, the more a crowd grew around. I tried to assuage her fears, to convince her that we were different and that she would soon see this when she started delivering the coffee. I could understand why she felt this way and all I hoped was that she would give us the opportunity to prove ourselves by delivering the coffee to our stores. She walked away without making a commitment. Other sceptical farmers looked on in amusement.

The next day, there was tremendous joy when Mzee Erikana Bwambale, a member of the Nyakabingo producer organisation, became our first farmer to deliver coffee to our stores. Two days later, as I mingled with staff outside the buying stores, I saw the woman from Mahango – the one who had given me that very public questioning – deliver 1 tonne of coffee. It was the largest single delivery by a farmer that month. I was grateful for her faith. Over the next six weeks we received over 6 tonnes of good quality coffees from over thirty producer groups of fifty farmers each.

Our first coffee consignment was loaded and taken to Kampala to the Cooperative Union in Kawempe for dehusking, cleaning and bagging. At that time, we didn't have a roaster in place and we were using a South African roaster for our coffees. The 6 tonnes we bought was not large enough to ship to South Africa. So, I found a local exporter who would buy the coffee from us, and we continued to buy Ugandan coffees from an importer in South Africa for our needs; a cruel irony that never left me.

After our first buying season, we continued to recruit farmers in producer organisations in other sub-counties. Our team expanded to include Bob Mugisha, a cousin of mine, who helped us with logistics. We recruited three interns from Kasese: Kabugho Judith, Didas Baluku and Ithungu Sadress. Our field trips continued using locally hired vehicles and *boda-bodas*, but their constant mechanical failures, especially in remote locations, began to affect our operations. On one occasion, a hired vehicle broke down on the way back from a training session in Mahango.

The team was stranded inside the Queen Elizabeth National Park for a whole night. Despite Janet and Didas' brave efforts – they walked seven kilometres trying to reach a trading centre where they would get assistance – they ended up sleeping in the saloon vehicle in a part of the park frequented by wild animals. The next day they managed to contact Sunday Mutabazi, who happened to be in Kasese town, and he came and picked them up. On another occasion, as the team drove back from high up in Kyarumba the vehicle they were travelling in lost its lights and the team had to use handheld torches as the vehicle crawled down the steep mountain. It would be a year later before we acquired our own pick-up truck and when we did even the farmers came down to the office to celebrate, excited at the acquisition and somewhat relieved too.

By the time the second coffee-buying season came around in August 2005, we had completed our registration of the farmer groups right up to the border with the Democratic Republic of Congo. In mid August we halted all our field visits to focus on the buying of coffee, and by the end of the season we had bought over 54 tonnes of coffee. This was a special season for us because in June 2005 we launched our coffees in Waitrose and became the first African-owned coffee brand to sell direct into British stores. This success gave the team tremendous encouragement. Then in January 2006, we acquired our first field office computer dedicated to our Management Information System (MIS), developed by our systems developer Tharcisse Maniraho. The system captured coffee deliveries by farmer, location, producer organisation and gender. Tharcisse brought both system and procedure to the large amounts of data we were collecting from the field. Not only was his arrival of great strategic value but, being older than most of us in the team, he became a source of wise counsel and encouragement for the younger team members.

In the field, we began to appreciate that given the seasonality of coffee, there was insufficient farmer group cohesion. Between seasons, farmers seldom met and some dropped out of the washed coffee programme altogether, while others complained that the pulpers were not enough for all the group members. Also, our field team-to-farmer ratio was very low; we only had five active field officers and one sub-county coordinator for over 14,000 farmers in seventeen sub-counties. This remained a big challenge. The issue of pulpers was also a constant strain. Initially, we had given the pulpers out as demonstration kits in the anticipation that once the technology was adopted the farmers would buy their own. But it was becoming evident that an increasing number of farmers were asking for the hand pulpers. We were now faced with the same dependency symptom we had earlier identified and critiqued.

We tried to increase our communication with the farmers and encouraged them to look to each other as the sustainable route to purchasing pulpers, through pooled savings in the Savings and Credit Cooperatives we helped them set up. We encouraged them to meet regularly and not just during the coffee season. The SACCOs were also the best strategy to dislodge the village loan sharks and their pernicious mortgaging of farmers' coffee farms and charging exorbitant interest rates. We supported the SACCOs with financial literacy training, basic office furniture and financial manuals and bookkeeping. By 2010, we had seventeen fully operational SACCOs boosting the farmers' savings culture and providing micro loans to those in need. The SACCOs were not only owned by the farmers but operated and managed by them too.

4 Markets

---

*Each generation must, out of relative obscurity, discover its
mission, fulfil it, or betray it.*
   Frantz Fanon

While logistical difficulties and poor infrastructure frustrate trade
between African countries, they also undermine the capabilities
of African exporters to competitively deliver goods and services
to the global market. According to the World Trade Organisation,
intra-African trade accounts for less than 10 per cent of total trade.[1]
African countries also maintain some of the highest tariffs in the
world, which contributes to this low intra-regional trade.
However, these problems are further compounded by tariff and
non-tariff barriers (NTBs) in the markets of the developed countries. While some progress has been made on eliminating a range
of tariff barriers through a number of trade agreements, like the
European Union Economic Partnership Agreements (EPAs),
Everything but Arms (EBA) and the United States' Africa Growth
Opportunities Act (AGOA), much remains to be done on
removing the many NTBs and subsidies given to the agricultural
sector in the developed countries that make international trade
unequal. The scale of OECD (Organisation for Economic
Cooperation and Development) member state subsidies to their

own farmers, for example, is approximately $350 billion per year, which is one-fifth of Africa's total GDP.[2] The Economic Commission for Africa states that 'there has been a resurgence of NTBs, especially regarding the use of a "new generation" of import controls by the industrialised nations, such as antidumping measures and phytosanitary, labour and environmental standards'.[3] As an Oxfam report on trade declared: 'The problem is not that international trade is inherently opposed to the needs and interests of the poor, but that the rules that govern it are rigged in favour of the rich.'[4]

There are other kinds of NTBs that are seldom mentioned in policy meetings or documented in any meaningful way, and yet they remain big barriers to trade for African exporters. These include restrictions on international movement of people through difficult entry visa procedures, entrenched negative perceptions of the continent and the attendant 'trust deficit', the cost of market entry, a 'knowledge deficit' that many exporters face when seeking market entry, and the constant shifting of technical goalposts regarding product packaging, labelling and certifications. I spent most of 2004 and 2005 trying to break into the South African and UK markets and experiencing many barriers that I hadn't anticipated – barriers that demanded perseverance and adaptability, barriers that undermine the efforts of many entrepreneurs.

SOUTH AFRICA

On Thursday 9 March 2004, we became the first Ugandan coffee brand to be sold in South Africa when Shoprite Checkers, the leading supermarket chain, agreed to retail our roast and ground coffees. Our three inaugural coffee products – 'Prestige', 'Gold' and 'Classic' – were branded under the 'Rwenzori Finest Coffee' label (which was the company's original name before it became Good African in 2005), and the roasting and packing of the coffee was outsourced to a roaster in Cape Town. The build-up to this entry into the South African market exposed us to the many challenges of a start-up export business and the realities of trading on the African continent. As pointed out earlier, trade between African states currently stands at less than 10 per cent of the region's total trade.[5] In comparison, 40 per cent of North America's trade is with regional partners, and the rate soars to 63 per cent in Western Europe.[6]

Over one hundred guests gathered on a cool March morning at the beautiful Arabella Sheraton hotel in Cape Town for our launch. After months of developing packaging designs, sourcing packing materials, finding a local roaster, getting the green light from Shoprite to list the product in their stores, what began a year before as a conversation with the Shoprite Checkers chief executive Whitey Basson in the back of my car from Entebbe airport to Kampala was now a reality.

Jackie and our kids had come down with me and so too did my mother and younger sister Judy. Several friends from Uganda also flew down to Cape Town. Henry Ngabirano, the managing director of UCDA, helped secure the attendance of the Minister of Trade and Industry from Uganda, Professor Edward Rugumayo, and his permanent secretary and the chairman of the UCDA, Paulo Mugambwa. On the South African side, the trade minister at the time, Alec Erwin, and members of his ministry attended the event. The Shoprite team, led by their chief executive, were also in attendance. The event management and publicity were handled by a small but extremely efficient company called Peridot Communications. Their media networks helped us get strong coverage in the South African papers after the event.

There were four brief speeches and the event gave me my first opportunity to unveil our 'trade not aid' message. Basson spoke about Shoprite's commitment to promoting more African products in its stores and his pride in working to get Ugandan coffees on their shelves. Both Alec Erwin and Professor Rugumayo spoke about strengthening trade between Uganda and South Africa; the South African minister even offered us the opportunity to set up a coffee shop at their Ministry of Trade campus in Pretoria. Peter Chappell, a film producer and long-time friend from London who helped us build our still and video archive, flew in from London to film the event and produce our first corporate video.

Our coffees could never have entered the South African market had it not been for my relationship with Shoprite Checkers. Social and commercial networks are so critical in building trading opportunities in any territory and it is one of the key determinants of market entry. Who you know and how you can leverage that relationship are critical elements in the building of commercial opportunities and highlight the importance of social networks. While at VR Promotions, I did some consultancy work for Shoprite; helping them with their investments in Uganda. Part of this work involved identifying ideal locations for their retail stores. In mid 2003, CEO Whitey Basson arrived in Kampala with his team. Part of their itinerary was to visit the site they had recently acquired for their second supermarket and also to pay a courtesy call to President Yoweri Museveni of Uganda at State House, Kampala. I had not met Basson before, but I knew that his visit to Uganda was important and that I had to make a good impression, first by ensuring a smooth arrival and, second, by doing everything possible to avoid the long waiting times that guests usually endured before seeing the president. To make matters worse for me, Basson would only be in town for about five hours.

Together with the Shoprite team in Kampala, I began making arrangements for this visit weeks in advance. Simon Ajiku, a protocol officer in the president's office, was particularly helpful in guiding me through the complicated process of arranging Basson's appointment with the president. If the protocol issues were not complex enough, the question of security caused a downright stir in my office on the day of Basson's arrival. That morning, three plain-clothes security personnel showed up at my office at 7.30 in the morning armed with AK-47s and asked my administrative secretary, Jennifer, where 'Director Rugasira' was. They were unwilling to discuss the reasons why they wanted to see me. On being told that I was not yet in, they then requested to be shown to a waiting room. Jennifer called me on my cellphone and nervously told me that there were men with guns waiting to see me, and she didn't know exactly what they wanted.

When I arrived I found three tall, slim young men seated in the boardroom looking very much out of place. Just then, as one of them introduced himself, I realised that they were the protective detail assigned to Basson for the duration of his visit. This was a privilege that was sometimes accorded to important VIPs visiting with the head of state. We headed to the airport.

Basson and his team arrived on their corporate jet and the immigration officials did a good job processing them quickly. As I rode with Basson in the back seat, I began to think when the right moment would be to ask him about whether he might consider retailing my coffee brand in his stores. Basson is a soft-spoken man with an unassuming manner. His eyes are focused and sharp but unintimidating. Sitting next to him, one would not imagine that this is the business titan that built Shoprite into a 600-plus-store retail giant across fifteen African countries and with an annual turnover equivalent to Uganda's GDP. I had many questions I wanted to ask him. But I had to contain myself, remain calm and wait for the right moment. Our first stop was the Shoprite store in downtown Kampala, where he chatted easily with the local team and toured the store. A couple of hours later we made the short journey to State House in Kampala, the president's official workplace and residence.

Driving into State House is quite an experience. Firstly, the place is a fortress of heavily armed guards and an impressive amount of defensive military hardware. The entry procedures are elaborate and so is the protocol. You are stopped at the main gate, your names checked against the guest list for the day. Further in, another gate awaits you where more checks are carried out. Despite all this, there was a calmness about the place that surprised me. People go about their work in a quiet and orderly manner. I expected the place to be a hive of frenetic activity, with people running up and down, stressed and harassed. Not here, it seemed.

Simon Ajiku met us at the gate, welcomed us, then walked us to the main building and up the stairs to the president's conference room. As soon as we arrived on the first floor, we were immediately ushered into a very large meeting room with a massive rectangular table that could accommodate close to fifty people. The president stood at one end of the table with his eyes fixed on us and his hand outstretched as we walked the fifteen or so paces it took to get from the entrance of the room to where he was standing. On his left was the minister of state responsible for investment in the Ministry of Finance, Hon Sam Kutesa, and one of the president's assistants.

Basson was excited to meet the president, having heard much about him and his stewardship of the impressive economic recovery of the country. By the time Museveni had been sworn in on 26 January 1986 as the eighth president of Uganda since independence from Britain in 1962, the economy was in a deep crisis. Rampant inflation had risen relentlessly to 150 per cent per annum; export earnings had collapsed and at one point amounted to only $320 million or $20 per capita. There was a cumulative drop in Gross National Product (GNP) with disastrous ramifications, giving rise to an economy of underutilisation, scarcity of consumer goods and low wages, which all had the aggregate impact of negating growth. When he took power, after waging a five-year guerrilla armed struggle, it was refreshing to see a president who was intellectually astute, serious about tackling national issues and keen on bringing the country together.

Museveni was credited with overseeing the economic recovery

and growth on average of 6 per cent per annum. This ushered in a tremendous amount of private-sector activity. Although his political groundings were leftist, he had immediately pivoted to the right and quickly embraced the Structural Adjustment Program and reform package designed by the IMF. In the process, he became not only the darling of the western donors, who showered his government with over $13 billion of foreign aid over the years, but also a champion for some of the reform prescriptions on the continent. Elective politics returned to Uganda in 1996 but Museveni continued to dominate the political landscape both by outsmarting his opponents and by being adept at presenting himself as the only serious option Ugandans could count on to further the peace and prosperity that was ushered in after 1986. Even when the war in Northern Uganda against the Lord's Resistance Army (LRA) continued to plague the government, he remained both popular and relatively well respected.

But the meeting in June 2003 was not about politics but about business – it was between a South African investor and a head of state. The latter strongly encouraged and supported investors to come to Uganda and the meeting was a courtesy call for Basson to show his appreciation of that support. It would also give him an opportunity to discuss several challenges to doing business in the country. The president seemed relaxed and he started the discussion enquiring whether the Shoprite that Whitey Basson headed was indeed the US-based Shoprite. Basson politely said it wasn't; this Shoprite was South African.

'Really? I thought you were part of the American group,' the president insisted.

Again, Basson gently said it was not.

'Oh, I thought you were the American group. I think I have seen Shoprite in America. Isn't it there?' he pressed.

Basson politely repeated his answer that Shoprite was a South African company.

'Ok.' The president seemed to reluctantly concede.

This wasn't the opening to the meeting I'd had in mind. The conversation moved on to the progress on the second Shoprite development, in which the president had intervened to cut the bureaucratic delays that had entangled the land acquisition for the project. An interesting discussion then followed about what Shoprite was doing to stock more Ugandan products. Basson assured him about his company's commitment to source more locally and also to consider exporting Ugandan products to the South African market.

As we walked back to the public car park outside the compound, I noticed how manicured the gardens were and again the calm and serene atmosphere. I almost forgot about those gleaming AK-47s on the shoulders of the young guards.

While heading back to the airport we talked a little about the meeting and I asked Basson about his impressions of President Museveni. He was clearly impressed and added that he was happy to find out that his views were consistent with what he had heard about the man. I then turned to the topic of my coffee project. I outlined my vision for working with small-scale farmers, developing a coffee brand built on a philosophy of trade as opposed to aid and with our key pillars being empowerment of the producer community and owning the value-addition processing in Uganda. With Shoprite behind us, we could build a truly African-owned and distributed brand. Basson listened attentively, and then asked me what experience I had in the coffee industry.

I did not have coffee industry experience, but what I did have was marketing and brand-building capabilities from my time at VR Promotions. I was sure that a brand with a social mission would be an attractive and viable commercial proposition. I was certain that I could build a successful coffee brand. I also said that we would initially outsource our roasting operations to a South African company as we built our knowledge and capacity to roast the coffees in Uganda. He promised to work on it and see how they could support us. 'I must warn you,' he added, 'the coffee business is not an easy one.'

With that conversation came my first break into the South African market. It took months of meetings with Shoprite buyers and presentations on brand design and strategy, which took me to Cape Town frequently. On several occasions, I would call on Basson to intervene when the project was losing momentum. During one such meeting with buyers in his office, I entered with a coffee brewer and some sample packs of our coffee and asked if I could make some for Basson. Watched by his team, I brewed and served the coffee. The atmosphere in the room that afternoon seemed to change for the better as we sipped our drinks.

Between August 2003 and the launch in March 2004, I worked with various service providers – brand designers, PR and marketing companies – as the project began to gain momentum. I was fortunate to meet an energetic and straight-talking coffee roaster in Cape Town called John Lear. John helped us beyond just roasting our coffee; he developed our first coffee roast profile and also connected us to the local packaging companies that were initially reluctant to deal with me because I lacked business roots in South Africa. I met John through Niell Coetzee, also a Cape Town-based entrepreneur who runs a family business exporting Rooibos tea and other herbal teas to Europe. Niell helped me manage the initial business set-up in Cape Town and the orders from Shoprite. He was also helpful in connecting me to other local service providers that enabled us to trade in the country.

The Cape Town launch brought with it tremendous publicity in both the South African and the Ugandan press. This was encouraging but never quite led to the level of sales that we expected. After several months of trading, it became clear that unless we could inject more capital into the business, to market, promote and activate the brand, our presence in South Africa was going to be very difficult. Shoprite themselves began to demand that we invest in marketing activities to generate repeat purchases and customer loyalty. We just didn't have the capital for this. And because our sales were not growing in line with projections, generating the interest and support of the bankers was a real challenge. Originally, my plan was to use the platform and credibility of the Shoprite launch to penetrate other retailers like Pick N Pay and SPAR quickly, while also looking to the massive market potential for single-serve coffees that were hugely successful in India and other Asian markets. I saw a big opportunity to introduce single-serve coffees in small packets, in places like Soweto, the most populous black urban residential area in the country, where I could target a huge pool of low-income consumers.

Eventually, the orders became more and more difficult to generate and fulfil, and I couldn't mount a meaningful marketing campaign. Sixteen months after our launch into Shoprite, and after much internal debate, I decided to withdraw from the South African market and set my eyes on the UK. It was not just a higher-value coffee market but it was also a territory that I was already familiar with, having lived there as a student. I also thought that our trade-not-aid message would resonate there. The withdrawal from South Africa was painful. So much effort, energy, trust and goodwill had gone into it. Withdrawing also undermined my own credibility and made me question whether it had been wrong to embark on a journey without adequate financial resources. I sought encouragement not just in my faith but in the numerous business stories that chronicled many entrepreneurs who struggled in the early years of their businesses. I resolved to fight on. The UK would be the breakthrough market I was looking for.

UNITED KINGDOM

We began planning for our UK launch in early 2005. Baroness Lynda Chalker graciously offered to host a reception for us at the Cholmondeley Room in the House of Lords in Westminster. Lynda has always been a friend and champion of many positive initiatives in Africa, right from the time when she was Minister for Overseas Development in the Conservative government of John Major. I met her at Swithin Munyantwali's house in Kampala in early 2004. Over dinner, I shared our plans for our coffee business and some of the challenges we were facing. Lynda immediately offered her support and promised that such an important initiative needed backing from Africa's friends in Britain. She became a staunch supporter; making introductions or co-inviting guests to the launch. When people received an invite from the office of Baroness Chalker of Wallasey it tended to have more impact than one from the desk of Andrew Rugasira, CEO of Good African Coffee.

The House of Lords was not an obvious venue for the UK launch of a small, untested African coffee company. Those who were sceptical found it difficult to believe we could pull it off. However, on Wednesday 8 June 2005, the day before our reception, the *Guardian* agreed to publish an op-ed article I wrote that summarised the speech I was to give at the launch. Until that point, I had never published an opinion piece. To write for a leading UK daily like the *Guardian* was nothing short of a miracle. This came out of a meeting Peter Chappell arranged for me with Duncan Campbell, a respected staff writer at the paper. On the afternoon of 7 June, I met with the engaging, silver-haired Duncan in central London. I gave him a rundown of the argument I would be making the next day, and he immediately agreed to speak to the editors at the paper and get back to me. Even after I had emailed him the speech, I didn't hold out much hope that anything would come of it.

That evening, Peter called me at my hotel frantically asking me to cut down the speech to about seven hundred words because the *Guardian* had agreed to run it. I was stunned. The timing couldn't have been better. Prime Minister Tony Blair was hosting the G8 Summit at the time and most of the discussions centred on getting the G8 countries to give more aid to Africa. A plethora of celebrities, from Bono to Bob Geldof, were all energetically doing Africa's bidding, either by hosting large concerts or by cajoling the leaders of the developed world to do more for the continent. My op-ed piece turned out to be a good opportunity to share a perspective that *Guardian* readers seldom came across: one from an African entrepreneur.

I had much to say. The billions of dollars that Africa has received in foreign aid after the Second World War has done more to stifle the creativity of the continent's entrepreneurs, creating a chronic dependency, than to foster sustainable economic growth. Conditionalities attached to aid disbursements typically become tools in an ideological warfare. Recipient countries have to adopt policy prescriptions designed by experts thousands of miles away or forfeit the handouts. This has undermined the sovereignty of many African governments. The politics of the aid industry demonstrate how enormous power and influence are conferred on the donor to the point that the leadership in African governments are more accountable to the donors than to their own citizens.

If an African finance minister in an aid-dependent country is really candid, they tell you that dealing with donors is closer to being told what to do than the collaborative partnership that is falsely presented in public. This paternalistic attitude of the donors invariably informs and determines the policy architecture in favour of donor politics and the outlook of their bureaucrats. Most key government departments in African countries – such as the Treasury, the Ministry of Finance and the Central Bank – have donor expatriates either as advisors or as overseers, or both. It therefore was not surprising that during the G8 Summit in Gleneagles, the voices that analysed and offered solutions to the continent's problems belonged to European specialists. There was no significant African voice to be heard at the time.

Most Africans are fed up with lectures, double standards and the paternalism of so-called 'African specialists' who reinforce the image of Africa as the 'white man's burden'. This attitude, which underpins much of the aid industry and its bureaucrats, will always compromise even those well-intentioned community interventions being undertaken by some NGOs. Development is a partnership, not an imposition, and the G8 countries never developed under such conditions. But African political leaders need to shape up, too. They continue to mortgage the future of our children through destructive systems of misrule that foster corruption, create conflict and undermine democracy and good governance. These kleptocrats prosecute useless and destructive wars that decimate communities and set their nations back for decades. They have significantly contributed to the current under-development on the continent and allowed the ease with which the donors can politically influence affairs on the continent.

Even when donors genuinely complain about the poor govern-ance and corruption of African states, Professor William Easterly observes that this itself creates 'an intractable dilemma: stick with the government as the primary partner and provide funds with no strings attached, even if it means money winding up propping auto-crats or attach strings and try to "fix" the government, meaning that outsiders with little local knowledge are dictating how other people should run their own societies.'[7] Aid further erodes accountability because aid agencies have an institutional incentive to disburse funds. Pressure to meet targets and even overlook procedural flaws in how donor programmes are structured have led to damaging results in some instances.[8] When borrowers know that donors will lend irrespective of their actions, the conditions attached to aid lose credibility. The *Economist* eloquently captured this point:

Over the past few years Kenya has performed a curious mating ritual with its aid donors. The steps are: one, Kenya wins its yearly pledges of foreign aid. Two, the government begins to misbehave, backtracking on economic reform and behaving in an authoritarian manner. Three, a new meeting of donor countries looms with exasperated foreign governments preparing their sharp rebukes. Four, Kenya pulls a placatory rabbit out of the hat. Five, the donors are mollified and the aid is pledged. The whole dance then repeated again.[9]

As an entrepreneur, I have witnessed first hand the transforming role of trade in creating wealth and fostering community development. When I started Good African Coffee, we set out to achieve four goals: one, to recognise our growers, customers, employees and shareholders as stakeholders and part of our quadruple bottom line; two, to bring the finest coffees to market bought directly from our growers at prices that ensure that they make a profitable return on their harvest; three, to transform the stereotypical 'basket case' image of Africa by being an example of entrepreneurial success and community transformation; and four, to create value for our stakeholders by re-investing a percentage of our net profits in sustainable community empowerment interventions in agronomy and the development of saving and credit cooperatives.

Africans do not sit around idle as they try to live on $1 a day. In fact, they wake up every morning seeking ways to create wealth for themselves and their families. Our farmers know they can get a better price for their coffee. So, even when we offer a premium price for their excellent arabica coffee, they bargain hard before they part with their precious beans. The business case is simple: my suppliers are my partners, and they impact my bottom line. Investing in them is investing in our business future. It is not smart marketing, it is just smart business.

But this all means nothing if African exporters cannot access high-value markets for their finished products. The most significant challenge to the export-led growth strategy is the limited access that Africa's few exporters have to foreign markets and the very nature of the markets themselves. Free and open markets are not the norm for most commodities that Africa exports, and nearly all those that are targeted, are controlled, distorted or simply closed. In the face of these controlled markets, African countries face the distinct problem of very little value addition on the continent. For example, even where European Union Economic Partnership Agreements with Africa are in place and they waive a whole range of tariffs, the cost of capital, technology transfer and lack of highly skilled personnel hampers African export opportunities. It is also likely that even under EPAs, exporters from Africa will face stringent rules-of-origin, which determine the number of exports that fall within the category preferential treatment. Ultimately they will also be competing with heavily subsidised European producers and manufacturers.[10]

The significance of value addition cannot be understated. Coffee illustrates this point well. One needs approximately 5 to 7 grams of ground coffee to brew a cup at your local coffee shop. An average cup of coffee sells for £2, which means that a kilogram of roasted and ground coffee would produce about 200 cups of coffee at a point-of-sale value of £400. Green coffee beans are bought on average by large multinational buyers for a top average price of £2 per kilo (at mid 2011 prices). Therefore, less than 0.5 per cent of the value of processed coffee sold in a café is retained at source by the producers. The United States – which doesn't grow much coffee (apart from in Hawaii) – is the largest coffee market, worth approximately $40 billion per year. Most of this consumption is supported by a huge value-addition industry that employs millions of people and keeps thousands of entrepreneurs in business.[11]

When African exporters compare their reception in the export markets with that given to western entrepreneurs travelling to Africa, there is a huge difference. The western investor is most likely to be welcomed by an official, if not a senior officer, from the local Investment Authority, with all the encouragement as to why this individual has made the right decision to come to the country to do business. Investors are then able to meet a relevant line minister and probably on the second or third trip even the president of the country. African leaders spend a lot of time meeting investors and while it is their responsibility as the head of state to encourage foreign direct investment, in many instances these are not investors but opportunists in fine clothing carrying

briefcases with business plans that rarely deliver on their promises. Not only is trade unfair in the western markets, this inequality
is exacerbated by the preferential treatment foreign entrepreneurs
receive when they visit many African capitals.

An exporter seeking to operate in most western capitals must
first get through the unpredictable process of obtaining an entry
visa, which must be the most offputting way of welcoming a
visitor to one's country. Applicants are peppered with seemingly
absurd questions and assumptions: to paraphrase one rejection
letter from the British Embassy communicated to me by a friend
who was married with four children, had a full-time job and refer-
ences from both his company and the people he was going to
visit: 'these documents lead me to doubt, on the balance of prob-
abilities, that you are a genuine visitor'. If, on the other hand, you
are a nurse or medical specialist whose skills are in demand in the
UK, then an entry visa is not an issue and of course you can be
entrusted with the most intimate physical care of British patients.
It seems that if it suits the government's needs, entry visas are not
a problem.

After the memorable encounter with Her Majesty's foreign
embassy, the next hurdle for the African exporter is trying to
reach a marketplace for their products. The UK supermarket
trade is valued at over £120 billion per annum. If African products
could obtain a 10 per cent market share of all products sold in the
UK supermarkets then that would represent £12 billion of annual
income, which is slightly over 30 per cent of the total foreign
direct investment that Africa received in 2008. If, on the other
hand, Africa's trade with the rest of the world increased to 1 per
cent of total world exports, it would be worth over $120 billion –
three times the total aid flows in 2008.[12]

The response to the *Guardian* op-ed piece was extraordinary. I
received over 1,000 emails expressing gratitude and encouragement. The article gave the company a good profile. I subsequently
wrote other pieces for the *Telegraph* and the *Financial Times*, the

latter with Michael Holman, the former Africa editor. The coverage was invaluable in building an awareness of the Good African brand in the UK. Now it was time to build on the success we'd had with Waitrose, and to get our products into more stores.

On a cold January morning in 2006, I walked into the London headquarters of J Sainsbury, the second largest retail chain in the United Kingdom. This was my first meeting with Sainsbury's and my mission that morning was to convince the buyers to retail our coffees throughout their network of supermarkets. Good African Coffee was poised to become the first African-owned coffee brand to be sold direct from Uganda to Sainsbury's.

Their London headquarters is an imposing glass building near the legal district and Lincoln's Inn. The magnificent St Paul's Cathedral looms in the background. Although it was winter, the sun was out and shone brightly through the building's glass facade, making the foyer inordinately bright. As I approached the entrance, I tugged at my rucksack, which held my laptop for my presentation, and neatened my suit and tie. First impressions matter a great deal, especially if you are a businessman from Africa.

I attended the meeting with Robert Wiltshire, the commercial director at LDH (La Doria), my distributors, and Peter Chappell. LDH is a major player in the supply of private label products (supermarket-branded) to most leading supermarkets in Britain. It was through LDH's retail connections that we had already managed to launch our coffees into Waitrose. Peter came along to explore the possibility of filming a documentary about our journey from the Rwenzori Mountains to the British supermarket shelf. We thought that the Good African story could make an interesting documentary.

Robert and Peter were already in the foyer by the time I arrived. We went straight to the front desk where we identified ourselves, and we were tagged and then ushered to the guest waiting area. I have often sensed a degree of anxiety in these waiting areas. The modest space is often filled with suppliers sitting patiently, clutching presentation folders or product samples, while others are engaged in last-minute presentation rehearsals. You can't help but contrast this with the brimming confidence of the supermarket buyers as they approach their visitors; and there is good reason for this. If your products are sold in supermarkets then the buyers are crucial to your business. They can make your day by listing your product, expanding your product range and store distribution – or break it by delisting your product, insisting on a higher margin or deeper commitments for product promotions. That morning, I didn't even have a foot in the door, so my anxiety was a little more accentuated than the other folks in the waiting area. I had many hopes pinned on this meeting and I thought that given our presence in Waitrose we would be able to close the deal quite quickly. However, that meeting was to be the first of five. The cost of travel to the UK was weighing heavily on our limited finances. Our market exploration costs, of which this meeting was emblematic, far outweighed the income we were receiving from our sales in Waitrose. Yet there was no cheaper way of doing it. Dispatching product samples with a covering letter just wouldn't do and I knew it, because I had spent several months writing letters to supermarkets and never once got a reply. It was clear that I needed to make these trips but they came at a cost.

My thoughts were interrupted by the arrival of the two gentlemen we were there to meet – a young buyer and his boss. They greeted Robert, whom they knew, and then Peter and me, and led the way down a short corridor to our meeting room. As we sat down, I took out my laptop to open my presentation while Michael Holman asked Peter what he did. As soon as Peter explained that he was exploring the possibility of filming a documentary on our coffee's journey to their shelves, it became apparent that neither Peter's presence nor his ideas were particularly welcome. Supermarkets are not very comfortable with film projects; especially those that they haven't originated. There is an inherent risk with such a project and the concern for the retailers is that they can end up looking bad. Michael resisted the suggestion and gently reminded us that we were getting ahead of ourselves because nothing had been agreed at that stage. It wasn't an auspicious start.

I began the presentation that I had made a dozen times: Africa needs trade opportunities and not aid handouts to create wealth for its people. The continent has received over one trillion dollars in the last five decades, with very little to show for it except chronic dependency on handouts, a stifling of the entrepreneurial spirit of its people and the perpetuation of the image of Africa as a basket case. Despite what many donors and celebrity activists say, the transformation of African economies can only be achieved by Africans; not from handouts and sympathy but through African creativity, innovation and hard work. If Sainsbury's lists Good African Coffee, you will be helping Africans help themselves and in the most sustainable way possible. I went on: African entrepreneurs have global business exposure and, given the chance, have the ability to deliver quality products that will meet your consumers' expectations. To date, Good African has managed to gain a listing in Waitrose stores and has shown that it is able to manage its UK supply chain efficiently. If only Sainsbury's can accept our coffees, it would allow the thousands of coffee farmers we work with in Uganda to make a profitable return on their harvest and enable us to bring about transformation in our farming communities. Charity is appreciated, but trade is better. Instead of feeling sorry for Africa, well-meaning celebrities should help us fight for better access to international markets.

I pointed out how, in all the celebrity-driven campaigns in the run up to the G8 Summit in Gleneagles in 2005, and the Live Aid concerts in Hyde Park, London, there was an embarrassing absence of African voices. Across television, radio and the press, the case for Africa was typically being made by non-

Africans. As I drew to a close, I handed out our coffee samples and hoped that I hadn't let my 'celebrities-for-Africa' critique cloud my presentation. Nevertheless, I felt it was an important point that needed to be made, as Paul Theroux had pointed out in an op-ed piece in the *New York Times* just a month before: '. . . because Africa seems unfinished and so different from the rest of the world, a landscape on which a person can sketch a new personality, it attracts mythomaniacs, people who wish to convince the world of their worth. Such people come in all forms and they loom large. White celebrities busybodying in Africa loom especially large.'

I thanked them for listening and waited for their feedback. The boss was the first to respond. 'Well done, that was an articulate presentation, and done in exactly twenty minutes as you promised, congratulations.' I suddenly felt like I was back in high school being patted on the back by my teacher. The room was quiet. He then put forward some of the reasons why African products found it difficult to enter supermarkets: poor quality, lack of consistency, reliability issues with supply among others. This was a genuine but familiar lament; and indeed I have heard of many situations where African businessmen have made a mess of good trade opportunities. I pushed back on this argument as gently as I could. I said that while I appreciated his concerns, each case needed to be judged on its own merit. In our case we were already stocked in Waitrose and therefore had a solid track record. We moved on to discuss the coffee category review dates, and when a possible opportunity to list a new product might arise. We closed the meeting with only their promise to get back to us 'soon'. As I folded my laptop, unplugged my power cables and began to pack up, I suggested that they go ahead of us as I didn't want to keep them waiting. 'We will wait because, you see, we English are polite,' the boss said and he held the door open for us. Robert and Peter glanced at each other. We left quietly, handed in our badges at the front desk and headed to the nearest café. I was unsure what the result of that meeting would be, but I was determined that Sainsbury's would stock our coffee on their shelves.

THE UNITED STATES OF AMERICA

In May 2000, the United States House of Congress passed trade support legislation to assist the economies in sub-Saharan Africa to access the lucrative US markets. President Clinton signed into law what became known as the African Growth Opportunities Act (AGOA). This initiative offered African economies incentives to promote free markets and also benefit from duty-free exports in the United States. It was well received not just by leaders in Africa but also by business executives who saw it as an opportunity to boost trade with the United States. However, very quickly it became clear to African entrepreneurs that it was one thing to pass such a commendable piece of legislation and quite another to operationalise its opportunity to generate business interest in African products. Unprocessed primary commodities, typically agricultural products, have always been imported into the US, processed in an environment of cheap capital and huge agricultural subsidies and then either consumed or re-exported as finished products. So African-processed and -branded products trying to enter the market are not only breaking decades of unequal, unjust and unfair trading systems, but even with their best efforts they will always be trying to catch up with much more advanced and sophisticated product manufacturing and delivery systems.

Part of the solution lies again in appreciating non-tariff barriers. Market access without production, logistical and marketing capabilities doesn't lead to the AGOA trade opportunity being fully realised. Since its enactment, AGOA countries have increased their exports from $23 billion in 2000 to a peak of $81 billion in 2008.[13] However, the majority of these exports are energy related, primarily oil and gas. AGOA could have more impact and stimulate African exports if it also addressed the constraints facing Africa's small to medium enterprises exporters. Mitigating trade asymmetries is a complex matter that goes beyond market access legislation; it must address historical distortions that undermine the market access of African countries.

Between April 2004 and March 2011, I made eleven trips to the US seeking to establish a presence in the North American market. Initially, my trips made sense because it was relatively cheap to cross the Atlantic from the UK. The short exploratory visits quickly evolved into more serious efforts to forge a business relationship with one of the most influential and oldest African–American church organisations, known as the Church of God in Christ (COGIC). This Memphis-based Episcopalian network of over 50,000 churches is headed by the influential Presiding Bishop Charles E. Blake. The concept was to link the African–American community with African business on the continent. In 2009, through a speaking engagement at the Global Leadership Summit at Pastor Bill Hybels' Willow Creek Community Church in Illinois, I came closer to the dream of our coffees being sold in the US. Our hosts during the visit, Jerry and Jan Kehe, became our connection to one of the largest distribution companies in the US and our eventual entry into the market. By the end of 2011, our coffee was available online throughout the US and also in Meijer Supermarkets, a Midwestern-based retailer. The American market represented a totally different set of challenges and opportunities for us. From the sheer size of its coffee economy, with over 150 million coffee consumers drinking up to 400 million cups of coffee a year, the challenge was both exciting and daunting.

In April 2004, I travelled to Los Angeles to meet Bishop Charles E. Blake, one of the leading African–American church ministers in the US. He is also a man with considerable social and political clout. The meeting was initiated by a friend of mine, Isaac Ruccibigango, who at the time was part of a US-based Ugandan gospel band, Limit X. My pastor, Michael Kyazze, Isaac and two other Ugandan friends huddled around the breakfast table at our hotel in Los Angeles as I made my presentation to the bishop. After giving him a brief overview of the contemporary socio-economic data from the continent, I moved to sharing my thoughts on Africa's economic experience over the last fifty years. I then presented my central idea of promoting trade linkages between African businesses and US customers. I reviewed the dynamics of the global coffee business and our company capabilities and demonstrated that we had the commitment and experience in the South African market to commercialise the opportunity.

In response, the bishop spoke deliberately and with his eyes steady and focused. He told us how he has always hoped for African-Americans to be to Africa what Jewish-Americans have been to Israel. Jewish-Americans have been a positive force for social-economic partnerships and cultural links with Israel. He envisioned a powerful relationship, especially given our shared history despite the fracture caused by a slave trade that saw over twelve million Africans shipped to Europe and the Americas. This tragic history has sometimes encouraged closer kin ties between the two communities, but at other times hindered solidarity. Nevertheless, there have been numerous efforts to heal, restore and even rebuild the historical memory of this experience. Hearing Blake speak in these terms, with conviction and focus, left a deep impression on me.

At the end of our meeting, we agreed that we would try to forge a partnership between his church community and the coffee business. This objective grew and sustained my relationship with Bishop Blake over the next seven years, until we finally signed the long-awaited partnership between COGIC and Good African Coffee in St Louis in November 2011.

On my next trip in October 2004, Blake hosted a meeting with business and civic leaders from his church, at the old West Angeles

Church, not far from the magnificent cathedral off Crenshaw Boulevard in south-western Los Angeles. During the event we served the guests with our coffees and I presented our company profile and the 'trade not aid' mission. Afterwards I held further meetings with actor/director Bill Duke, who encouraged me to package my message into a short corporate video. He emphasised the importance of an audio-visual aid in the early stages of the business and its role in communicating a strong message. On the same trip I tried to meet former NBA basketball star Magic Johnson's people, who were aggressively expanding their Starbucks franchise operation at the time. I hoped the connection would help us gain a supply opportunity into his stores but, as I later learned, Starbucks only sold their own coffees through their outlets. They buy green coffee from all over the world, but roast it themselves before distributing it through their coffee shops and other retail outlets.

Darryl Smith, who worked with Bishop Blake in their charity focusing on children in Africa, introduced me to another church elder, Phil Hart, an architect who had some good retail contacts in California, particularly at Gelsons, a California-based chain of supermarkets. In our discussions with Chris Fromm, the grocery category manager, I came face to face with the tough retail entry requirements. They typically charged high costs for introducing new items into their distribution system. This would then guarantee a six-month supply window from that time for an acceptable sales performance to be established. There were other marketing costs that we would be required to pay for and we were expected to produce a six-month marketing plan that included shelf display in-store demonstrations of the products, discount pricing and coupons for their in-store magazine.

However, even before shelf presence could be given, a supplier needed to be set up with a local distributor who was prepared to accept their products, as most retailers were not interested in buying direct into their distribution centres. Once a distributor was confirmed then a buyer, together with their buying committee, would confirm acceptance of the new product.

This posed two challenges. One was a cost-of-sales issue, which while surmountable, demanded deeper financial commitments than we could make. The other was logistical – the issue of securing a distributor, which ultimately became our biggest challenge. I contacted all the distributors suggested by Chris but with little success. I just couldn't find any interested in taking on our products. They all suggested that we needed to get more interest from retailers before they could get involved with us. I wrote numerous emails and made several phone calls, but I wasn't making headway. I was quickly beginning to appreciate the gap between all the trade rhetoric and market realities.

In 2005, Bishop Blake recommended that part of building our US trading opportunity involved strengthening my social networks. He suggested I go up to Boston and meet with Reverend Eugene Rivers III, who would assist me in making some helpful introductions on the east coast. I had met Reverend Rivers before with the bishop during their visit to Uganda. Rivers is the energetic, sharp and quick-witted founder and pastor of Azusa Christian Community in Boston. He has a well-established reputation as one of the most effective community organisers and crusaders against gang violence and other community problems in the worst inner-city neighbourhoods in America and he once appeared on the cover of *Newsweek*.

Jackie and I met up with the silver-haired reverend in downtown Boston and he suggested that we go see Professor Louis 'Skip' Gates at Harvard University. A leading American literary critic and the head of WEB Dubois Institute for African and African-American Research, he is one of the country's most influential African-American scholars. Skip Gates had good contacts in corporate America, and Rivers thought it was important for me to share our 'trade not aid' vision with him to see what connections he could help us with.

We arrived at the professor's office fifteen minutes early. I was excited to meet him as I had read so much about him during my undergraduate years at the University of London, especially his strident critique of the 'Eurocentric literary canon'. Gates postulates that black literature ought to be assessed by its own aesthetic criteria that are rooted in its culture and not through paradigms imported from western cultural traditions. The latter, he argues, has led to a damaging and enduring intellectual racism and unfair privileging of western thought over others. Gates would later become a household name when he was arrested by the Cambridge police after they received a tip-off from a neighbour that a black man was attempting to break in to a property; the problem was that the property happened to be Skip Gates' house. When the officers arrived an altercation ensued, the good professor was arrested and the media circus came to town. When cool heads prevailed, the fracas was brought to a 'teachable moment' over beers with the professor, the arresting officer, Vice-President Biden and President Obama in the gardens of the White House.

After the professor had welcomed us into his office, with mischievous humour he made a wisecrack about being surprised to meet an African businessman who wasn't a drug dealer. I didn't find this funny. He then told me about his friends in Uganda, who included the Kabaka of Buganda. The rest of the meeting meandered across several topics without much traction on any next steps. I left the meeting uncertain about how much value we had gained from the interaction.

We spent the rest of the afternoon visiting the engaging Charles Stith, a former US ambassador to Tanzania. Ambassador Stith directs Boston University's African Presidential Archives and Research Center (APARC), which studies democratisation and free market reforms in Africa and, through a programme for retired democratically elected African leaders, motivates them to write papers on their experiences in government and share them with the current leadership and wider academic and policy audience. He gave me some valuable contacts on the east coast and also promised to make introductions with friends he had in the venture capital sector. He also offered me an opportunity to participate in several of his APARC events in South Africa as a good platform for generating publicity on the continent.

Between 2005 and 2007, I made three more trips to the US, meeting with the bishop and trying to bring the COGIC partnership to a signing. But I also realised that COGIC could not deliver Good African Coffee to the US market but rather would become a valuable marketing opportunity once we had established a retail presence. These were financially lean years, and on the face of it, justifying the trips was difficult. I was conflicted between the obvious and logical choice of not travelling due to limited finances and the faith and persistence to keep knocking on doors and investing in personal relationships that would bear fruit in the future. These trips also exposed me to the American marketplace – its complexity, culture, business etiquette and knowledge; it was a valuable and necessary investment to make.

5 Capital

Remember that there is nothing stable in human affairs; therefore avoid undue elation in prosperity, or undue depression in adversity.
  Socrates

Accessing affordable and patient capital for Good African Coffee has been my biggest challenge since inception. It has not only been a major constraint for my business growth but it also represents the reason a majority of small to medium enterprises (SMEs) in Africa fail to take off. A World Bank report of 2010, estimates that only twenty-eight persons per 1,000 borrowing adults in sub-Saharan Africa get access to credit.[1] I believe this statistic doesn't fully capture the magnitude of the problem. There are many non-borrowing adults who are simply discouraged from even entering the formal credit market, and many more who access loans in the massive, informal and unregulated short-term finance market that is dominated by loan sharks and money lenders that charge up to 20 per cent interest per month. Poor access to capital is the single biggest constraint to entrepreneurship everywhere.

The shallow financial markets in sub-Saharan Africa are also compounded by foreign aid inflows that create significant market distortions. In Uganda, for example, foreign aid accounts for over 26 per cent of the national budget and a large proportion of development budgets for projects like infrastructure, health and education.[2] Large foreign exchange inflows of aid have to be converted into the local currency before they can be spent. This process increases the volume of Uganda shillings in circulation and due to the potential inflationary impact of this the Central Bank intervenes to 'mop up' the excess liquidity by selling monetary policy instruments like Treasury Bills (TBs) and bonds on the local market. This process is also known as 'sterilisation', where the Central Bank attracts individuals and institutions to purchase Treasury Bills at competitive interest rates. The effect of this is to crowd out capital from the private sector and the commercial banks into TBs – a very unproductive relocation of resources. This has also led to a spiralling of domestic interest costs of approximately 300 billion Ugandan shillings per annum and ultimately translates to a high domestic debt stock.[3] In Uganda, interest costs alone have increased by over 1,000 per cent in the last six years while the domestic debt stock is currently around 10 per cent of GDP.[4] This large government debt position means that each year the government has to spend more and more in this deficit-financing cycle. This has a negative impact on economic growth. Treasury Bills are essentially 'risk free' investments and commercial banks are more inclined to invest depositors' funds in them as opposed to other riskier projects. Statistics from the Central Bank of Uganda for the 2010 period show that out of the total stock of government securities, commercial banks held the largest portfolio, 65 per cent.[5] TBs over the years have offered attractive interest rates as high as 15 per cent per annum.

This problem of access of capital is exacerbated further by the local banks' emphasis on securitisation of loans rather than managing risk through project viability or other available risk-mitigating options. Venture capital and other long-term credit products are in short supply and, where available, prefer large infrastructure projects and established firms to 'greenfield' and 'brownfield' projects, and definitely not agribusiness. Almost all capital available in the banking sector is short term yet the sector with the highest impact on economic growth, the agriculture sector, needs capital with long-term horizons.

The financial sector in Uganda, like in many sub-Saharan countries, is still underdeveloped. Only 4 per cent of all bank credit goes to agriculture, and of the twenty-eight or so registered financial institutions in the country, all are commercial banks except two development banks; however, these two might as well be called commercial banks given their loan terms, cost of borrowing and risk aversion.[6] The market for venture capital is still small and the few companies that exist, despite claiming to be seeking out small social enterprises, tend in practice to work with mature and profitable firms. The commercial banks, with their short-term outlook and risk aversion, prefer to lend to import traders, commodity exporters, multinationals, large corporates and NGOs. The bank culture for establishing one's credibility is essentially historical data and past performance and not the innovativeness and future viability of an enterprise. New and innovative projects are seen as high risk, leaving many entrepreneurs discouraged and driven to be job seekers as opposed to becoming job makers.

The issue of access to capital is not just a Ugandan or African problem but one also faced by many entrepreneurs in the global marketplace. South-east Asian countries made it central to their development strategies. For these countries, availability of capital was seen as a critical necessity if they were to unlock their private sector and accelerate economic growth. The success of China's powerful conglomerates is not a result of the efficient allocation of capital by the financial markets but of a deliberate and decisive provision of capital for industries that are both strategic and key to the modernisation of the economy.

Western economies have always championed the role of free

markets in Africa and have highlighted the distorting influence of state intervention while cynically ignoring the difference to their own development, which had the distinct feature of a very powerful and determined role of the state in matters of allocating capital and technologies in the early stages. As Cambridge professor of economics Ha-Joon Chang observes, 'contrary to the conventional wisdom, the historical fact is that the rich countries did not develop on the basis of the policies and the institutions that they now recommend to, and often force upon, the developing countries. Unfortunately, this fact is little known these days because the "official historians" of capitalism have been very successful in re-writing its history'.[7] Yet, in the 1980s, two World Bank documents – the 1981 Berg Report, named after its principal author, and a 1989 report – articulated and established the World Bank's key ideological perspective of the African economic crisis. The policies of African governments, which distorted the proper workings of the market, were identified as a key cause of this crisis. Distortions were manifest in these policies of excessive and 'overcommitted' government expenditure, overvalued exchange rates, government controls – on prices, imports, wages and more – and the excessive costs of import-substitution industrialisation. These policies became part of the package of reforms that constituted the Structural Adjustment Programs (SAPs) adopted by many African countries in the 1980s and 90s, with mixed results at best. At worst, massive social unrest and dislocations resulted from the program's austerity measures.

Robert Wade, a leading economist, has pointed out the hypocrisy of western policy recommendations in his seminal book *Governing the Market*. Wade argues that none of the industrialised economies of Europe and America ever subjected their nascent industries and firms to the vagaries of the free market. Instead, they had a very deliberate industrial-assistance policy that included making capital available widely and cheaply, the provision of technology, massive subsidies and the support of export market expansion. It was only when the capabilities of firms had reached a level of efficiency that the economies were willing to subject them to free trade. Alexander Hamilton, the first United States Secretary of the Treasury between 1789 and 1795, laid out a very clear strategy for protecting American industry through tariffs and capital incentives until such time that they were strong enough to compete with foreign firms. Wade points out that this strategy was promoted until after the Second World War, by which time American industry had achieved a general level of supremacy.

Western donors' neoliberal commitment to 'market fundamentalism' as an aid conditionality has undermined Africa's opportunities in international trade and its share of world merchandise export. Liberalised economies have become net importers rather than export economies. There has been hardly any benefit from the global boom in manufactured exports over the last thirty years, with the continent's share in world manufactured exports changing by 0.1 per cent in thirty years from 0.8 per cent in 1980 to 0.9 in 2010.[8] Furthermore, in 2010 alone only 18.6 per cent of Africa's exports were manufactured products, meaning that over 80 per cent of the exports from Africa were in raw form.[9] As has been shown, Intra-African trade has also remained very low over the past decades.[10]

Put in context, 40 per cent of North American trade is with other North American countries, and 63 per cent of trade by countries in Western Europe is with other nations in Western Europe. Low intra-African trade implies that many opportunities for using trade within the continent to enhance the prospects for specialisation among African countries are lost. This is certainly not the foundation upon which rapid economic growth and wealth creation for the majority of Africans can be built. By comparison, Asia's contribution to global trade over the last thirty years has increased substantially from 15 per cent of global exports in 1980 to over 33 per cent in 2010.[11] The Asian Tigers – Hong Kong,

Singapore, South Korea and Taiwan – offer an interesting example of unique economic strategies and tactical choices that have led to tremendous growth.

Therefore, what is known as the 'Washington Consensus', a set of policies believed by some economists to be the formula for promoting economic growth in developing countries – policies, including privatisation, trade liberalisation and deregulation, which were vigorously advocated by the Washington-based IMF, the World Bank and the US Treasury in the 1990s – are hypocritical, empty of the historical realities of how the advanced economies themselves developed. The perspective of the free markets does not consider 'markets' beyond their abstract form, as shown by the Berg Report's understanding of the concept.

A fairer treatment of the early stages of development requirements would instead emphasise the responsibility of governments in Africa to create capital where the markets clearly have failed to provide it. Of course, it is critical that this is done within clear frameworks of private–public partnerships or within strategic industry guidelines that provide sector-wide support, as opposed to individuals on the basis of cronyism. The south-east Asian countries that embarked on the process of industrialisation during the 1960s, 70s and 80s did so on the basis of home-grown, structured blueprints and by a process of significant market intervention, whether directly or through systems of incentives and disincentives. More importantly, all of the south-east Asian countries resorted to domestic liberalisation far ahead of external liberalisation. A dynamic role for the state, supported by a system of targeted import substitution, was an integral part of that strategy.

The quality of economic management has also been one of Asia's key achievements and in this respect, the coordination of economic policies through the instrumentality of state and private-sector cooperation should be largely credited. In the case of China, it was particularly careful to ensure that development strategy was gradually implemented and carefully sequenced. The economic reforms in the newly industrialised Asian economies was based on heightened and broadened protection for domestic industries, which brought government directly into industrial decision-making. These reforms included a bias towards industrial interventionist policies and were knowingly based on the existence of market distortions and / or market failure.

It is revealing how, for example, the South Korean government steadfastly pursued an industrial policy based on a strategy of heavy and chemical industrialisation (steel, metal, machine, building, electronics, chemical and ship building) and targeted intense government support and development, despite stiff opposition from the IMF and the World Bank. The World Bank country report in early 1974, for example, voiced grave reservations regarding South Korea's development strategy and governance. It argued instead for a strategy of growth focusing on light-manufacturing industries and textiles on the ground of comparative advantage. That the World Bank was subsequently proved wrong is a relevant lesson for Africa.

Japan is another example. Since the early 1950s, Japanese economic development has consistently been guided by what have become known as long-range economic plans, which serve as guideposts for economic operation within the basic institutional framework of free enterprise and a free market. A crucial area of economic success was the decision-making process characterised by an informal process of consensus-seeking between the state and the private sector. Through this process, the Japanese government tended to achieve positive responses to its reform initiatives. This is unlike what took place in many African countries, which under structural adjustment were forced to swallow the bitter pill of adjustment and hope for recovery in the long term. As the entire world has seen, the Japanese strategy has led to a more efficient prioritisation of investments and incentives to investors.

The methods of technological acquisition by the South Korean state bear important lessons for Africa. The first thing the South Korean government did was to create an institutional context for the transfer of technology; it did this through licensing agreements. Strategic partnerships through joint ventures in both technological development and ownership offered opportunities for this development to be on equal or near equal partnership with foreign firms (importantly, foreign investment that competed with local producers was rejected). There were informal means of technological acquisition through foreign-educated research personnel. These well-trained people returned from abroad to form part of the influential Korean Institute for Development. This brings to mind the Iwakura Mission, a Meiji-dynasty example of the planning foresight that informed the Japanese state. Waves of Japanese diplomats, bureaucrats and academics traversed the cities of Europe for two years learning what they could about their civilisation and economic development.[12] The Korean state also heavily promoted local firm manufacture of component parts or sub-assembly for foreign manufacturing firms located either within or outside the country. This policy contributed significantly to the domestic development of an equipment manufacturing capacity, a vital and necessary component in the industrialisation process.

One clear policy adopted by the majority of south-east Asian countries was that the market could not be left alone to allocate resources efficiently. This was not a blind rejection of the market, but an appreciation that markets can fail and therefore need an interventionist mechanism in the early stages of economic development. With this came a clearly defined proactive role for the state. This intervention, however, increasingly relied upon dense institutional linkages between politically insulated state bureaucracies and organised business.

Dambisa Moyo, in her influential book *Dead Aid*, offers a robust critique of the aid industry, and proposes for aid to be cut off in the immediate term and for African governments to seek financing from the global capital markets. Although this remedy offers an interesting solution to a systemic problem, it has also met with a fair amount of scepticism, especially given the financial markets meltdown in 2008. My own take is that what is actually lacking is not always insufficient capital but a problem of access and absorption. So often we learn how locally available capital is not being adequately utilised. The National Social Security Fund (NSSF) in Uganda is a good example. They collect over $150 million per month in workers' contributions and, until recently, in return offered workers 5 per cent interest on their money per annum. It is estimated that the NSSF holds over 20 per cent of the money supply in the Ugandan economy, and yet most of this capital sits in commercial banks earning little interest and boosting the balance sheets of the banks rather than spurring economic activity. Ironically, the Ugandan government will seek dollarised interest-bearing loans for large public-sector projects like dams, roads and other infrastructures instead of utilising the huge pool of domestic savings available. There is something fundamentally wrong with this picture. Observers have complained that past corruption scandals, political interference and governance issues have created a culture of risk aversion when it comes to NSSF resources. In my view, as long as the private sector is small, the state institutions will remain vectors for corruption because they will be seen as one of the few spheres of available capital. But as the private sector strengthens, alternative modes of accumulation become available and predation by elites becomes less prevalent.

THE RUBBER HITS THE TARMAC

Between 2003 and 2008 I met with over two dozen financial institutions in Uganda and several outside the country in an effort to raise capital. There seemed to be a real disconnect between the excitement about the Good African Coffee model and my ability to close on the fundraising. Different financiers had different reasons for declining to support us. For some, it was that I was an 'unknown quantity' – what I was proposing sounded interesting but not fully assuring. For others, the model was just too complex. Controlling the whole coffee value chain, from the garden to the retail shelves, seemed like a stretch. It hadn't been done before, so how could I be sure that I would succeed now? Kampala is a small town, and banks talk to one another about potential clients. As I racked up rejection after rejection, it became clear that chatter was fossilising into an opinion – I was not worth the risk.

I had something of a breakthrough in 2005 when, through Crane Bank, I was able to access the Ugandan Central Bank's Export Credit Guarantee Scheme (ECGS). Crane Bank is a locally owned bank belonging to Sudhir Ruparelia, a Ugandan Asian tycoon with a diverse business portfolio. He is also one of the wealthiest, most hardnosed businessmen I know. He has established his empire through a combination of business acumen and street smarts. I first met him in the mid eighties when he ran a foreign exchange bureau in his shop on the main Kampala road. At the beginning of my UK school term, I would go to his shop and queue with other travellers and traders, to buy either US dollars or pound sterling on what was then an informal Forex market. Sudhir would be seated behind the counter doing the trades himself. He moved from informal financial services to establish a foreign exchange bureau after the liberalisation of the sector. He then set up a commercial bank, and built a diversified business portfolio that included numerous commercial and industrial properties, hotels and rose farms. Crane Bank quickly became adept at addressing the financial needs of many traders and other small to medium businesses; they did this through the speed of their loan-processing system, which had little bureaucracy. Of course, the speed with which loans are accessed is consistent with the swiftness with which defaulters are pursued.

The ECGS facility was created by the Central Bank to promote exports by providing guarantees for loans to enable exporters to fulfil their orders. The only problem was that it was a very short-term facility – a maximum of 180 days. It was designed for and utilised by traders and other commodity exporters who were able to complete their transactions within six-month cycles. Good African Coffee was a seriously long-term business in need of long-term and affordable capital. But at that time, we were not able to raise any capital and I was getting desperate. The UK launch was fast approaching and I didn't have the funds to keep up with the frequent travel and the necessary set-up costs. I had to develop the brand design and promotional strategy and this was very expensive. Outsourcing the roasting of our coffees in the UK, combined with the local field operational expenses, all levied a heavy burden on our cash flow.

I set about trying to access the ECGS facility first by writing to the Central Bank to seek their approval that we would be eligible. Between the end of 2004 and early 2005, I held meetings with the bank's officer in charge of development, Mrs Naomi Nasasira. Although she was sympathetic and supportive, the available options didn't look hopeful. When this didn't go anywhere, I decided to change strategy and wrote to the governor of the Central Bank directly. This was risky because it could mean the door being firmly closed in front of me; but I thought that it might force a way out of my predicament.

The governor, Emmanuel Mutebile, is a well-respected economist and has been credited with being one of the key architects of Uganda's economic recovery. He is also a man known for a level of candour that can take some getting used to. Even though I knew him as a friend of the family, it did not stop him from being very forthright with me. After he got my first application letter, he immediately wrote back saying that the ECGS was not the facility I needed as it was short term and I should consider alternative, longer-term products and should speak to the lending institutions directly. I responded, saying that the problem was that long-term products required large securities, which I didn't have, and that the attractiveness of the ECGS was that the need for collateral was diminished by the guarantee the Central Bank provided. He wouldn't budge. We exchanged two more letters before I decided to call him, in desperation, at his office. In a sympathetic but candid way he said there really was nothing more he could do. And there the conversation ended.

Three weeks later, I decided to seek an audience with him at his home in Kololo, one of the plush suburbs of Kampala, to plead my case outside the bank environment, where I knew his schedule was tight. That evening, as I climbed the steep drive to the top of 'Summit view', the name given to the hilltop location with a magnificent view of the city, I wondered if he would even see me. The guard at the gate told me to wait outside as he called the house to get clearance for me to enter. As I waited, I began to rehearse the apology I would need to start with before presenting my case. Then I heard a loud click as the gate latch unlocked. I was ushered into the house and down a flight of stairs to the living room. I was told by one of the governor's staff that he wasn't yet home but that they had contacted him and he had asked that I wait as he was heading back. I took that as a positive sign.

Given the layout of the building on the side of hill, with the parking on the top floor, I didn't hear the governor come in. As he came down the staircase, our eyes met and we exchanged greetings. I quickly apologised for intruding on him at home, explaining that I was desperate to speak with him. He seemed relaxed and in a good mood. I began by recounting the journey from Kasese to our launch in South Africa and how we were on the verge of getting onto the UK retail shelves. I shared my frustrations with the inability to raise capital and acknowledged that whilst the ECGS was a short-term facility, it would give us the critical momentum to launch the coffee and then enable us to seek alternative refinancing. Not getting the capital now would be disastrous, and we stood to lose much more in terms of the development infrastructure we had put in place in Kasese as well as all our hard work in creating the brand. He listened and then said, 'But this facility will cause you problems soon. It really is meant for exporters with contracts and not for you. Can you really turn it around within six months?'

Without flinching, I replied: 'Yes'. But in my heart I knew that I was making a high-stakes gamble. He was silent for a moment then said: 'Look, I don't want to be the one in your way. Find a local bank willing to support your application and let them submit it and let's see what can be done.' As I unclasped my hands, I noticed how moist my palms had become; I hadn't realised the level of tension I was under during the discussion.

The next day, I went to Crane Bank to formally present our proposal and also hint at the Central Bank's tacit support for the project. For the next six weeks, we worked to put together the necessary paperwork and documents for the ECGS; I signed the last batch of documents on my way to the airport as I rushed to catch a flight to London. Three days before the UK launch, Crane Bank released $200,000, which was a portion of the facility approved under the ECGS, and the balance of $500,000 was used to refinance a loan I already had with the bank. Even with this facility we still found that the working capital was insufficient. But because I was desperate to get the launch into the UK market underway, and there was so much credibility on the line, I ignored the future consequences of the facility expiring in 180 days. All I was focused on was launching in the UK. With the released funds we immediately made payments for the branding designs, materials, the launch event, and other operational costs in Kampala and Kasese. No sooner had the funds come in, they were swallowed up.

From early 2006 to the middle of 2008, I was under tremendous pressure from Crane Bank to repay the loan or refinance it from another bank. In all, I must have received close to two dozen letters from the bank or their lawyers. Initially these letters asked me to urgently regularise the account by paying outstanding interest on the loan: in time they became letters demanding that I repay the whole loan. With a satisfactory response not forthcoming, the lawyers then began dispatching letters with threats of legal action. Eventually these escalated to foreclosure notices and the potential appointment of auctioneers. In addition, the bank made regular phone calls; with each, I tried to buy some more time. I quickly learned that tough situations with banks require giving constant feedback and updates, even when the banker looks at you with the 'I don't believe your excuses or your stories any more' stare. I had gambled everything on Waitrose and now I was scrambling to find another retailer to salvage our paltry revenues. But this too was a moving target. To get another retailer required more capital; capital to travel to the UK for the pitches that I was not even certain would result in a listing on the shelves. The challenge with pioneering projects with long gestation periods is that those listening to your story don't have much to build their confidence on other than your words and actions. I quickly appreciated that candour and feedback were very valuable. On many occasions Sudhir himself would call to establish what was going on.

But the pressure from the bank was unrelenting. I would be in the middle of a meeting and my phone would flash with a call from the bank. I began to think that the bank inundated me with calls to keep me focused on nothing else but them. One afternoon in early 2007, as I was driving in Kampala, I got a call from the managing director, Kalan, and something just snapped. I called Jackie to say that I had had enough with the calls, letters and threats. She too was tired of the constant pressure and our inability to meet the bank's demands. She said, 'This has become too much. If they want to sell the house then let them go ahead. Enough of these sleepless nights, enough of this pressure.' I turned the car around and headed straight to Crane Bank in order to share my frustration with Sudhir.

Sudhir's office is a very large room with wide glass windows overlooking City Square, the central point in Kampala. Marble tiles cover the whole floor and a conference table is set on the right-hand side as you enter the room. Sudhir sits between two large columns, at a large desk. As I approached and greeted him, I felt a welling up of so much emotion that I almost couldn't speak.

'I have had enough, Sudhir,' I said. 'I have had enough of the phone calls and all the pressure.' My vocal cords were so constrained that I felt as though I was whispering.

Sudhir looked at me a little perplexed and asked, 'What's the problem?'

I wasn't making headway with the bank loan, and yet the pressure from the bank was unrelenting – I was fed up. I even offered him the house to buy, but he rejected.

'Look, you seem like you need a rest. Why don't you take a few days off?' he said. I was surprised that the person whose managers called me relentlessly was now advising me to take time off. When I got up to leave I was not sure what I had achieved; but I felt somewhat relieved.

Not only was the bank situation tough but so too was the operational environment. On several occasions we failed to make payroll on time and each time I had to sit down with the team and explain why we couldn't pay them. I learned that candid discussions about shared challenges build both trust and understanding. I shared my own struggles with meeting my own needs on time, such as my children's school fees and other personal obligations. In addition, during this period, I had to forgo my salary so we could cover the rest of the team. Without a regular salary, I lived on the allowances from a coffee shop that Jackie ran in Kampala. From the time I started my first business in 1995, I had never suffered such a financial drought for so long a period and I drew on every reserve of my faith and also the recognition that while mine was a temporary discomfort, there were farmers who knew no other lifestyle but one of constant lack.

One of the key challenges for Good African was the mismatch between long-term funding requirements and the short-term products available on the market. This was costly and a recipe for disaster. The investments we were making in Kasese included providing farmers with inputs, training on harvesting and washing their coffee cherries, organic certification, financial literacy training, and start-up costs for SACCOs. These investments could not be entirely funded by internal resources, and yet to build a sustainable and solid business we needed to get the Kasese supply side right – and right from day one. Upon this solid foundation, we could build our commercial activities. Another challenge lay in trying to build the supply side of the business; activating the demand side by investing in brand-building activities like sales and trade marketing was very quickly exhausting any resources. The African Development Bank represented the opportunity to access long-term, affordable capital, and they had grants they could offer for technical support and organisational capacity building. They also seemed interested in projects that were sensitive to the community. In early 2006, I flew to meet with the bank's president, Donald Kaberuka. However, nothing came of the meeting or the subsequent correspondence.

Through all this our staff was magnificent. They were strong, dedicated and courageous. In one meeting I suggested that members of the team take leave until a time when I was able to secure the capital to continue with our operations. During the discussion that followed, I was surprised by their resoluteness and commitment to stay the course. This was a great source of encouragement to me and others. We spent most of our lunch breaks at the office in prayer and fellowship, encouraging one another. Many staff members committed themselves to long periods of fasting and intense prayer during this time and in many ways it was a privilege to witness this level of commitment and faith. The team's hopes weren't tied to material comfort but on a rich fellowship that could only be born out of a struggle for something bigger than individual needs at the time. This commitment was also not due to my persuasiveness or logic of argument but rather because they recognised the value of their labour and sacrifice and how important it was for the thousands of farmers we worked with. Whenever I felt that I needed to encourage my family, we would all jump into a minivan and drive down to Kasese and visit some of our farmers in Maliba, Rukoki and Kilembe. The kids always loved to visit and Jackie drew strength and encouragement from the work that was being done and remained to be done for transformation to become tangible. She worked with some of the local women's groups in Rukoki, providing them with tailoring machines that would generate a sustainable income for them producing and selling school uniforms and other clothing. We always returned from these trips refreshed and energised.

One of the ironies of Good African was how the external perception of the brand tended to be positive – that it was a strong business making great strides in the marketplace. This conflicted with the internal fragility of our financial situation. Given that coffee buying is a cash business, the buying season required significant financial resources, and as volumes began to grow so did the working capital requirement. The cash-on-delivery procurement system also presented an ongoing struggle, as engaging with the farmer community became a daily requirement. Our local team helped to mitigate some of these challenges and to generate a good level of trust between us and the farmers. I later learned from some of the farmers that our continued operations in the face of glaring financial constraints actually showed them the depth of our commitment and resolve to the mission. This was news to me – I had never looked at it this way, though I got a glimpse of it when we bought our first field pick-up truck and the farmers celebrated this acquisition.

Whenever I met with banks or other funding institutions, they frequently challenged me on the sustainability of our business model, and the debate always centred on defining the gestation period. Our take-off required long-term investments that we needed to marshal, and yet the expectation was that Good African needed to prove its viability very early on in the cycle. This constant tension underlined the reticence of many financial institutions that I came across. There was also the concern that our model seemed to favour social impact over commercial return. Our counter argument was that community empowerment made absolute business sense and could be profitable if we looked at the community not only as our trading partners but also as a huge reservoir of social economic capital. However, for the banks it all tended to boil down to profit. Despite the talk of growth of the private equity sector in East Africa, most private equity firms seek large infrastructure projects. Yet the majority of those seeking capital are small to medium enterprises with much smaller capital requirements.

The importance of investing in the green coffee supply side of the business was made clear to me early on. For many years, international coffee buyers of Ugandan coffees had complained that while the country's coffee had great potential, the crop handling was poor and had affected the market potential. I remember writing to a Starbucks executive in 2004, through a friend in California, Kevin Reylea, to explore the potential for a coffee partnership. As premature as that might have been at the time, it exposed me to the perception problems that Ugandan coffees had in the global market and why improvement of quality was imperative if we were to build a viable business. Starbucks responded by saying that they last attempted to use a Ugandan coffee in 1999 and that the coffee was neither good nor had the quality controls improved. They went on to say that they had used the coffee in a decaf blend due to the high amounts of off flavours and that they thought a 'no' was prudent at this point.

Ironically, in 2007, we did sell some of our surplus green coffee to Starbucks through our relationship with Kyagalanyi Coffee, a Ugandan-based coffee exporter. Starbucks had come to recognise the improved quality of the coffees and the potential.

In 2006 we developed the partnership that would help us address our working capital needs for buying green coffee. This strategic relationship was with Kyagalanyi Coffee Limited (KCL), a local subsidiary of Volcafe, Switzerland, which is one of the largest coffee-trading companies in the world. Volcafe is in turn owned by EDF MAN, a global commodities trading giant. KCL is the second largest green coffee buyer by volume in Uganda, buying over 2,500 tonnes of coffee a month from across the country before hulling, cleaning and sorting the raw beans for export. I met KCL's chief executive David Barry in 2005, together with the head of finance, Robert Whitwam, and Gabriel Artunduaga, the production manager. They all became a critical source of support for our operations. David is a tall, courteous Englishmen with slightly puffy eyes caused by the long hours he works in front of his computer monitor, managing the trades. When I met him, I was excited to find someone who not only was a leading coffee trader with enormous experience at the commodity level but who also understood our business model and appreciated its value to the community. He was sensitive to the challenges we faced and quickly leveraged his company's resources and knowledge to support us.

KCL began to fund our coffee purchases in Kasese and this immediately ameliorated the stress on our cash-flow. An arrangement was structured where KCL would advance the cash to buy the coffee and then take in the purchased coffee as collateral. We would then buy the coffee back at cost plus interest and processing charges when we needed to roast it for export. KCL essentially became the financing arm of our green coffee operation. They also rented us a warehouse next door to their plant where we eventually set up our roasting factory. Both David and his division head from Switzerland, Peter Moser, became important supporters within the Volcafe group.

Their financial support enabled us to generate our largest volume of coffee purchases at the end of the second season in 2006. The volume of coffee we purchased from our farmer groups totalled 310 tonnes of quality parchment coffee, with the leading farmer alone producing over 15 tonnes. In December that year, we held an awards ceremony at the Catholic Gardens in Kasese town to recognise the best farmers and farmer groups by quality and volume over the year. We were honoured to have Minister of Finance Dr Ezra Suruma, Minister for Agriculture Hillary Onek, and local MP and Minister for Defence Dr Crispus Kiyonga in attendance. Robert from LDH flew down from London, as did Peter Chappell and Alex Walford, a friend working at the European Union office in Brussels.

Over 2,000 farmer leaders trekked down the mountains to attend the function. There were individual farmer prizes, group prizes and location prizes for both production and quality of coffee. The farmers put on a play with a strong message about transformation in the community and the pitfalls of economic prosperity without values; it was not just aimed at their fellow farmers but spoke eloquently of the dangers of increased income and the potential for destructive social habits; it spoke to everyone.

In 2005, I approached the government of Uganda for a loan to refinance the Crane Bank loan and also to purchase roasting and packaging equipment. Dr Ezra Suruma, a US-trained professor of economics, had been appointed the new Minister of Finance and Economic Planning earlier that year. I had encountered Dr Suruma in 2002 during a public debate on the economy at Makerere University, and immediately recognised that he had an appreciation for many of the challenges being faced by farmers in the rural agriculture economy. Shortly after his appointment, I wrote to him, inviting him to visit our coffee farmers in Kasese and to see some of the opportunities and challenges we were facing. He accepted and visited the area with another senior ministry official, Peter Ngategize, who headed the competitiveness desk at the Ministry of Finance at the time. By the end of the visit they both seemed sympathetic to some of our challenges and also appreciative of the progress made. I wrote a follow-up email laying out our constraints and future plans and areas where we needed government support.

The degree to which one has to engage with a wide array of government officials demands well-honed interpersonal skills and some diplomacy. The key decision-makers must be always engaged, and by many accounts sometimes cajoled or placated, before they will give your project due attention. Given the many competing demands on government resources, and the reality that the government constitutes the largest pool of capital, there is a risk of abuse of the system, influence peddling and corruption. I was fortunate with the officials I engaged with and never saw any sign of this. And I was grateful that I had the goodwill not only of the minister who championed the initiative but also of his key technocrats, who shepherded it through. Officials in the ministry like Deputy Secretary to the Treasury and Deputy Permanent Secretary Keith Muhakanizi, tolerated my incessant phone calls for status updates and my frequent and unannounced visits to his office. Charles Byaruhanga, Technical Advisor for Budget, became our point of contact on the project and with a methodical, calm and candid approach helped us navigate the intricacies of dealing with government bureaucracy. Many other officials in the budget department helped make a long interaction process manageable and conclusive. In December 2007, after the necessary reviews and internal ministry approvals, Dr Suruma wrote to the president seeking his approval for the transaction. Three months later, the reply came back giving the project the green light. The president's approval was not just a vital endorsement, it spoke of his belief in the importance of value-addition in the Ugandan coffee sector.

After two years of negotiations, review and detailed supplementary requests for information from the Attorney General's office, in 2008 Phillip Karugaba, my legal counsel who had worked on this project, presented me with the final copies of the memorandum of understanding for signing. The agreement was for a five-year loan facility of $820,000 at the June 2012 exchange rate. Interest was set at the Treasury bill rate plus 300 basis points. This was not a cheap loan by any means but it was the best we could get. We would have preferred to borrow much more, but the budgetary constraints at the time limited the resources available. In exchange for the financing we gave the government preference shares, which could be redeemed at the end of the loan period with interest or converted into shares for the farmers in Kasese. When we received the funds we immediately paid off the Crane Bank loan and used the balance of the funds to buy the roasting and packing equipment. The challenge with private–public projects in Uganda is that there isn't a clear, established framework in place governing the procedure and outcomes of such partnerships. I was grateful for the goodwill and support of the many people who were involved in the process.

By 2011, it was clear that we needed to exercise the redemption option of converting the loan into farmer shares sooner rather than later, as the TB rate soared and the interest burden on the loan was becoming heavy. We embarked on a programme of strengthening the governance structures of our farmer groups as we explored the idea of them becoming shareholders. Together with my very dedicated and efficient colleague Musarait Kashmiri, who had worked with me in the VR days and rejoined me as our new general manager, we developed a plan for bringing the farmers into the shareholding structure of the company.

Procurement of the roasting equipment took me to Izmir in Turkey. I visited a company with a strong export record all over the world and quickly settled on the size of plant and the cost. I then flew to China to source the packaging equipment. This visit was a result of discussions I had with a friend, Solomon Rutega, who worked at the Ugandan Embassy in China at the time. Solomon and I were childhood friends and he had spent four years in Beijing and was fluent in Mandarin. Together we went to several cities including Shanghai, Nanjing, Shenzhen and Ningbo, where we met many manufacturers and suppliers of equipment. Solomon also introduced me to a young Chinese lady, Sonic Hao, who became our liaison in China, helping us get around the language barrier during our visits and for the subsequent export of the machinery.

Plant installation and commissioning in Africa can be challenging. Our roasting and packing facility was not commissioned until nine months after it was ordered and paid for in 2008. In fact, the supplier from Izmir never showed up to install the plant. Claims of illness and schedule constraints seemed to conspire against his arrival; it seemed he was uncomfortable travelling to Uganda. I pressed and pushed and even threatened to no avail, and for several weeks I just stared at the crates of equipment on our premises. We were stuck without the technical support to install the machinery for four months before I was finally put in touch with a Brazilian-trained engineer who had installed several coffee hullers; he assured us the setting-up of the roaster wouldn't be a problem. Again, KCL helped us renovate the building we rented from them and supported the civil works that would allow the installation work to commence.

In March 2009, I and several board members agreed to send out an invitation to the President of Uganda to be our guest of honour at the launch of our factory. Given the extent to which he had been championing the case of value addition for exports from Uganda it seemed only right to ask him. We delivered a letter to the president's office on Parliament Avenue in Kampala and within three weeks, I was surprised to receive a written confirmation from his private secretary that the president was willing to officiate at the function. The launch of the roasting factory represented a significant milestone for us. For too long, African economies have exported unprocessed raw materials, meaning the developed countries that carry out the processing keep the lion's share of the added value. Our roasting plant in Uganda not only addressed our commitment to capturing the full value addition of our coffee exports in Uganda, it also enabled us to employ local staff and to empower our farmers and their communities in a meaningful and sustainable way.

Soon after we launched the roasting factory, Jackie and I took a decision to formally invite friends to buy equity in the company. I also met Jonathan Friedman, a master's student at London School of Economics who had written to me seeking job opportunities at Good African Coffee once he graduated. Jonathan would eventually connect me to a young Italian graduate student at LSE called Luca Faloni, who volunteered to come to Uganda and write our business plan. Luca spent almost two weeks in Kampala and put together one of the most robust business plans we had ever seen. But after nine months of fundraising we had only managed to raise $485,000 from three shareholders: Ndema Rukandema, Peter Chappell and Hans Paulsen. All were friends for many years and supporters of the company. As gratifying as the initial support was, 2011 was spent trying to source more capital for our market expansion and opportunities with the US market.

PART THREE
Lessons

_____

6 Perseverance

Success is the ability to go from one failure to another with no loss of enthusiasm.
Sir Winston Churchill

The 30th President of the United States, Calvin Coolidge, had this to say about persistence: 'Nothing in the world can take the place of persistence, talent will not; nothing is more common than unsuccessful men with talent. Genius will not; unrewarded genius is almost a proverb. Education will not; the world is full of educated derelicts. Persistence and determination alone are omnipotent. The slogan "press on" has solved, and always will solve, the problems of the human race.' Coolidge placed persistence at the heart of what not only drives human effort but determines human solutions. Now if we are to accept Coolidge's definition of persistence, then it seems to me, two key questions emerge: are there times when we are to persist and others when not to? Are some people better equipped and able to persist than others?

I have often been faced with the first question. When is persistence the correct strategy and when is it misguided? The truth is, I haven't found one correct answer. Some people are stirred up by challenges, persist and overcome them, while others resign or give up. I believe that persistence – defined variously as steadfastness, tenacity, constancy, indefatigability, resolution, grit, stamina and endurance – is the substance of our life journey and a capability in all of us. We choose either to deploy it or not; deploying it has never been painless. We all have the inner energy to persist through circumstances that are painful, embarrassing, disappointing and challenging. Persistence is not just about trying to overcome an obstacle that one faces in business or enduring through a tough situation; it sometimes involves receiving neither appreciation nor support – or sometimes even acknowledgement – for what you are trying to achieve. Do persistent people with solid goals lose battles? Of course they do. The challenges that confront people who are weak also confront those who are strong. The difference is not what battles we lose, but what we do about the challenges that confront us. To paraphrase Martin Luther King, the mark of a leader is not his conduct at the height of his success but how he manages the lows of his challenges and failures.

With hindsight, I have questioned where the energy to keep going comes from and I have settled on three lessons: the first is that everyone faces challenges in their lives so it is neither special nor peculiar; the second, that conquering obstacles is best done by a continuing persistence because very few successful people start successful, they attain success by persisting in the face of failure or great challenges; and third, always try to take advantage of adversity and not to let adversity take advantage of you. Use the challenge as an opportunity to learn and appreciate your inner strengths and weaknesses. Draw strength from adversity; learn, regroup and move forward again. A crisis doesn't make a person, it reveals who you are; you don't always know who someone is until you can appreciate their character and drive in the face of adversity. To persist or not isn't about whether we have it in us or not; rather, it is a question of choice. Choice is also defined by how we view the world – and what we view as our purpose in life.

I have found that perseverance and passion can achieve, in business, what finances may not. The only thing I had to rely on in convincing supermarket buyers or vendors or financiers was my passion and my commitment to making the argument over and over again. Howard Schultz, the current CEO of Starbucks, tells a story of the dozens of bankers and venture capitalists he approached, and the constant rejection, disappointment and stress he suffered. He persevered and ultimately succeeded, going on to build one of the world's biggest-ever retail coffee brands.

Back in 2004, a month after our South African launch I was already beginning to think about Britain as a potential market. For a start-up like ours, market expansion is an important route to profitability. Between April 2004 and August 2005, I made over a dozen trips to Britain from Uganda; all this was to build the commercial opportunity with Waitrose, who of course in June 2005 became the first UK supermarket to retail our coffees.

After the initial meeting with Sainsbury's, I met with them on two more occasions before they decided that listing our coffees was not a priority. At 7.07 p.m. on 17 July 2006, a brief email delivered the devastating news. They were working on a new approach, with a hundred or so stores used to introduce lines to customers; but until this was implemented it would be difficult for them to introduce Good African coffees into Sainsbury's.

It was polite speak for: 'We shall not be listing your coffees in our stores any time soon.' I stared at my computer screen, rereading the email as the implications of its contents dawned on me. My first thought was the realisation of a loss of a much needed revenue opportunity. My second was a question of sorts: 'Why, Lord?' Our sales at Waitrose were a paltry £66,000. Our cash flow was bad. We needed Sainsbury's and, if possible, Tesco too. We were spending more on field operations like agronomy and financial literacy training than we were receiving in sales revenues. At the time, our costs outweighed our revenue by a factor of almost two to one; and the reality of being poorly capitalised was constraining us terribly. We were quickly exhausting the goodwill of most of our suppliers with our assurances of an imminent turnaround in our financial circumstances.

I had taken out the ECGS loan by this time and the facility was already in the dangerous 'non-performing asset' territory. The letters from Crane Bank about overdue interest payments and the need to 'regularise' the account were arriving with increasing frequency. I was trying hard to keep up the hopes of the bank managers with updates on our market-development efforts, but market-development efforts aren't quite tangible enough. I couldn't walk into yet another meeting and say, 'Well, I have spent the past ten months developing the UK retail market opportunity, we have had several meetings and I am hopeful that we will get our products on their shelves soon.' Market development is a story; people want to see results, full stop. I was fast becoming known as a storyteller.

My other concern was that I was losing credibility not just with the bank, but also with many of my friends and business colleagues. For them, the project was beginning to look like a pipe dream. For how long, many asked, would I continue to haemorrhage cash I didn't have on a so-called 'opportunity'? My insistence on putting an African-owned coffee brand on the inter- national stage for the first time didn't cut it for many, because it might just mean that there was wisdom in not venturing where others had feared to tread. Wasn't I just being stubborn and refusing to accept reality? Friends and family told me I was squan- dering goodwill: 'Everyone is talking, Andrew, they say the project is unlendable'. I was even surprised to see that someone took the time to go and see my mother to find out if all was well with me: 'Martha, we hear Andrew is in so much debt and is ruining his good name in town. He was always a smart boy: what happened?'

As if that were not enough, the effect of all this uncertainty was starting to take its toll on my wife. Jackie always stood by me steadfastly. As my business partner and closest friend, she had never questioned our vision nor wavered in her commitment to what she invariably knew to be a difficult journey. But even she too was beginning to wonder how long this breakthrough would take. The constant travel and the creditors phoning at odd hours with impatient messages accusing me of intentionally holding up their payments were affecting her. 'How do you get to travel so often but fail to pay us?' one asked me. It was tough having your integrity constantly questioned. Yet, I knew that I had to soldier on. Throwing in the towel was not an option.

I read the email again. My instinct was to get back to London, meet Sainsbury's and salvage the situation. More challenges were headed my way, though. The coffee-buying season would start soon. In Uganda, we have two main seasons for the arabica coffees. The first is a short season known as the 'fly crop', and generally runs from February to April, while the main season starts at the end of August and finishes in December. Green coffee purchases are a cash-hungry business and it is no coincidence that the leading green coffee buyers in producer countries tend to be very well-funded businesses with good access to international capital. We initially financed our coffee purchases through a loan from the bank and by diverting the revenues from the coffee shop we run in Kampala. Meeting payroll was still a problem. The team I worked with had always displayed incredible patience and resilience. They persevered, insisting that they, too, had invested too much to quit and that it was as much their project as it was mine. Transforming the lives of the farmers, as one employee told me, was more important than our short-term challenges. Others who couldn't handle the uncertainty moved on to other jobs.

I paced up and down the open-plan office; I hadn't felt this stressed in a while. I got down on my knees and began to pray. I don't remember how long I was on my knees but as I got up, a thought suddenly crossed my mind: what if I was to write directly to Justin King, CEO of Sainsbury's, and ask him to reverse the decision? What would such an appeal say about my company vision? More importantly, how would I go about getting my appeal to him?

I called Peter Chappell in London and asked him if he had any idea how I could get hold of Justin King's email address. He suggested I call a mutual friend who, as a journalist, had interviewed King a few months earlier. I called him and asked him if he had the email address and he said yes in such a laid-back manner that I thought that he was joking. It was only when he read it out to me that I knew he was serious. I was speechless.

By 9.05 p.m., I had drafted an email to the chief executive of Sainsbury's and it went like this:

As the only African exporter of coffee to the UK, I naturally want to have our Good African Coffees on the shelves of J. Sainsbury. However, given Sainsbury's commitment to fairer trade with African suppliers I am increasingly surprised by how difficult that is proving.

Over the last several months we have met and corresponded with your category buyers and in the process established the viability of the Good African Coffee brand. We have also designed new packaging exclusively for your company and your buyers have acknowledged the need to give retail opportunities to African-owned and ethically traded brands (we share 50 per cent of our profits with our farming communities). To date, we have not received any commitment on listing our products.

We launched our range of Good African Coffees into Waitrose supermarkets in June 2005. Prior to that, I made a total of thirteen trips before the product eventually was listed. For a small-to-medium African exporter like our company, development costs such as these are not only prohibitive but can be crippling. I have spent much time giving lectures and speeches to British media, business and academic audiences arguing that Africans do not need handouts but opportunities to trade themselves out of poverty. We understand international business dynamics and product delivery standards, but for trade to become a viable strategy we need to sell our products in supermarkets like yours.

If African products could obtain just 3 per cent market share of products sold in UK supermarkets, it would represent approximately £7.2 billion per annum, which is just under the total foreign direct investment the whole continent of Africa received last year! J. Sainsbury has a long tradition of social responsibility evidenced by the amount of work and resources you have invested in Comic Relief. However, the only viable and sustainable way Africa can develop is for its people to help themselves through trade and not aid. However honorable the motivation and the objectives, if there is one lesson history has taught us about human development, it is that a people, working in partnership with companies like yours, will only lift themselves out of poverty by their own energy, creativity, hard work and commitment.

At home we have a saying, that if you give a person a fish you feed them for a day but if you teach them to fish you feed them for life. I hope you will consider our product listing in your supermarkets and give us the opportunity to help our people and ourselves. We have an excellent product, with a unique selling proposition and a proven sales record.

I hope that you will support this proposition. I am available to discuss this matter with you further at your convenience.

I clicked the 'send' button. A few minutes later, I reread the email and, to my horror, I discovered some typos; I hadn't done a spell-check. I tried to recall the message several times, but failed. Now, not only would the CEO of Sainsbury's receive an appeal from a person he didn't know, but he would receive an appeal letter with spelling errors. I packed up my laptop, closed the office and went home.

A reply from Justin King's PA arrived a couple of weeks later and it carried encouraging news: Sainsbury's were planning an autumn launch of three lines of our coffee, including one exclusive to their stores.

There was tremendous relief and excitement all round. Our coffees were finally stocked in over 200 Sainsbury's stores in September 2006 and we became the first African-owned coffee brand to be sold in their stores. I sent out around a hundred emails to friends and family thanking them for all their support, and for standing with us.

The same year, Tesco supermarkets agreed to retail our coffee in their stores. They were the last retailer to take us on but soon became out biggest supporter, keeping the product on the shelves even when sales were low. Despite having a reputation for being very tough on suppliers who didn't meet their sales targets, their various buyers encouraged me to keep persevering and to innovate within our limited resources. I made numerous trips with Barry Fine from LDH to their headquarters in Cheshunt, thirty minutes by train from London. We frequently walked into the meeting room apprehensive that we were going to be delisted, only to come out stunned by their understanding and even compassion. In my view there was a real disconnect from the image Tesco had in the UK marketplace as a hard-nosed retailer. They were tough but compassionate, and willing to take a risk on us.

All this was a long way from my first coffee trip to Britain in April 2004, when I had set about trying to arrange meetings with the major supermarkets. I made several calls, wrote emails and even letters to Tesco, Sainsbury's, ASDA and Waitrose, all to no avail. I just couldn't get beyond the switchboard operator or get a reply to mail. The only appointment we managed to secure was with Londis, a convenience store franchise operator. The gentleman I met sat quietly through my presentation as I went on about the opportunities of trading with African-owned brands. In the end, not wanting to discourage us much, he gently suggested that our products would be a better fit for the large retailers and once we were in there, we could then make another pitch to Londis. I returned from that first trip having accumulated nothing more than hotel bills, cab and train receipts, and a good dose of reality.

The following month, I called a South African contact, Grant McGregor, the chief executive of Berfin, a Cape Town-based distributor, for advice on getting into the retailers in the UK. By coincidence, one of his shareholders, Roy Fine, had a brother, David, who he said might be able to help me.

An intense, no-nonsense businessman, David Fine is the managing director of LDH (La Doria) a leading UK private label supplier of canned tomato products, dried pasta and other selected ambient foods to major supermarkets. We met in the lounge of the Four Seasons hotel on Hyde Park Corner. I sensed he was curious as to why we were meeting in such a posh hotel, though he said nothing. Two years later, I confessed to him that my brother-in-law Evode worked in the finance department at the hotel and had a 'friends and family' rate that I dutifully took advantage of.

My agenda for the meeting was to talk about the philosophy of Good African Coffee and the commercial opportunities for our brand; why Africa needed trade and not aid; and how a major challenge facing African brands was under-representation in global markets. Knowledge and access to the retailers was critical to market presence, and we lacked this. I assured David that we could be relied upon to bring a quality coffee product with strong brand values to the market. Our launch in South Africa showed we were serious and could deliver the product to market.

Throughout my presentation, David didn't say anything. He just listened and, when I was done, asked me why I was doing this. I told him how my faith journey and commitment to bringing transformation to our rural communities defined my aspirations. I added that it was incumbent on us, the new generation of African entrepreneurs, to puncture the stifling conversations about Africa; its litany of failures, its unending misery and hopelessness.

He wanted to know if there were any other people I was talking to. Given the great difficulties I had encountered on my first trip, with no retailer willing to speak with me, there was no one else. I was encouraged by David's acknowledgement that the timing was right for the 'trade not aid' message in Britain – he felt it could resonate with the consumers and the decision-makers in the supermarkets, assuming of course that the quality of the coffee was as good as I claimed it to be. Two days later he sent me an email requesting pricing structures and other logistical information. A month later, he sent me another email saying that both Sainsbury's and Waitrose had samples, and that he was expecting feedback in the next two weeks.

A month later he relayed the feedback from Waitrose. While there was no immediate prospect of them taking our coffee on as a new range, they had been impressed by the taste and packaging. However, they had been concerned about freshness, as by this point the coffee was still being roasted in South Africa, and thought that the 'trade not aid' stance was not special enough on its own to distinguish our coffee from the others that promoted the same message. There was a huge positive to take away from their comments, however, as they promised to give us further consideration in a few months' time.

This motivated the next dozen trips to Britain where I made the case over and over again as to why Good African should be retailed in Waitrose. At the same time, all this travel was placing a terrible strain on our finances. My credit facilities with the travel agents became maxed out, as were their patience and goodwill. The banks, too, were very unresponsive. They couldn't take their minds off the risk involved with controlling the whole value chain and they were not convinced that as innovative as the model was, a social entrepreneurial model could be pulled off. This is even before we explained that the processing was done in South Africa and the coffee would then be exported to Britain. Supermarkets operate largely without contracts and on an ordering system, which wasn't a risk many banks were willing to accept. By contrast, raw coffee transactions are straightforward, with contracts signed on a Freight on Truck (FOT), Freight on Board (FOB) or Cost Insurance Freight (CIF) basis. By the time I got to explain the role of LDH as our distributor and order fulfilment company, I had lost the attention of most.

Re-engineering the coffee value chain was proving difficult to sell to bankers and bureaucrats in government too. I attended numerous export strategy meetings, competitiveness workshops and public–private discussion groups in an effort to sensitise participants about access to capital, and other export issues. The problem of appreciating private sector constraints is reinforced by these institutions being dominated by people who have never run their own business, let alone exported a product. Issues like brand development, the difficulties of market penetration and the political will that is necessary to create meaningful trade linkages always remain at the level of rhetoric and never translate into actionable, deliverable and measurable initiatives.

African politicians and technocrats are only now beginning to appreciate that the global competitiveness of the products the continent produces rests heavily on branding and marketing. The economies of the Newly Industrialised Countries of Asia, such as China, Thailand, South Korea, Taiwan and Malaysia, have all embraced the importance in brand development. Today, many of these countries have spearheaded the branding of their countries as tourist destinations. Colombia is a classic study in how a nation can brand coffee. Thirty years ago, when you mentioned Colombia, you would be forgiven for thinking of right-wing death squads, drug kingpin Pablo Escobar, and the Medellin drug cartel and their lucrative cocaine export business. Today, we have all heard of Colombian coffee and many of us are aware of 'Juan Valdez': the famous fictional character used in adverts and marketing materials for the National Federation of Coffee Growers of Colombia. The Juan Valdez marketing campaign has been very successful in distinguishing Colombian coffees from those originating in other South and Latin American countries.

Appearing alongside his mule Conchita and carrying sacks of harvested coffee beans, 'Juan Valdez' has become a global icon, instantly recognisable as a sign of quality and provenance. Yet mention the importance of branding to most of our bureaucrats in Uganda and you are likely to receive a tepid response.

I met Ted McFadyen, the Waitrose buyer, twice in 2004 and just as we were beginning to develop a relationship and rapport that could lead to the potential listing of our coffees, he moved to another department. A new buyer came in and we started all over again. Richard James replaced Ted and quickly became our biggest supporter within Waitrose. A man of great warmth and humility, he also was genuinely interested in what we were trying to accomplish and he always encouraged me to keep going throughout our interactions. During this period, Robert Wiltshire and I were making monthly or six-weekly trips down to Waitrose headquarters in Bracknell, 45 kilometres west of London.

All the other supermarkets remained hesitant to commit to us so I focused all my energies on Waitrose. Richard James was promoted to category director and he handed us over to the new buyer, Michael Simpson-Jones. Richard continued to support us but sadly passed away, succumbing to cancer in 2010. Michael was very supportive too and oversaw the launch into the chain.

On 9 June 2005, I woke up early with a very pressing concern on my mind; it was the day of our UK launch, and a money transfer from Uganda needed to facilitate the payments of some of the branding and event materials had not yet credited on my UK account. The items, including gift bags, brochures, banners and name tags, were all ready but the printer had refused to release them without payment. Without these items there would be no launch. Forty-eight hours earlier, I had frantically tried to get confirmation of the funds transfer from Crane Bank in Kampala but all I was being told by the manager was that the transfer had happened. I must have checked my account balance on an hourly basis the day before. When that proved futile, I resorted to calling the bank's call centre. Nothing. As the hours ticked by, I began to get desperate and called the branch manager, who simply said he couldn't do anything and I should just keep checking on the account.

I walked down to the hotel dining room to meet a Ugandan journalist friend, Andrew Mwenda, for breakfast. Andrew had flown in from the US on his way back to Uganda, stopping over in London to attend the event. As we chatted over breakfast, my mind kept drifting to the transfer. If there was ever a time I needed a miracle, it was then. I jumped into a taxi and headed to my bank branch to make one last enquiry in person. When I got there, I explained to the assistant that I was expecting a transfer and wondered if she would check my account or establish if there were any funds waiting to be credited. She took my bank card, went through a side door and to the back of the teller counter to check. I prayed hard.

Several minutes later she returned, handed me the card and said the words I thought I would never hear: 'Twenty-three thousand pounds has just been credited to your account this morning, sir. Are those the funds you were expecting?' I thanked her profusely – I almost wanted to hug her – and made an immediate transfer to the design company for the materials.

Together with my mum, my wife Jackie, my sister Cathy and her husband Evode, I made my way to the House of Lords in Westminster. We arrived at the side entrance on the western wing of the building, went through security and up to the event room. It was such a relief to see the registration table laid out with the name tags, gift bags containing coffee and our corporate brochure, all in readiness for our guests' arrival.

The Cholmondeley room is rectangular with small chandeliers that run along the centre of the ceiling which is draped with white satin cloth. The most attractive aspect of the room, though, is its beautiful terrace that overlooks the Thames, Big Ben and the

London Eye. It was a beautiful summer afternoon and for a moment the pressures and stress of the past few months seemed to be suspended.

The guest list was diverse and ran to close to 120 names. Some of the invitees were Lynda Chalker's fellow peers and colleagues in the current government; others were African diplomats from their embassies in London and business leaders. Media personalities like Jon Snow from Channel 4 News, Tim Adams from the *Observer*, Duncan Campbell from the *Guardian*, Stuart Hall from the *Telegraph*, Claire Bolderson from the BBC World Service and Stuart Price from *African Business Magazine* were there too. I had also invited the senior buyers from Waitrose, Sainsbury's and Tesco. David and Robert from LDH were there along with Colin Smith, our UK contract roaster at the time. There were also a few church leaders and friends from the UK and Uganda and a representative from the Fairtrade Foundation.

I restricted the speakers to three: Lynda, Michael Holman, former Africa Editor at the *Financial Times*, and me. At 3.45 p.m., I stepped up to the podium; behind me was a pull-up banner acting as a backdrop with the words, in bold, 'Africa needs Trade not Aid to fight Poverty.'

I thought a joke would calm my nerves and relax the audience too: 'As my wife and I were preparing to come here for this function, my son was saddened that we weren't bringing him with us. When I tried to explain to him why he said, "But, Dad, you always take me with you when you go to the House of the Lord, why not this time?" "Well, son," I replied, "it is not the House of the Lord but the House of Lords."

'"What's the difference?" he asked.

'"Big difference," I said.'

As I was just beginning to thank the guests for attending, the handheld microphone I was using went dead. The sound technician couldn't get it to work and, curiously, they didn't have a spare one. I really didn't need this to happen to me on such an occasion and in such a place. I decided to speak without a microphone.

I summarised the key elements I had included in the op-ed article in the *Guardian* into a fifteen-minute speech and concluded by imploring the audience to become ambassadors advocating trade for Africa, and to become consumers of Good African coffee. This is how they would directly impact and empower the producers and their communities in Africa more so than any aid programme could ever do. The speech was well received, with many people coming to tell me in person how they felt about it.

Lynda Chalker was wearing a bright blue trouser suit with a floral white blouse that seemed to brighten up the podium as she stepped up to make her address. Her speech was supportive. She recounted the many years she had been working in Africa and the wonderful relationships she had built. She emphasised her continued confidence and hope in the future for Africa. She then touched on our relationship and the importance she saw in our work and suggested that initiatives like Good African would be key to the continent's future development. She reminded the audience that opportunities like the G8 Summit and the Commission for Africa focused a lot of attention and goodwill on Africa, and that this needed to be harnessed and it was important to keep the attention on the things that impeded trade. She promised to take up those issues in her work in the House of Lords.

Lynda's endorsement was important; it went a long way in strengthening our credibility in the circles where we were unknown. She didn't just champion our cause in the UK but also when on her numerous travels across Africa, where she offered both advisory and consulting support to many government leaders and private sector organisations. That evening after the launch she called me to say how proud of me she was; I sensed in her voice that she, too, had been looking for an emerging and positive story from Africa.

Michael Holman then gave a vote of thanks. As he talked, my mind went back to the time I went with Peter Chappell to visit him at the *Financial Times* in the summer of 2000. I was looking for capital for a mineral water project at the time, and Peter thought that Michael would have good contacts in the financial district. Back then he was the Africa editor but was struggling with the debilitating effects of Parkinson's disease. Having never been close up to a Parkinson's sufferer, when I saw how Michael moved, shuffled and twitched constantly, I was shocked by the symptoms of the disease. I couldn't quite reconcile the reflexive movements of his body with his sharp, incisive and knowledgeable arguments on African politics. After our visit, Michael introduced me to Joel Kibazo, a Ugandan working at the *Financial Times*, and also suggested some equity firms we could visit.

As Peter and I walked out of the *Financial Times'* London Bridge offices, I commented about the disconnect between Michael's mind and body. The mind was sharp, controlled but encased in an uncontrolled and disobedient body. Peter told me about a revolutionary operation in Grenoble in the Swiss Alps that Michael was due to undergo that would significantly reduce the tremors and control Michael's involuntary movements. I would meet Michael four years later at a summer party at the journalist and writer Richard Dowden's house in north London. I couldn't believe that this was the Michael I had met at the *Financial Times* offices years earlier. In many ways, he had not changed: he was warm, funny and sharp. But physically he was a new person, steady and controlled. I was stunned by the transformation.

Once Michael had ended his speech, I spent the next thirty minutes mingling with the guests, saw Jon Snow on the terrace on his cell phone on a call that, as I subsequently learned, led to my Channel 4 interview in Uganda. Tim Adams promised to get in touch with me later about coming down to Uganda to do a story; this became a profile story in the *Observer* that gave us great exposure in the UK, and it is still read and quoted to this day.

The launch not only raised the profile of the Good African brand but also my profile as its promoter. Immediately, a gap developed between our external image and profile and our internal capacity and condition. What people seemed to take away from the public functions was an exaggerated sense of my personal profile. For this to be so high in the context of a business that was still fragile was risky. Publicity was good, but I feared that too much of it could be dangerous. Soon after the launch we held a SWOT analysis on the company, and one of the key threats we identified was the reputational risk that I represented. If something damaging were to happen to me it would definitely negatively affect the young brand we were building. This issue remained a lingering concern.

Over the course of the next three weeks, however, I tried to generate more awareness by doing interviews and speaking events. On 5 July 2005, the Commonwealth Business Council (CBC) asked me if I would speak at the G8 Business Action for Africa Summit in London, which preceded the G8 Summit in Gleneagles, Scotland. The invitation letter reflected my fears of how exaggerated my profile was becoming.

Following on from our discussions, it gives me great pleasure to invite Rwenzori Coffee to be one of the supporters of the G-8: Business Action Group for Africa organised by the Commission for Africa with the Commonwealth Business Council. As one of the Uganda's largest coffee exporting organisations, the CBC believes that Rwenzori Coffee are well positioned to make a valuable contribution to the debates taking place at the Summit concerning the economic development of Africa and the importance of the Agriculture sector in this process. We would like you to provide thought leadership through case study examples, identifying how [to form] smart partnerships between business and government and how to successfully implement projects to unlock Africa's natural resources to support regional economic development.

As delighted as I was about the prospect of speaking at the event, I was concerned about the disconnect between perception and reality. I was put on a plenary panel with several industry leaders like Titus Naikuni, the CEO of Kenya Airways, the chairman of Royal Dutch Shell Company and the chairman of Zenith Bank in Nigeria. In my speech I revisited the themes I had been talking about all summer: the need to be a focus on trade for Africa and the importance of addressing the constraints African businesses face when trying to export products to developed markets in the West. I pointed out that foreign investors to Africa spend a lot of their time focusing on what is wrong with Africa instead of promoting what works and what motivates their investments on the continent in the first place. In part, I was responding to the speech by the chairman of Shell, who raised corruption, poor governance and bureaucracy as the key impediments to invest-ment in Africa. Shell is a major investor in the energy sector in Africa and the operations there contribute to a significant portion of its global revenues; yet the chairman was overly focused on the negative aspects. It is not fair to focus on these things alone and to underplay the positive elements that many investors enjoy on the continent. A friend in the audience later joked that I had squan-dered any hope of getting support from the Shell Foundation. After my speech, a South African entrepreneur involved in banking and telecommunications, who was seated next to me, asked me what the annual turnover of my company was since it sounded like Good African Coffee was a very big and promising company. I smiled and said: 'Probably the equivalent of your annual salary.' We both laughed, only I wasn't joking.

Soon after the business summit, I was invited to Dublin to meet Bewley's, a coffee roasting company. I had met their managing director earlier in London where we had explored the idea of shifting Good African's roasting operations to their much larger facility in Ireland. Bewley's was a much bigger operation with greater capacity than any other roasters that I had met and they could also handle our packaging requirements instead of us sourcing packaging separately as we were then doing with a company in Leicester. A one-stop shop operation was what we really needed. Both the managing director, Jim Corbett, and the commercial director, Brendan McDonnell, were keen to develop the opportunity and by 2006, we had completed the transfer of our roasting operation to them. The relationship lasted until 2008, when we set up our own roasting facility in Kampala.

On this particular trip, Bewley's and the Irish ambassador to Uganda, Aine Hearns, arranged a welcome dinner for me and the next day I had a business interview with Dublin's premier radio station, RTE Radio 1. I was also hosted at a breakfast with some of the private sector development people in the Irish Development Agency. My radio interview generated some chuckles when I talked of us 'wanting to expand our brand to Ireland and other parts of the UK'; of course Ireland is an independent country and it is Northern Ireland that is part of the United Kingdom. I also did an interview with the *Irish Times*, which opened with: 'Andrew Rugasira is fast becoming a poster boy for Africa's new generation of entrepreneurs.'

In March 2007, I decided that I would not do any more media interviews until the business had really built some solid traction. Nevertheless, in February 2010, I was surprised to find out that I had been nominated for the *Financial Times*/ArcelorMittal Boldness in Business Awards. This new award, promoted in conjunction with Indian steel magnet Lakshmi Mittal, recognised several categories: drivers of change, corporate responsibility, environment, emerging markets, entrepreneurship, newcomer, and person of the year. Good African was nominated in the Social Responsibility category together with GlaxoSmithKline, Natura, Standard Chartered Bank and Triodos Bank. The award unsurprisingly went to Standard Chartered Bank.

In an invitation-only gathering of industry titans at the Tate Modern gallery, as far as I could see, there were only four black guests, including me. We had more in common with the numerous black waiters and waitresses at this high-profile gala. I feared that I would be asked by a passing guest for a champagne refill or a tray of canapés. In hindsight, it was curious how Good African even got nominated for this award. I was struck by the irony of the presence of many corporate leaders who run huge conglomerates that do business in Africa while there wasn't a single African corporate leader with large-scale operations in the West in the room.

My break in the US came in August 2009, when I was invited to speak at the annual Global Leadership Summit, organised by the Willow Creek Community Church in Barrington, Illinois. Willow is the mega church pastored by Bill Hybels, a prolific author, renowned Bible teacher, thought leader and mentor to many leaders in the market place. I spoke on my perennial theme of Trade for Africa and the Good African case study.

Over lunch at the magnificent Signature Room restaurant, which is on the ninety-fifth floor of the Hancock Center in downtown Chicago, our hosts Jerry and Jan Kehe talked about their business life and retirement from active operations with Kehe Distributors, the company where Jerry was now the chairman. We shared stories about supermarkets and the challenges of getting products listed. They had obviously read up on me but for some reason I hadn't Googled them as I usually did before my meetings. If I had, I would have found out that Kehe Distributors was one of the largest distribution companies in America, servicing some of the largest retailers in the country.

The night before my presentation, Jerry and Jan invited us to dinner with a group of Kehe company executives. The dinner was an annual tradition and it brought the team together to celebrate some of the social initiatives the company had engaged in over the year. Many of the executives present were also due to attend the Summit. I was intrigued to find out that Kehe contributes 10 per cent of its pre-tax profits to its community programmes that provide a million meals to poor and struggling communities and repair community buildings. The senior leadership included Brandon Barnholt, the president and CEO; Mark Kroencke, who handles the gourmet and specialty products; Ted Beilman, VP for marketing and merchandising; Eric Fields; and many others. This was not the modest company Jerry had described over lunch. I got to hear about the hundreds of trucks that distributed thousands of products to retailers across the country. I was excited; was this finally the company that would pull our dream across the Atlantic and make it a reality?

My speaking slot was on the second day of the conference. On the first day there were some powerful presentations on leadership, change management and nurturing one's team. Past speakers included personalities such as Bill Clinton, Tony Blair, the musician Bono, business guru Jim Collins, and the former General Electric CEO Jack Welch. Everyone in the organising team was incredibly efficient and friendly. They all kept assuring me that I would do great and that they were praying for me. If they had some anxiety about my speaking there for the first time, they didn't show it, and if they were indeed praying for me because of the daunting task that lay ahead, I would never know.

On the day, I was led from the front row of the auditorium by an event producer and up a short staircase leading to the podium on a massive but darkened stage. The audience could not see me as Jim Mellado, the head of the WCA and master of ceremonies, introduced me. The auditorium is so massive that you can barely see the people seated in the upper breaches. The event was being broadcast on giant jumbotron screens on either side of the stage, and as I stood there on the stage looking at the 7,500 – mostly white – faces in front of me, there were another 100,000 people viewing the event via podcast. Jim finished his introductory remarks and with a loud applause that followed, the stage lights came on and the clock timer on the floor below the stage started its countdown.

'Thank you, Jim, and good morning, ladies and gentlemen,' I began. 'Before I get into the substance of my presentation this morning, I would like to ask what comes into your mind when I say the word "Africa".'

I then described the general perceptions many westerners had about Africa. It is not often that when one thinks about Africa positive thoughts come to mind (as opposed to what people in Africa would think when asked about America). Images of poverty, misery, warlordism, corruption and despair tend to cloud the mind. There is a good reason for this: the media's preoccupation with the perspective of a destitute continent ravaged by poverty and conflict.

I outlined how Good African Coffee had set out to try to change the conversation on this subject. We argued that only Africans are best placed to help themselves through hard work, discipline and innovation. With competent leaders at home and development partners who treat us with respect and dignity, we can chart a more sustainable course to prosperity for the people on the continent. We have introduced the principle of investing 50 per cent of our profits in sustainable community programmes like savings and credit cooperatives and farmer training programmes not because it is something exceptional but rather, sharing and caring for the community is part of our African value system and heritage. As African entrepreneurs, we want the same things that American, European and Asian entrepreneurs are looking for: markets and the opportunities to do business and create value. We don't seek to be pitied but to be treated equally and fairly. Compassion is important and a critical part of my own faith, but it must always be tempered with respect otherwise it undermines the dignity of the very people we seek to help and they end up being seen, and viewing themselves, as perpetual burdens.

It is time to paint a different portrait of Africa, I told them; a continent with a market of 900 million consumers and blessed with huge natural endowments, a land of extraordinary cultural and historical diversity. We can do it. We can change the narrative. We all can make a big difference today. You can buy an African garment, you can drink Good African Coffee, eat African fruits and enjoy great African music. This way you empower producers, create employment, and contribute to the growth of the continent.

The speech seemed well-received by the audience. I was met at the steps by Bill Hybels, who hugged me and said: 'That was a very brave speech.' Coming from Bill this reaction was really something; the few times I met him over the summit he seemed like a man very much in control and not taken to being effusive.

Over the next two weeks, I received over 1,500 emails expressing support and enquiring about how to buy our product. Some supporters went as far as writing to retailers requesting that they put our coffees on their shelves. One lady even wrote to Whole Foods introducing our coffee and our business model, insisting that they carry our coffees in their supermarket. They declined. A great number of the emails came from churches and church communities, who generously offered to try the coffee and encourage their congregations to buy it. This was a stunning reversal from the many years of lacklustre interest. We were now being asked for coffee that we didn't even have in the US yet.

The day after the GLS speech, Jerry drove me to see the Kehe operations in Romeoville, Illinois, which was an hour's drive south from Barrington. He seemed touched by the arguments for more trade for Africa and asked many questions about the trade barriers that deny African products entry into the American market. He mentioned how he hoped that Kehe might help us to bring our coffees to the US. The Kehe Distributors facility sits on sixty-five acres of land and their operations are housed within 1,200,000 square feet of built-up space. The company operates a massive fleet of trucks that bring products into the warehouses one way and take out consolidated pallets to retailers direct or via retail distribution centres across the country. The company has been employee-owned since 2001, when Jerry and his leadership team passed ownership to the 4,000-strong staff. Jerry's dad, Art Kehe, had founded the company in 1952. When he began, he operated the business out of his basement, with his wife and children as the first employees. Jerry joined after graduating from Bradley University and took over the company in 1975 when his dad retired.

We walked into the lobby of the Kehe building to a friendly welcome from the lady at the front desk and as we walked down the corridor we passed several work stations where people greeted Jerry warmly. Some of the staff were from a period when he had been CEO, others were second- and even third-generation employees whose parents and grandparents had worked with the company. I was struck by the culture of collegial interaction. Jerry gave me a tour of the key operational areas; the most impressive aspect of the facilities by far was the eight-mile set of conveyors that moved products at a high speed to different parts of the building. The maze of conveyors transported an assortment of products across the facility ready for palletising, consolidation and sorting for specific orders. Products zoomed past along the track as a small guiding block cut across the short track to push a box or two to a siding conveyor that takes the product to another destination. This happened all along the conveyor, which uses a sophisticated infrared object-identification system to transport and guide the products. I had never seen a logistics management system this elaborate and complex before.

After the tour of the plant, we went into the boardroom for a meeting that Brandon had organised with his team. Without wasting time, he launched into a discussion about how Kehe could help GAC enter the US market. We discussed some of the work I had done with COGIC and reiterated how if we could set up an online order-fulfilment capability, we could bring the coffee to the US. Online sales were my preferred entry strategy. Walter

Roy – the head of Eye Level Solutions, Kehe's online division – explained how they deliver products by the unit or case to customers across America and how because they had good relationships with leading couriers in the US they could offer a good price on freight costs with short turnarounds.

The logistics of getting products to the US were complicated. From shipping and Food and Drug Administration (FDA) authorisation to freight clearance from the port of entry, much work needed to be done. In the meeting, I was not just the promoter but also the student, as I learned many things including the differences between the US and UK barcodes – something I had never realised was an issue. The product weight measures were also different. Our UK standard coffee packs weigh 250 grams, while in the US the measure tends to be either 1 pound or 8, 10 or 12 ounces. This meant that we would have to change the packaging for the US market, and all this would have cost implications. The meeting ended with a firm commitment from Kehe to begin working on the logistics necessary to bring the coffees to the US. I would go back home and work on the supply side of the product: roasting, packaging and supply.

I had come to Chicago to give a speech and was now leaving with a real possibility of bringing our coffees to the American market. Yet still it took another sixteen months before we were able to finally ship our maiden container to the US. The container arrived at the port in New York in February 2011 and we went 'live' with our online store the following month. Within those sixteen months, I travelled to the US five times, working with the Kehe team and our dynamic new territory sales representative, Darryl Humphrey. Our focus had been getting the logistics right.

Jerry has sharply defined business instincts. Coming from a distribution background and with a strong appreciation for the retail industry, he was aware of the financial implications of trying to develop a presence in the US. He began to take an interest in our finances, having become aware of the difficulty we were having accessing capital. In February 2010, Jerry tried to secure a facility under his name for $250,000. The bank responded with alarm: was Jerry sure he hadn't fallen victim to some business scam? They only calmed down after Jerry asked them to do an internet search on me. They returned to pronounce that indeed, it seemed that I was 'legit'. However, because my business was not based in the US, they couldn't advance me a loan as requested. Jerry then decided to take out the loan himself and immediately wired the whole amount to us in Kampala. No agreement was signed, only a commitment to pay it back in the future. It was an extraordinary gesture of support and friendship.

Jerry's lifeline was nothing short of a miracle. Without it, we would not have been able to meet many of the commitments we needed to get going in the US market. It once again taught me that goodwill comes from unexpected places and is motivated when we share some of our challenges with those who are committed to our success. Frank and transparent discussions reveal where people stand on important issues for you. Pride is worthless, candour priceless.

Our online sales began in March 2011 with slow momentum and in June that year, I participated in our first American Food show at the massive McCormick Center in Chicago. I was invited to speak before Kehe's 2,000 key account managers who would be bringing their clients, major retailers, to the show to see the thousands of products being exhibited by various suppliers. Brandon and I spoke before this important audience, and several key account managers brought their retail customers to our booth. Darryl then followed up with samples and product literature, and together with Mark Kroencke and the Kehe account manager he helped to get us listed in over fifty Meijer stores. In November 2011, we finally signed the COGIC/Good African Coffee partnership agreement in St Louis, Missouri. What began as a dream back in 2004 was now a reality; with it came new challenges and opportunities, celebrations and frustrations but, ultimately, the proof was there – it could be done. A small African business could enter the competitive coffee market in America. And if we could do it, through the challenges and the mistakes, the hopes and the discouragements, many others on the African continent can and will do too.

7 The Good African Way

Overcoming poverty is not a task of charity, it is an act of justice.
Like Slavery and Apartheid, poverty is not natural. It is man-
made and it can be overcome and eradicated by the actions of
human beings.
  Nelson Mandela

THE BUILDING BLOCKS

In developing our business objectives, my first concern was to
ensure that we could buy quality coffees direct from the farmers
at prices that ensured that they would make a profitable return on
their harvest. This was of critical concern given the very low
farmgate prices that we encountered when I began the industry
research in 2003. The year before, the UK charity Oxfam published
a blistering critique of the coffee industry titled: *Mugged: Poverty
in your coffee cup*. This report exposed the unfair trading structure
of the coffee market, the power imbalance between the producers
and giant multinational buyers and the devastating impact of
low coffee prices on farmers and their communities in the
coffee-exporting countries in Africa. The report went on to detail
how large multinational coffee-processing companies used new
technologies to remove the bitter taste and other poor coffee

attributes that normally come with low-priced and low-grade coffees. Low prices didn't just have a devastating impact on the livelihood of poor farmers, but took away any incentives to produce quality coffees. Our primary goal would be to provide farmers with agronomy training, enabling them to produce quality coffees for which we would pay a good price so that they would make a profit on their harvest.

My second concern was the issue of what constitutes the bottom line. In a lot of business literature we hear about the bottom line; as well as double, triple and even quadruple bottom lines. This is an attempt to communicate an expanded stakeholder that goes beyond the traditional corporate shareholder model of the 1980s and 90s. In the late 1990s, there was an increased recognition for Community Social Responsibility (CSR). Large profitable companies began to find it difficult to justify raking in huge profits while doing nothing for the environment or the communities where they worked. The era of Gordon Gekko, the protagonist in Oliver Stone's movie *Wall Street,* who advocated greed being good, was over; that brand of business philosophy had become distinctly unpalatable. Companies began publishing their annual accounts with a section dedicated to their CSR initiatives. From tobacco companies to mining companies, pharmaceutical companies to financial institutions, as well as many small and medium sized business, all started dedicating a large amount of ink to documenting their CSR efforts.

For me, two defining issues stood out as far as CSR was concerned. The first of these was the issue of dignity. Every time a company spoke of its good works, it did so from the vantage point of privilege. The relationship between the companies engaged in CSR initiatives and the recipient communities often lacked dignity. In many instances, the designs of CSR programmes don't include the views of the target communities but are conceived and designed by the CSR divisions of the giving companies, NGOs and charities. A friend once told me a story about a water project in rural Ghana that posed an interesting dilemma. In a bid to alleviate the long distances that women in a particular village had to walk to collect clean water and do their washing, an NGO built an expensive clean-water system in the village for the community. But after a few months it became apparent that the women were still trekking the several miles to the river to do their laundry and collect water. After some focused group discussions it became clear that the reason the women still travelled the long distance for their water was because collection of water and doing their laundry was an activity where they also socialised, fellowshipped and counselled one another. Doing this in the midst of the village men was not ideal, nor did it allow them privacy; the water project repiped the water a short distance away from the village and immediately the women flocked to it.

Sharing and caring for the community is something that is intrinsic to the African way of life; an unofficial welfare system in the absence of a public sector that delivers effective community services. Just like many other African families, my family provides support to extended family members and many others. This commitment is not unique but is a normal way of life. My ambition with Good African was to entrench this commitment to the community as a fundamental element of our business model as opposed to just being something we would do once we had plenty of money to throw around. I therefore sought to recognise our coffee growers, our employees, our shareholders and the environment as our business stakeholders – our quadruple bottom line.

When we started in 2004, I first called the company Rwenzori Finest Coffee (RFC) before changing it to Good African Coffee in 2005. Whilst the Rwenzori name had provenance value, it nevertheless was difficult to pronounce for many and also too geographically specific to capture our ambition of buying coffees from other regions. I met a London-based design agency called Thinkfarm who began helping us with our brand migration from

RFC to Good African Coffee. They did a brilliant job in developing a design framework that captured our 'trade not aid' vision and ethical-trading platform and communicated it to the consumer. The Good African name enabled us to build a brand platform that would allow us to extend to other products like tea and chocolate in the future.

In 2005, Good African unveiled its new coffee packaging with two of our key values placed prominently on the front of the packaging: 'Africa Needs Trade not Aid' and '50% profit shared'. This was radical and risky. It was radical because we were the first African brand that openly communicated our core values on the packaging of our products. The risk lay in the possibility that we might end up generating more debate than purchases. But I felt that part of establishing our dignity in the global market place was to be candid about our values and aspirations. The issue wasn't that we wanted to be drawn into a debate about whether aid should be stopped immediately, but rather to draw attention to the argument that African farmers are the real engine for transformation. The irony wasn't lost on many that what we were proposing was merely the basis of western prosperity for the last 300 years. However, up to 2005, Good African Coffee was the only African-owned coffee brand in the UK supermarkets.

But the profit-share commitment was even riskier. Here we were stating on the front of our coffee packets a commitment to share half of our profits with our farmers and their communities by investing in financial literacy and agronomy training. We were making a pledge on an issue we didn't have full control over. A business can have sound and well-thought-out strategy, have a competent team and all the capital they need but still fail to make the profits they projected. Furthermore, we didn't have very much going for us in terms of resources, nor the team or the capital to make such a bold commitment. Suppose it was interpreted as a gimmick or a ploy; suppose it took longer than we anticipated to turn a profit; would the commitment be emptied of its value and seem overly ambitious?

I spent many hours sharing these concerns with Jackie, and also discussed it with friends and colleagues. In the end, I resolved to stick to the decision for two reasons: first, it related directly to my faith and the value of sharing and caring for my community. As I once read in a book by John Stott, the influential Anglican theologian and clergymen, there is an old adage that the heart of the human condition is a problem with the human heart. Getting our 'heart' right was the first step on which we could build the profit-share commitment, aligning our values to our aspirations and securing the commitment to deliver on them. Second, it was not enough to announce such a major commitment once we had the resources on hand. Many rich people announce the giving away of their extraordinary wealth at the peak of their careers or in retirement. I believe that the key issue is putting the stake in the ground very early on.

Another objective was to confront the image of Africa as a 'basket case'. For many, Africa is characterised as a place full of conflict and violence, poverty, disease and senseless death. The negative images that fill our television screens and the apocalyptic metaphors that define most of the writing on Africa have done much damage. Africa has many critical challenges but they do not define the continent or its entire people. Part of the problem stems from a lack of sufficient airtime given to positive examples from the continent. I thought a good place to start would be to brand our coffee with a positive name and attributes that are lacking in the narrative on Africa. We chose to champion self-help, integrity, product excellence and commitment to the community, as well as transformation through trade and not handouts.

Karen Rothmyer, a contributing editor to *The Nation (US)* and an award-winning writer, has made insightful observations regarding the historical and contemporary mischaracterisation of

Africa in the media. She writes: 'Other indicators suggest that the continent, while beset by many problems, is on a trajectory of progress. Yet images and stories emanating from sub-Saharan Africa continue to portray a region of unending horrors. In June, 2010, for example, *Time* magazine published graphic pictures of a naked Sierra Leonean woman dying in childbirth.'[1] It is impossible to imagine a similar image of a European or North American woman in similar circumstances on the cover of *Time* magazine.

The data she provides is disturbing: 'A survey of Africa coverage in the top 10 US newspapers and magazines between May and September of 2010 found 245 articles mentioning poverty but only five mentioning GDP growth. Similarly, a survey of major western television reports on Africa between mid 2008 and mid 2009 by Media Tenor, a media monitoring organisation, found that crime and violence took top billing, but the economy didn't even feature in the top 10 issues. This occurred despite the fact that 2008 was a strong year for sub-Saharan Africa, whose GDP grew 5 per cent to $1.6 trillion – spurred by advances in many sectors, not just natural resources – even as US GDP growth dropped to zero.'[2]

Rothmyer captures the heart of the enduring phenomenon of how Africa is represented in the popular conscience. This distorted image has powerful incentives. It keeps empathy and aid money flowing to western-based NGOs operating in Africa and African governments and also keeps attention on the continent. As Tony Blair put it when promoting his Commission for Africa initiative, Africa 'is a scar on the conscience of the world'. In this environment, context and breadth are sacrificed for a sound bite and the result is 'global appropriation of suffering, one that sells both their [Africa's] suffering and our [western] power to ameliorate it'.[3] This influences philanthropic initiatives aimed at raising resources to 'solve' Africa's problem while at the same time reinforcing the image of hopelessness and dependency. Celebrities have been catapulted into the international development arena through initiatives where 'consumption becomes the mechanism for compassion and new forms of value.' [4] Complex and systemic issues facing many African economies are ignored and instead feel-good opportunities of consumption-based philanthropy are championed.

A good example of this was the 'Kony 2012' video that went viral with over 100 million viewings in March 2012, created by the US charity organisation 'Invisible Children'. This video and the merchandising that followed created a massive awareness about Joseph Kony, his brutal abductions of children in northern Uganda, and his diabolical brand of violence that includes torture, such as maiming and padlocking people's lips. The video reduced a deeply complex issue into a simple narrative juxtaposing the western opportunity and privilege of the producer's child with the consigned misery and fatalism of a child victim of the conflict. It is not in dispute that Kony has terrorised northern Uganda and caused great havoc, but he hasn't been in Uganda for over four years now and the north of the country is beginning to heal and move forward. Also, despite the intentions of the producers to bring attention to the plight of the victims of the conflict, the video itself erodes the dignity of the people of northern Uganda, presenting them only as victims and reinforcing the view that solutions lie in the hands of well-meaning people and organisations in the west. Never mind the fact that international attention is precisely what this nearly extinguished tyrant wants: now he can still claim relevance.

The negative branding of Africa is not a recent phenomenon but has its roots in Africa's long history of exploitation by foreign powers. It is evident in the justifications for slavery and colonial domination and is rooted in the image of African primitiveness and the urgent need to be brought into modernity. The enduring nature of this misrepresentation can be seen in the modern absence of African voices in the contemporary development debate. The popular champions for Africa tend to be white male

Europeans or Americans who are celebrities, academics, policy experts, politicians or philanthropists. This advances two impressions: that Africa is 'The White Man's burden', as leading economist William Easterly's book is titled, unable to do much for itself and needing others to champion its recovery and development; and that western civilisation represents the 'standard' model for Africa's development. Thus the solutions promoted are unquestionably western in concept, design and application.

Africa's misrepresentation has been captured in western notions of the continent being 'inferior', 'primordial', and 'backward'. In the view of the late Edward Said, the accomplished Palestinian-American literary theorist, the presentation of 'otherness' by the colonialist of the colonised was a justification for power and domination of the oppressed. From racist works like Joseph Conrad's *Heart of Darkness* and Helen Bannerman's 1898 children's book *Little Black Sambo* to Hollywood films like *The Birth of a Nation* by D. W. Griffith, which showed the Ku Klux Klansmen as saviours of the nation, and characters like the bug-eyed Dudley Dickerson appearing in the 'Three Stooges' films – all furthered the characterisation of the black stereotype as primitive, exotic, lazy, joyous, naive, superstitious and ignorant. When Joseph Conrad's novella was published in 1903, it was celebrated as a masterpiece in several academic circles. Chinua Achebe, Nigerian writer and author of the continent's most widely read novel *Things Fall Apart* wrote an essay in 1977 in which he questioned the attention given to Conrad's writings, which in his view were nothing more than the 'parodying of prejudices and insults and the questioning of the humanity of black people'.[5] Whether it was via cartography, literature or history, a strong thread of positioning Europe above Africa was woven in the fabric of western thought and knowledge. English historian Hugh Trevor-Roper once said that Africa had no history – the only history was European, and the rest was darkness.

As a child growing up in Uganda, I found very little in school or in the community that celebrated our history. If it was there, it had more to do with legend and folklore and was never documented nor systematically taught. Much of the history taught in our schools begins with the advent of colonialism – essentially 11 April 1894, when Uganda officially became a British protectorate. When my parents sent me to school in England, there too I found nothing in the history classes or literature that documented a history of Africa that wasn't written by Europeans. It was only at university that I discovered material on Africa written by either Africans or people of African origin. For example, the Senegalese historian, anthropologist, physicist and politician Cheikh Anta Diop advanced the theory of Black African roots of civilisation by building an impressive body of scientific material that showed that the ancient Egyptians were in fact black Africans, and it was from them that the Greeks sought knowledge and culture.

This challenged my many years of inculcation that African history began with the Berlin Conference of 1884 and the subsequent Scramble for Africa, which saw the continent partitioned by European powers. Many other thinkers and respected scholars like Ali Mazrui, Leopold Senghor, Aime Cesaire, Kwame Nkrumah, Julius Nyerere, Mahmood Mamdani, Wole Soyinka, Valentin Mudimbe, Amilcar Cabral, Frantz Fanon and Walter Rodney opened my mind to the reality that there was an Africa with a history far richer and deeper, more complex and worth celebrating than what was marketed as 'official history'. Most children born on the continent today will not find much history from which they can draw inspiration and build confidence about their past. Every epoch studied carries with it an indictment against the Africans – whether it is slavery or the despotism of the old kings, domination and colonial rule or the autocracy and kleptomania of post-independence rulers – fossilising into a durable and damaging narrative that robs us of our sense of pride and dignity.

★

This lack of dignity was evident even among our coffee farmers. When we first went to the Rwenzori Mountains, the farmers looked at us with great suspicion. The notion that a Ugandan company could advocate for a business relationship that considered farmer empowerment as a key goal was simply not believable. They told me and my team on many occasions that they thought that Good African belonged to 'a white person' and I was just 'a worker'. It took a long time to convince them that one of their own could actually own the company that exported their coffee to Europe. I readily admit that there is much going on in Uganda to justify their suspicions, but what I hadn't bargained for was this degree of cynicism. Years of exploitation by middlemen and loan sharks led most in the community to frown upon home-grown initiatives.

A critical pillar of the Good African model became the advocacy that we Africans had to become the solution to our own problems. We need to believe it and act on it. Breaking barriers and selling processed coffees in western supermarkets became an example of the milestones we could attain if we worked together and had faith in ourselves and our capabilities. My focus on dignity as a critical element of our business model is not meant to ignore the many structural constraints on the continent; neither do I seek to romanticise the past in an effort to promote a fictional image of Africa, one that Professor Mazrui, the US-based Kenyan scholar and political analyst, terms 'primitive romanticism'. Rather, I believe that a key value that needs to be restored if we are to have a fighting chance at developing our communities is a belief that together we Africans are actually a large part of the solution. We reject the cliché that history must repeat itself. Many in Africa have become fatalistic about the future; there is a resignation that current conditions will continue because that is how they have always known things to be.

At Good African we see the rural economy as a place with huge potential and rich social capital – land, labour and knowledge – in which we have made three principal interventions: knowledge transfer (agronomy training), technology provision (hand pulpers, improved crop varieties) and institutional capacity building (savings and credit cooperatives and producer groups). The results have also been tremendous: improved quality of harvest and a growth in volumes of coffee delivered from 7 tonnes in 2004, supplied by several hundred farmers, to 430 tonnes in 2011, supplied by over 7,000 farmers. The price for the quality coffee purchased also increased, from $1.25 per kilogram in 2004 to $4.25 per kilogram in 2011.

A key element of our business model was ensuring that as much of the value addition was carried out at source as possible. It was important that we reversed the historical trend of exporting much of the value of our agriculture commodities. The launch of our coffee factory in Kampala in 2009 was a major milestone that validated this key component of our vision. Earlier, I had felt constrained talking about value addition in Uganda while we were using facilities in the UK to roast and pack our coffees. When I travelled to China in 2008 to look for packaging equipment, I was astonished at the level of sophistication in the manufacturing sector; as well as its size and diversity. The Chinese story is simply extraordinary in this regard. Between 1978 and 2008, China's economy grew at an annual average rate of about 9 per cent.[6] China's share of global manufactured exports has since grown from 0.79 per cent in 1980 to 14.83 per cent by 2010.[7] This has generated huge foreign exchange reserves that have enabled China to take advantage of global acquisitions during economic downturns in the West. In 1980, China's foreign exchange reserves amounted to just $2.5 billion; by 2011, this amount grew to over $3 trillion.[8] At the moment, China boasts the highest foreign exchange reserves in the world and this can be attributed not only to international trade but also to the value addition of its exports.

AGRONOMY

As 2004 drew to a close, I met officers from a United States Agency for International Development (USAID) project in Kasese called 'Productive Resource Investments for Managing the Environment in Western Region' (PRIME/WEST). USAID contractors do an outstanding job coming up with memorable acronyms: SPEED (Support Program for Economic and Enterprise Development) and SCOPE (Strengthening the Competitiveness of Private Enterprise), among others. PRIME/WEST was established to promote biodiversity and conservation in several districts in western Uganda including Kasese. By sheer coincidence their Kasese offices were right next to ours. I met the chief of party, Dr Jim Seyler, in Kampala after a couple of exploratory talks between our logistics officer Mathias and their field officers in both Kasese and Kabale. PRIME/WEST was interested in our introduction of the washed coffee processing method and wanted to find ways in which they could support our farmer training and the provision of farm inputs. Our critical challenge was providing a sufficient number of inputs like hand pulpers and drying meshes for the coffee. Negotiations progressed to a level where a number of farmer training workshops were facilitated and paid for by PRIME/WEST. They also supported the provision of several hand pulpers for the farmer groups across the district in return for us expanding our training to include biodiversity and conser- vation aspects and expanding the participation of farmers near the Queen Elizabeth National Park. Part of the effort to stem poaching in the park was to provide alternative sources of income for the communities living close by. Coffee was seen as a good opportunity. Also, the toll of those killed while poaching game was very high and I was stunned when I found out that there was an association of 3,000 widows whose husbands had been killed while poaching.

My interactions with Jim were always cordial and supportive, although I never seemed to be able to convince him that while supporting farmer workshops did enable the farmers to increase their knowledge, what we really needed was to establish a roasting and packing operation in Uganda, which would incentivise higher coffee prices for the farmers. He said PRIME/WEST couldn't do it because it was not part of their mandate. Donor strategic interest on many occasions ignores the logic of what would have wider impact and be more sustainable. Nevertheless, Jim and his team provided an important contribution to the training of our farmers in 2005 and 2006. The lesson for me is that recipients are just that – recipients. However much donors make claims of 'country-owned programmes' or 'partner-owned programmes', a significant degree of conformity is expected and received. This can be viewed as quite reasonable and even justified from the viewpoint of the one giving the grant or support. The bigger lesson, though, is that economic freedom is only for the empowered. It is only through financial independence that one can enjoy financial freedom. This issue goes to the heart of the aid debate. There is an intractable dilemma here: donors expect certain conditions tied to aid, but those very conditions undermine the sovereignty and independence of the recipient. The recipients lack other immediate sources of capital and reluctantly agree to conditions they would otherwise reject. The donors also consider the conditionalities to be important markers for improved accountability but they end up being significant weapons of policy leverage and control. Later, in 2009, we would work with another USAID project called LEAD (Livelihoods and Enterprises for Agricultural Development), which generously supported our brand-development activities and helped us acquire washing stations for our farmer group areas. There was greater flexibility with this programme and the relational aspects of the project were greatly enhanced by the leadership of Susan Corning, the managing director and chief of party, and her technical team.

In 2008, Good African was chosen as one of several Ugandan

companies to access funding from the International Trade Center (ITC) under the Uganda Organic Export Initiative (UOEXI) project so that we could obtain organic-certification status for our farmers. I signed a memorandum of understanding with the National Organic Movement Uganda (NOGAMU) and Agro Eco East Africa that implementation of this project would include training farmers in organic production as well as the set-up of Internal Control System (ICS). We recruited Patrick Byensi as our new organic coffee training officer; he and Tharcisse, the systems developer, started field activities to promote organic farming methods in Kasese district. In reality, most of the coffee was already grown organically but it was just not certified. We embarked on training workshops and internal organic standards were maintained. We identified seventeen coordinators and GAC staff for this exercise. Farmer registration for organic production was completed in 2008 by our field coordinators and trained field officers and thereafter, several other training workshops on internal control systems and organic pest management were conducted. We then began the compilation of the organic internal control system manual and by the end of the year we had carried out all the farmers' training for internal organic standards in all the sub-counties. On 5 December 2008, we submitted our application for certification to the Soil Association Certification Limited in the UK for 2,028 farmers. The certification contract was signed soon after and our organic status was obtained after an eighteen-month conversion period. Sustaining this status proved quite costly, and we had to suspend renewal in 2010 until we had the necessary resources in hand.

FINANCIAL LITERACY AND SAVINGS AND CREDIT COOPERATIVES

After a round of field research in 2005, we established that access to capital, specifically micro-loans, was a major constraint for our farmers. The two coffee seasons represented a total of six months in a year for farmers to earn an income. One of the key areas of intervention for our profit-share commitment would be financial intermediation: helping the farmers set up Savings and Credit Cooperatives (SACCOs). We carried out financial literacy training of the farmers based on location across the seventeen sub-counties in the district. I then invited George Kariithi, a Kenyan with extensive microfinance experience, to advise us on how to set up the training programmes. Both George and his brother Kibby, a former Good African Coffee board member, helped us appreciate the opportunity that SACCOs would represent in transforming the lives of the farmers. We then recruited Mohamed Mokili, a young graduate with training in microfinance, and immediately placed him in the field to carry out training support for the farmers. Once the farmers had gone through several rounds of financial literacy training, we encouraged them to elect their SACCO leaders and formally resolve to set up the SACCO. We helped them draw up the guidelines, process their applications with the government regulatory authority and facilitate their registration.

When all the SACCOs were registered, we embarked on securing modest office space and furniture for them. The condition was that we would not give any further financial support beyond training costs, provision of basic office infrastructure and the payment of their office rent for the first year alone. In turn they would commit to making savings from their coffee sales and other activities. These savings would then form a pool of resources that farmers in the SACCO could use as loans in a well-documented and communally agreed process. A core element in this initiative was empowerment through ownership. The farmers own their SACCOs outright as a partnership and are responsible for how they progress. Our contribution is limited to set up support, training and provision of operational materials like ledger books and savings and banking account books and provision for initial office costs. It was important that the farmers owned and operated their SACCOs. There can be little empowerment without ownership. Ownership gives the farmers equity, it exposes them to the complexities and dynamics of the financial sector, which raises the farmers' level of ambition and aspirations. As George kept pointing out to me, Kenya is one of the classic success stories for SACCOs and the Cooperative Movement in Kenya has played a big role in the development of financial literacy and enabling the pooling of resources for investments and wealth creation. The total SACCO subsector in Kenya was worth $2.5 billion in 2010 with 5,544 registered SACCOs and controlling almost 10 per cent of Kenya's GDP.[9] And the cooperative sector employed over 300,000 Kenyans directly and many more indirectly.[10]

In 2011, we took the decision to separate our community activities from the business operations by setting up the Good African Foundation. I felt that the foundation would best serve the community initiatives in a focused way while the business did the work of selling coffee. This would mean that the profit-share commitment from the business would go directly to the foundation that then carries out the two principal activities of farmer agronomy training and SACCO training and strengthening. The foundation allows for more specialised interventions like business development skills training that we, up to this point, have not had the resources to carry out.

SELLING THE MODEL

By 2007, Good African as a brand had received considerable media attention. The *Financial Times*, *Telegraph* and *Guardian* had given me the opportunity not just to make the argument for trade but also to advocate our business model as a sustainable route for community empowerment and transformation.

In February 2007, two further media opportunities widened the awareness for our model. The first was an invitation to speak at the prestigious RSA (Royal Society for the encouragement of Arts, Manufactures and Commerce) in London, the other was an interview with Stephen Sackur for the renowned BBC current affairs programme *Hardtalk*. The former offered me the chance to articulate some of my thoughts on our business model in front of a high-profile audience, while the latter gave me access to a huge television audience. After the BBC interview, I received several hundred emails of encouragement and support that indicated a resonance with the model.

I remember clearly where I was on 20 February 2007, the day the BBC interview was aired. I was up in the Rwenzori Mountains with a group of Japanese coffee officials from the Ueshima Coffee Co., Ltd (UCC). UCC is the leading coffee company in Japan and their team was in Uganda to visit David Barry at Kyagalanyi Coffee in Kampala and then visit our field operations in Kasese. We set off from the Magherita Hotel in Kasese and travelled to Mahango, Rukoki and Kyarumba sub-counties, where we visited several farmers and the UCC officials were able to see first hand the washing techniques being used. Back at the hotel that evening, tired from the drive on the rough mountain roads, we sat on the balcony that overlooked the garden, facing a television set. We had only been sitting down for ten minutes when *Hardtalk* came on air – and the presenter introduced me as his guest. I hadn't actually known when the programme was scheduled to be aired, so I was as surprised as my guests when I appeared onscreen. As the interview progressed, the UCC guys began to speak with each other in excited tones. Obviously seeing me on the screen was as unexpected for them as it was fortuitous for me. Some even took out their cameras and started taking pictures; another phoned his wife in Japan to tell her to watch the programme.

After the interview, the atmosphere, which had been one of slight fatigue from the day's travels, was energised. An hour later, when my uncle John Sendanyoye who works at the ILO in Geneva phoned me to say he had seen the interview, I told him about my guests and their reaction. Having lived in Japan for many years, he laughed and assured me that it was probably the interview that would give me credibility rather than any field visits I had arranged for them in the mountains.

Although the *Hardtalk* interview garnered significant publicity, somehow it didn't translate into product sales. There was an increase in the number of personal invitations or commendations, and this caused me some concern. The business was still very young and I felt that some of the recognition was premature. The operating environment remained very challenging, with continued financial pressures and the day-to-day struggle of making ends meet. Two events in 2007 captured the dilemma. The first was my nomination by the World Economic Forum (WEF) to become a Young Global Leader (YGL). As their website says: 'The Forum of Young Global Leaders is a unique, multistakeholder community of more than 700 exceptional young leaders who share a commitment to shaping the global future'. Thousands are nominated each year, from which between 100 and 200 are honoured with the invitation to become YGLs. That year I was nominated to join what was an esteemed club of high-profile individuals, including Larry Page and Sergey Brin, the co-founders of Google; Mikheil Saakashvili, the president of Georgia; Marjorie Scardino, chief executive of Pearson; Arthur Sulzberger, chairman and publisher of the *New York Times*; Jimmy Wales, the founder and promoter of online encyclopedia Wikipedia; Tom Glocer, chief executive officer of Reuters, and Hisashi Hieda, chairman and chief executive officer of Fuji Television Network. I travelled to Dalian, China, in September 2007 for my maiden meeting with some of the YGLs and there met a group of wonderful, highly intelligent and successful individuals from diverse walks of life. It was a great opportunity to share and network.

Then in October 2007, I received an even more surprising

invitation: to attend a reception at Buckingham Palace. The reception was in recognition of diaspora Africans in various fields – business, academia, and those in the social sector – and was hosted by the Queen during the year of the biennial Commonwealth Heads of Government Meeting (CHOGM), which was to be held in Uganda. I agonised over whether to attend this reception, as I didn't really have the funds to spend on a trip to the UK. Eventually, I decided that the trip was worth it, as it might result in something positive. I flew to London and a friend of mine, Richard, who works as the deputy head concierge at a five-star hotel, offered me a chauffeur-driven vehicle free of charge. As he put it, 'It is difficult accessing Buckingham Palace using the underground train. You must go there with dignity.' The reception turned out to be an occasion to mingle and network with the many guests, before queuing to meet the Queen and the Duke of Edinburgh. As I sat back in the car on the way back from the Palace, I reflected on how the invitation had turned out to be a balm, a tonic for the soul in a season of business challenges.

REFLECTIONS ON THE FAIRTRADE MODEL

In February 2007, I gave my talk at the Royal Society for the Encouragement of Arts, Manufactures and Commerce in London. The presentation focused on the barriers to trade between Africa and the rest of the world and the lessons we could learn from the rapidly industrialising economies of Asia.

Afterwards we had a question and answer session and among the dozen or so questions that I was asked that evening, one of the audience sought out my thoughts on the Fairtrade organisation that certifies producers, often smallholder farmer groups, and has been at the forefront of campaigning for better prices for third-world growers for the last two decades. The question was asked by Harriet Lamb, the energetic executive director for the Fairtrade

Foundation, and later over dinner she asked me whether I would consider Fairtrade certification. Since we launched our coffee in the UK, we have received several enquiries into why Good African Coffee is not certified. In the past I responded to these questions with a brief and standard response: working with the farmers directly and being based in Uganda, processing our coffee locally and having a profit-share commitment, we didn't need to be Fairtrade-certified; in other words, we were more than fair trade. However, a more detailed response is now necessary because Fairtrade is increasingly becoming the ethical standard for well-meaning consumers seeking to do something against third-world poverty. They have become the modern litmus test of one's commitment to tackling unjust and unfair trading conditions in the third world and, by inference, if you are not certified then you probably are not doing very much to address third-world poverty.

Fairtrade is a European-based social movement that was shaped by the student activism and political consciousness of the 1960s and became popular during the crisis of low coffee prices in the 1990s with its strong advocacy for better prices for poor farmers in producer nations. Fairtrade seeks to help producers in third-world countries by improving trading conditions through the payment of higher prices for a variety of products, notably bananas, honey, cotton, coffee, chocolate, flowers, cocoa, sugar, tea and fresh fruit. It does this by a certification process. The movement has become popular in Europe and North America where consumers see it as providing a traceable model for impacting poor producers in third-world countries. It wields together consumption, trade and philanthropy into a broad narrative of doing good through your shopping choices. The idea is that Fairtrade protects against exploitation in international trade and reconnects consumers with producers. And it seeks to do this by setting minimum prices, direct trading mechanisms, and a social premium paid to producer groups.

The sales for Fairtrade products in Europe have grown tremendously. In the UK, roast and ground Fairtrade coffees sold through retail outlets have increased exponentially in value over the last fifteen years. In 1998, for example, retail sales for Fairtrade coffees were valued at £13.7 million and by the time we launched our coffees in the UK in 2005, sales had grown to £65.8 million. In 2009, they jumped to £157 million.[11] The market for Fairtrade coffees and other products grows by almost 50 per cent year on year. Even during the recession period from 2009, growth has remained strong. However, they remain, for most commodities, a very small percentage of total global sales. And most farmers who are members of the Fairtrade cooperatives only sell a portion (sometimes small) of their output through Fairtrade channels. Nevertheless, the Fairtrade movement doesn't just have a large following, it also has a significant brand presence that is reinforced through activities like 'Fairtrade Fortnight' and partnerships with community networks.

However, underpinning this advocacy for the improvement of third-world living conditions is a western model of trade that I believe does more to further the entrenched commercial interests of the advanced economies without altering the structural dynamics that are keeping third-world producer countries poor and advanced economies rich. Fairtrade is overly generous about their value and is not far from the old charity model, which encourages consumers to pay a few extra cents for products with the in-built assumption that transformation of the producer communities will happen as a result.

Fairtrade advocates state that it is the distortions and impediments of the free market that make trade unfair. They then address these problems through their price premiums and social good works. In reality, though, this is only partly true. There are structural distortions and asymmetries inherent in the free market, but Fairtrade has an in-built distortion of its own. With free trade, the distortion is in the nature of the markets themselves; they are neither free nor fair, for subsidies, tariffs and non-tariff barriers define the environment for producers from Africa. Fairtrade, on the other hand, presents a false panacea to this systemic problem by, as I see it, claiming that by paying a few extra cents for pounds of coffee, for example, western consumers are having a significant and sustainable effect on the third world. This might be well-meaning but in my view it is also self-serving. It is a Eurocentric model for compassionate consumption that defines Africa and other third-world producers as deserving of western generosity, which will lift them out of their poverty and misery. It diverts attention from the structural issues that make trade between third-world producers and the developed world unfair and unjust.

Through the use of labels, certification, a brigade of celebrities and other 'moral sovereigns', Fairtrade can become a shortcut for complex and systemic socio-economic issues that keep poor producer countries poor. Consumption becomes a tithe, through which social value is created by appropriating the corporate social responsibility of a developed country's manufacturers or retailers. Consumers can then relax in the knowledge that they are doing well by purchasing products in their retail stores.

A failure to recognise the dynamics that keep poor countries poor is exemplified in the case of coffee. Coffee farmers in Africa are poor not just because world commodity prices have been low, but fundamentally because these farmers operate at the bottom of the coffee value chain, have little crop diversification and limited access to farm inputs and other appropriate technologies. They engage in low-quality coffee production, low productivity and low output farming, have poor access to technology and capital, and have poor ownership of their productive assets. They face these structural impediments every day and Fairtrade does not even begin to address them. Empowerment and community transformation require more than just better prices for third-world growers, they necessitate linking African farmers to African processors, who then add value and supply the global marketplace with value-added products. Along this value chain, jobs are created, entrepreneurs are encouraged, tax revenues grow and wealth is created. This is how prosperity was achieved in the industrialised countries of Europe, North America and Asia.

It is not by accident that today's developed economies, including those of the BRIC countries (Brazil, Russia, India and China), have rapidly transformed through the export of finished goods. In 2011, China became the world's second largest economy with a GDP of $10 trillion behind the USA with $14.6 trillion. Brazil overtook the UK to become the seventh largest economy in the world with a GDP of $2.1 trillion. In the next eight years, China will overtake the US economy, and by 2020, Russia will have overtaken Germany. All this rapid development by former so-called developing economies has been largely built on aggressively developing the manufacturing and processing sectors. Yet, while most Fairtrade products that are sold in the retail outlets of developed countries are processed in those countries, very little value-addition manufacturing takes place in the producer countries. This is the reason why, for a long time, we remained the only African-based coffee company exporting roasted and packed coffees direct to British retail stores. It was not because we possess greater capabilities or opportunities than other enterprises; it was just that it is so difficult to penetrate these markets with finished products that entrepreneurs either give up or find other more rewarding engagements.

The Fairtrade model has argued for the importance of its payment of a minimum floor price for a variety of products, but in reality this price minimum works at best as a price protection mechanism when commodity prices are depressed. In an environment of sustained high prices, this proposition ends up proving less attractive to roasters who are contending with already shrinking margins. This minimum floor price has increased over time, from US$1.20 per pound of coffee at one time to its current level of US$1.40 per pound of coffee in mid 2010. This minimum price is not necessarily linked to a guaranteed volume of coffee and there is no evidence I have seen that Fairtrade farmers get higher prices on average. As coffee prices for example continued to rise – as they did for most of 2010 and 2011 – to a thirty-five-year high, there was little incentive to pay a premium price for coffee and because approximately only 5 per cent of coffee sales in the UK are Fairtrade, the overall impact on the producers in aggregate terms is minimal.

The Fairtrade minimum price could also be described as a reward for nothing. It serves, in effect, as a price-fixing concept to bolster farmer incomes in the absence of any linkage to sustainable coffee quality. The lack of a strong price-quality linkage means that farmers do not necessarily capture high-value niche markets and other gourmet buyers, who are very quality conscious. This opportunity failure reinforces farmer vulnerability to price-sensitive buyers. Also, for small-scale farmers, sustaining high-quality produce remains a major challenge. When we started buying coffees from our farmers in Kasese, we paid a high price, in most instances about 30 per cent higher than the prevailing market price. The reason: the quality of the coffee. We told the farmers that we were paying the premium price for quality washed arabica coffees and we would not compensate them for low quality. It is important that farmers are not rewarded in sympathy but rather for quality. Sympathy is not sustainable, quality is. The result has been higher coffee prices and improved quality of coffees from the area, even those bought by our competitors.

For sustainable empowerment, specific interventions are needed. Farmers need to be linked to the formal financial markets by financial literacy training, creating savings and credit know-how through the intermediation of savings and credit cooperatives. Farmers need to move up the value chain by engaging in some form of value-added processing at source. Through agronomy best practices training, farmers can improve the quality of their crops and yields and so fetch better prices. Processing at source and building brands on the continent develop intellectual property, dignity, motivate business aspirations and increase exposure. More processing at source will lead to deeper and wider economic impact through increased employment and growth in the domestic tax base. When we set up our roasting and packing facility in Kampala and took the finished products to the farmers in Kasese to drink, there was a shift in their mindset. There was an appreciation that they don't just produce coffee as a commodity, but actually contribute to a finished product that is tangible and which they themselves can consume. A 'can do' attitude emerges and spreads across other economic activities. Sustainability is established when the farmers can continue to access the best prices for the best quality coffees outside the costly certification models like Fairtrade.

To me, the Fairtrade movement has been largely preoccupied with celebrating African producers for their small-scale and rural idyll, as though this is really worth celebrating. To be a small-holder farmer means to be vulnerable and exploited, with little access to inputs, capital and technology. These farmers are tied to their land in relations of production that are unfair and unjust; and the burden is worse when it comes to women who have unequal access to the assets within their own communities. Only by increasing farm sizes, through land consolidation and communal farming where technologies can be applied across bigger tracts of land generating efficiency and economies of scale, can output and productivity increase. Good African's experience in managing a large pool of small-scale farmers has exposed us to the myriad challenges of operating in this area. We struggle to maintain a reasonably low ratio of extension workers to farmers. Also, the management of quality on so many small-scale plots of land is problematic. We have learned to encourage farmers to consolidate their land rather than managing very small plots of land. Agricultural modernisation is a result of scale and efficient deployment of capital, labour and technology. But this ultimately is a political question and something that the Fairtrade movement sidesteps through their rhetoric of 'Better deals for third-world growers . . .'

Conclusion

Our experience has shown us that in the general framework of daily struggle, this battle against ourselves, this struggle against our own weaknesses . . . is the most difficult of all.
  Amilcar Cabral

The Good African story has been a journey of tremendous privilege and it continues to unfold in unexpected ways. In the introduction I said that I decided to write this book because very few African entrepreneurs write about their business experiences. By neglecting to do this, they deny the historical memory that is of critical intellectual value to the next generation. Returning to my American friend's comment that his mission was to make mistakes and then help others avoid them, as the reader will have invariably established, I have made many mistakes along the way and learned many wonderful lessons. Some mistakes became apparent immediately, while others took time to emerge.

There is a tendency in business leadership literature to celebrate the factors that lead to success and place less emphasis on those that can lead to failure. We can learn as much from our mistakes as we can from our success. In fact, it is the lessons we take away from failure that offer us the insights and encouragement to improve and to become better people. I don't share these lessons as timeless truths, or as coming from some wise sage; rather, I share them by way of reflection and encouragement for the next generation of social entrepreneurs. Every day, we meet obstacles and challenges that threaten us, discourage us and even sometimes dislodge us, and yet we must continue to strive to help transform our community. Transformation is a rough, messy and difficult engagement. The thing the social entrepreneur recognises when he embarks on his journey is that he is largely dealing with structures. Transformation begins when we change social structures and relationship frameworks among the economic actors in the community. To do this, the social entrepreneur must seek to improve the values in the community, and in the process align his personal values too. To do this is to embrace a goal larger than self. The social entrepreneur must therefore be willing to pay a price that involves personal sacrifice. But the returns are immensely rewarding.

BIG VISIONS MEAN BIG SACRIFICES

If there is a lesson that has left an indelible mark on me over the last seven years, it is that big visions demand big sacrifices. It might sound like an obvious point but it is an issue that challenges entrepreneurs all the time. Big visions always sound improbable to others and the entrepreneur has to be willing to make significant sacrifices along the way before they get buy-in, acceptance and even support from the wider community. When I started our coffee business in 2003, I was naive in my assumption that because there was so much talk in the policy circles and in the business community about the opportunities for processed and branded coffees, our model would generate immediate support from banks, governments, supermarkets and even the farmers themselves. Yet from the outset, the farmers were cynical and even reticent. The banks were not just uninterested but went even further, sharing their scepticism with fellow bankers. The supermarkets were equally sceptical and that's why it took over a dozen trips before they first put our coffees on their shelves. Many friends and colleagues were unconvinced that the project would succeed. Seven years on, and with hindsight, I can see that my biggest challenge was to maintain my self-confidence and commitment to the project. Negative and cynical people became a no-go area for me because, like the flu virus, negativity is contagious. I also sought and engaged with people on various paths in life who were facing different struggles; people from whose experiences I could learn and gain wisdom. You are a product of who you surround yourself with.

I learned to appreciate that I was not owed a sympathetic ear by anyone and that while a pioneering vision rarely elicits much support in its infancy, with time, and as people see you make your own commitments and sacrifices, they buy in to your vision. Investors, whether of capital or of their time, are really investing in the entrepreneur and their capacity to deliver on the business plan. As the business matures, investors will look more to the company and its performance. The key focus for the social entrepreneur is to define clearly where the company is going and then align all the key constituencies on that course; be it people, resources or operations.

An entrepreneur's journey might be a lonely one at times but they rarely carry the mantle alone; they have a team that walks alongside them. Your team will make sacrifices if they see you do the same. I remember calling a staff meeting in 2007, during a difficult time for the business, to let the team know that I would have to let them go because we just couldn't continue to delay salaries and I couldn't guarantee when our cash flow would stabilise. This was a very difficult meeting for me, given how much the team had already sacrificed. Once I had finished talking, one of my colleagues spoke and said that they too had made sacrifices and they had a stake in the vision, and they were willing to continue until the situation turned around. In their eyes, letting them go was not a solution and would just mean that they had made sacrifices for nothing.

It is very important to be candid with your team. Candour develops trust and confidence. In the beginning, I tended to shield the team from some of the difficulties I was grappling with but in the end I found this to be a poor strategy for handling challenges. Candour generates buy-in and allows others to contribute ideas about how to solve problems. Without it, the team looks at you like the proverbial weatherman, expecting you to announce when the rains are due.

INSPIRATION

A social entrepreneur can learn from and be inspired by a person, or a cause in their line of interest. Most leaders have accomplished great things by faith, self-belief and courage. It is not that they lacked fear and self-doubt; rather, they were inspired to do things beyond the constraints and limitations of their environment. Inspiration drives you, and encourages perseverance and resilience. It is the substance of our hope and commitment.

INTEGRITY

Integrity is not just being open and accountable about one's situation; it is also appreciating the truth about what it will take for you to get to your objective. Leonard Sweet – author, pastor, scholar and professor of Evangelism at Drew Theological School in Madison, New Jersey – has an interesting perspective on integrity.[1] For him, it is the willingness to do anything you ask those working with you to do. It is about being who you say you are even when it costs you. On several occasions, I have found myself in a situation where I was being asked by a potential financier to compromise on a key element of our model, such as the profit-share commitment to the farmers and their communities, or even to sell the business and be done with the daily cash-flow challenges. Despite the desperate circumstances the company frequently found itself in, for me, integrity meant rejecting such offers even when the cost was undoubtedly going to be high. As my good friend Arthur Burk often remarks, most people cannot visualise the joys of freedom as clearly as they can visualise the pain of their current challenges. This paralyses many entrepreneurial initiatives. We eschew walking the talk for pain relief and surrender.

An entrepreneur is like an evangelist: preaching his message to anyone who will care to listen and rejoicing when a few make the altar call. To speak openly about one's failures as well as successes attracts people's attention because that is what their own journeys have been like.

The British Antarctic explorer Ernest Shackleton, who from 1914 to 1917 attempted the crossing of the continent from sea to sea via the South Pole, displayed extraordinary bravery and leadership even though he ultimately never accomplished his goal. He became a role model for leadership, motivating his men and keeping them safe through the most adverse conditions imaginable. The advert he placed in *The Times* of London must have been the most candid and transparent recruitment drive ever:

Men wanted for hazardous journey. Small wages, bitter cold, long months of complete darkness, constant danger, safe return doubtful. Honour and recognition in case of success.

The response was overwhelming.[2]

WE ALL HAVE BEEN GIVEN TALENTS

Poverty is not just defined by a lack of material resources but also a lack of opportunities. In the early days of development economics, a popular concept used in the analysis of poor communities was known as the 'vicious cycle of poverty'. People are poor because they are poor and will remain poor as the cycle reinforces itself. But one thing I have learned about the peasant farmers is that once they have the opportunity, the tools and the knowledge to work and earn an income, they can break this cycle and lift themselves out of poverty. Lack of opportunities, rather than lack of money, is the critical constraint. We are all born equipped with talents, whatever our circumstances. It is what we do with these talents that is key.

Money facilitates, circumstances can also be conducive, but talent is the intrinsic infrastructure that can shape opportunities and circumstances for the good. Most people that today we celebrate as successful had less than ideal circumstances in the beginning of their lives. I love watching South African athlete Oscar Pistorius, the 'Blade Runner', compete in races. Pistorius was born with a deformity in both his legs and had them amputated from the knees down at eleven months. Nevertheless, he went to school, played tennis, rugby and water polo; today, he is known as the fastest man on no legs. His parents and coach believed in him, but more importantly he believed in himself.

TESTIMONIALS

Over the years that Good African Coffee has been operating in Kasese, we have seen and documented tremendous transformation in the socio-economic lives of many of our farmers. The three testimonies that follow capture some of this transformation.

*

Muhindo Perezi is a widow and mother of five children from Rukoki sub-county. Three of her children attend school while two are still at home. Two of her other children passed away. She has a coffee farm that is approximately half an acre. Before we went to Kasese, Muhindo usually mortgaged her coffee farm at the flowering stage to cater for her consumption needs. When she harvested her coffee she usually processed the cherries by drying them, which was costly and time consuming. Muhindo had never kept any records on her farm yields. She joined a SACCO in her area and was able to borrow money and repay it after she sold her coffee.

When we first met Muhindo she was not sure that the prices we promised to pay would be a reality or that the coffee they delivered would be paid for. Before we began trading with her, Muhindo would sell each kilo of coffee for about 1,800 Uganda shillings per kilogram, which is equivalent to $0.80. That same year, with improved coffee quality Good African paid 3,300 Uganda shillings per kilogram ($1.50) at the farmgate price for parchment coffee.

Baluku Bwanandeke Exevier is from Maliba sub-county, a married father of seven children. One of our most successful farmers, he is emblematic of the transformation that has occurred as a result of our model. Exevier has one of the best organised producer groups with the highest deliveries of coffees in the programme. His sub-county SACCO is one of the fastest growing in our programme. Two of his children have gone through institutions of higher learning and when I asked his eldest son whether he wanted to be a coffee farmer too, he said no; he wanted to be an engineer. In Katabukene, the village where Exevier and his family reside high up in the Rwenzoris, they now have five university graduates. In 2004 they had none. Exevier has a three-acre coffee farm and he used to get very little for his coffee. He found the drying method for his cherries very involved and time consuming.

When we met he told me that it would take him over thirty days to dry his coffee. The hygiene in his home declined during harvesting time and drying and most seasons he mortgaged a large chunk of his farm at flowering stage, which in his words kept him a slave on his own farm. The traders who used to buy his coffee direct from his farm didn't have much coffee knowledge and spoilt the flowering for the next season. Like most of the other farmers he also had trust issues: would we pay for the coffee delivered to our stores or even pay the price that we promised on the board outside the office?

When I first met Exevier in 2004, he was staying in a mud-and-wattle house and made the long journey from Katabukene to Kasese town by bicycle. Today, he travels around on a *boda-boda* and lives in a bricks-and-mortar house with a corrugated iron-sheet roof with stores and extra rooms built at the back. He and his community have built a store for their coffee, and their SACCO averages fifty new members each month. By December 2011, his SACCO had savings amounting to Uganda shillings 18,245,488 (US$7,300), and a loan portfolio of Uganda shillings 12,445,970 (US$ 5,000). When I spoke to him in December 2011, he told me that he had Uganda shillings 2,780,000 (US$1,200) as savings on his SACCO account; he had never saved this kind of money before. Through our agronomy training programmes, Exevier no longer sprays his coffee with pesticides and has learned to use local herbs. One of the challenges he finds is our inability to give the farmers loans directly. As much as we would like to help capitalise the SACCOs, we just don't have the resources to do this.

Masereka Sylvester is our leading coordinator in Kitholhu sub-county near the border with the Democratic Republic of Congo. He is a father of seven children, five of whom attend school while the other two are still infants. Our field team first met Sylvester at Kanyasti primary school where they were carrying out a farmer training programme. Like Muhindo and Exevier, Sylvester mortgaged his farm to middlemen traders during the flowering season for the coffee. He didn't keep much by way of records by the time we met him and his coffee was fetching very low prices. Sylvester and his fellow farmers also quickly adopted many of the coffee agronomy best practices we taught them, such as mulching, stumping, pruning, the planting of shade trees and the use of manure from their animals for fertiliser.

When we first met Sylvester he complained about being discouraged by the low prices for his coffee at 1,800 Uganda shillings per kilogram (US $0.80 dollars) – his commitment to growing coffee was waning. But as the quality and value of his coffee grew, he helped open up offices for the farmer producer group and also the SACCO in his area and he mobilised farmers to join the savings programme.

These are only a few of the many transformations that Good African Coffee has been privileged to witness. Their stories have encouraged me, taught me valuable lessons, and exposed me to the timeless truth that once innate talents are tapped by opportunity, transformation can occur. Muhindo, Exevier, Sylvester and others like them are all reasons why I have walked this Good African journey; been blessed, fulfilled and honoured by it.

Notes

INTRODUCTION

1   Amina Mama, 'Is It Ethical to Study Africa? Preliminary Thoughts on Scholarship and Freedom', *African Studies Review*, vol. 50, no. 1, April 2007, pp. 1–26.

2   Ibid.

3   Calestous Juma, *The New Harvest: Agricultural Innovations in Africa* (Oxford University Press, 2011).

4   Ibid.

5   Ibid.

6   Ibid.

7   G. Denning, P. Kabambe, P. Sanchez, A. Malik, R. Flor et al., 'Input Subsidies to Improve Smallholder Maize Productivity in Malawi: Toward an African Green Revolution', *PLoS Biology*, 7(1): e1000023. doi:10.1371/journal.pbio.1000023, 2009.

8   Ibid.

9   Ibid.

10 Ha-Joon Chang, *Kicking Away the Ladder: Development Strategy in Historical Perspective* (Anthem Press, 2002).

11 Nicholas D. Kristof, 'Aid: Can It Work?', *New York Review of Books*, 5 October 2006.

12 Jeffrey Sachs, *The End of Poverty: Economic Possibilities for Our Time* (Penguin Press, 2005).

13 William Easterly, *The Elusive Quest for Growth: Economists'*

Adventures and Misadventures in the Tropics (MIT Press, 2002); Dambisa Moyo, *Dead Aid: Why Aid is Not Working and How There is Another Way for Africa* (London: Allen Lane, 2009).

14 Samuel Huntington, 'The clash of civilizations' in: *Foreign Affairs*, 27: 3, p. 34.

15 Chalmers A. Johnson, *MITI and the Japanese Miracle* (Stanford University Press, 1982); Robert Wade, *Governing the Market: Economic Theory and the Role of Government in East Asian Industrialization* (Princeton University Press, 1990); Peter Evans, *Embedded Autonomy: States and Industrial Transformation* (Princeton University Press, 1995).

16 Chalmers A. Johnson, *MITI and the Japanese Miracle*.

17 World Trade Organisation data, 2011.

18 Ibid.

19 D. P. Chiwandamira, 'A Review of the Negotiation of Economic Partnership Agreements (EPAS) Between the European Union & SADC and the Implication for Small Scale Farmers, IFAD, Working Paper (November 2006).

20 Ibid.

21 Ibid.

22 Otsuki et al., 'A Race to the Top? A Case Study of Food Safety Standards and African Exports', Working Paper 2536 (World Bank, 2001).

CHAPTER ONE

1 This formulation has its roots in Douglas C. North's classic formulation. However, it is not only formal institutions that define the opportunities or constraints of the state but also the informal institutions, and in the post-colonial African context some have observed the eminence of the latter.

2 *Cuba: an African Odyssey*, ARTE France, 2007.

3 Robert Craig Johnson, *Heart of Darkness: the Tragedy of the Congo, 1960–67*, part of a series first published, in abbreviated

form, in *Eagle Droppings*, the Newsletter of the Rocky Mountain Chapter, IPMS/USA, 1997.

4   Odd Arne Westad, *The Global Cold War: Third World Interventions and the Making of Our Times* (Cambridge University Press, 2006).

5   Ibid.

6   Daron Acemoglu and James A. Robinson, *Why Nations Fail: The Origins of Power, Prosperity and Poverty* (London: Profile Books, 2012).

7   Ibid., p. 91.

8   Peter Forbes, 'Why Nations Fail by Daron Acemoglu and James A. Robinson', *Independent*, 26 May 2012.

9   Daron Acemoglu and James A. Robinson, *Why Nations Fail*, p. 68.

10   Jared Diamond, *Guns, Germs and Steel: The Fates of Human Societies* (London: Vintage, 2005).

11   Daron Acemoglu and James A. Robinson, *Why Nations Fail*, p. 50.

12   Jeffrey Herbst, *States and Power in Africa: Comparative Lessons in Authority and Control* (Princeton: Princeton University Press, 2000).

13   World Bank Data, 2011.

14   Robert H. Bates, *When Things Fell Apart: State Failure in Late-Century Africa* (Cambridge: Cambridge University Press, 2008).

15   Patrick Manning, *Slavery and African Life: Occidental Oriental and African Slave Trades* (Cambridge University Press, 1990).

16   B. A. Ogot, 'Hadith, History and social change in East Africa', proceedings of the 1974 conference of the Historical Association of Kenya, vol. 6 (East African Literature Bureau for the Historical Association of Kenya, 1976).

17   Mahmood Mamdani, *Citizen and Subject: Contemporary Africa and the Legacy of Late Colonialism* (Princeton: Princeton University Press, 1996).

18   Sam C. Nolutshungu, *Limits of Anarchy: Intervention and*

State Formation in Chad (Charlottesville & London: University Press of Virginia, 1991).

19 Frederick D. Lugard, *The rise of our East African Empire: Early Efforts in Nyasaland and Uganda* (London: Cass, 1968).

20 Frederick Cooper, *Africa Since 1940: The Past of the Present* (Cambridge University Press, 2002).

21 Joel S. Migdal, *Strong Societies, Weak States: State-Society Relations & State Capabilities in the Third World* (Princeton: Princeton University Press, 1988).

22 Patrick Chabal and Jean-Pascal Daloz, *Africa Works: Disorder as Political Instrument* (International African Institute and Indiana University Press, 1999).

23 Ibid.

24 Jean-François Bayart, *The State in Africa: the Politics of the Belly* (Malden: MA Polity Press, 2010).

25 Nicolas van de Walle, 'Presidentialism and Clientelism in Africa's Emerging Party Systems', *Journal of Modern African Studies*, 41, June 2003, p. 310.

26 Patrick Chabal and Jean-Pascal Daloz, *Africa Works: Disorder as Political Instrument*, p. xv.

27 Ibid., p. xviii.

28 Ibid., p. 11.

29 Jeffrey Herbst, *States and Power in Africa: Comparative Lessons in Authority and Control.*

30 Chris Allen, 'Understanding African Politics', *Review of African Political Economy*, vol. 22, no. 65, September 1995.

31 *Independent*, 21 December 2010 (Kampala, Uganda).

CHAPTER TWO

1 Republic of Uganda. *Statistical Abstract 1971*, Entebbe, 1972, 13. The 1969 population census recorded the citizenship status of the members of the Asian community as: 36,593 British citizens, 8,890 Indian, 253 Pakistani and 25,657

Ugandan, bringing the total to 71,393. Here, the term Asians is used to define people originating from the Indian subcontinent, and including subsequent generations born in Uganda. 'Asians' is the popularly used term in the literature. We use the term Indian and Asian interchangeably.

2   Mahmood Mamdani, *From Citizen to Refugee: Ugandan Asians come to Britain* (London: Francis Pinter, 1973).

3   Mahmood Mamdani, 'The Uganda Asian Expulsion: Twenty Years After', paper presented at workshop on *Ugandan Asians Twenty Years after the Expulsion* (Queen Elizabeth House, Oxford University, 1992).

4   *New Vision*, 12 April 2007.

5   Ibid.

6   Mahmood Mamdani, 'The Asian Question Again: A reflection', *Pambazuka News*, issue 303, http://pambazuka.org/en/category/comment/41273.

7   V. Jamal, 'Asians in Uganda 1880–1972: Inequality and Expulsion' in: *Economic History Review*, 19 (4) New Series, 29, no. 4, November 1976, pp. 602–616, 609.

8   Michael A. Tribe, 'Economic Aspects of the Expulsion' in: *Expulsion of a Minority* (London: Athlone Press, 1975).

9   John S. Galbraith, *Mackinnon and East Africa 1878–1895: A Study in the New Imperialism* (Cambridge University Press, 1972).

10 E. A. Brett, *Colonialism and Underdevelopment in East Africa: The Politics of Economic Change 1919–1939* (London: Heinemann, 1973).

11 Mahmood Mamdani, *Politics and Class Formation in Uganda* (New York: Monthly Review Press, 1976), p. 76.

12 V. Jamal, 'Asians in Uganda 1880–1972: Inequality and Expulsion'.

13 E. A. Brett, *Colonialism and Underdevelopment in East Africa*, p. 239.

14 Mahmood Mamdani, *Politics and Class Formation in Uganda*, p. 86.

15 Ibid., p.86.

16 V. Jamal, 'Asians in Uganda 1880–1972: Inequality and Expulsion', p. 604.

17 House of Commons, Debates; see E. A. Brett, *Colonialism and underdevelopment in East Africa*, p. 239.

18 E. A. Brett, *Colonialism and Underdevelopment in East Africa*, p. 239.

19 Ibid., p. 240.

20 Mahmood Mamdani, *Politics and Class Formation in Uganda*, p. 198.

21 Ibid., p. 87.

22 Manubhai Madhvani, *Tide of Fortune: A Family Tale* (London: Manubhai Madhvani Bermuda Trusts, 2008), p. 12.

23 Ibid., p. 26.

24 Mahmood Mamdani, *Politics and Class Formation in Uganda*, p. 81.

25 Manubhai Madhvani, *Tide of Fortune: A Family Tale*, p. 27.

26 V. Jamal, 'Asians in Uganda 1880–1972: Inequality and Expulsion', p. 604.

27 Ibid., p. 604.

28 Ram R. Ramchandani, *Uganda Asians: The End of an Enterprise: a study of the role of the people of Indian origin in the economic development of Uganda and their expulsion, 1894–1972* (United Asia Publications, 1976).

29 Ibid.

30 Nizar Motani, 'The Ugandan Civil Service' (1979), p. 99; Mahmood Mamdani, *Citizen and Subject*.

31 Michael Twaddle, *Expulsion of a Minority* (London: Athlone Press, 1975), p. 100.

32 *Uganda Herald*, 16 April 1920.

33 Manubhai Madhvani, *Tide of Fortune: A Family Tale*, p. 76.

34 Ibid., p. 76.

35 Milton Obote, 'The Common Man's Charter' (Entebbe: Government Printer, 1970).

36 Ryan D. Selwyn, *Economic Nationalism and Socialism in Uganda* (York University, Toronto, 1973), p. 143.

37 Report of the committee on Advancement of Africans in trade and commerce, Parliamentary Debates.

38 Ryan D. Selwyn, *Economic Nationalism and Socialism in Uganda*, p. 143.

39 Michael A. Tribe, *Expulsion of a Minority* (London: Athlone Press, 1975).

40 Ibid.

41 Ibid.

42 Ibid.

43 E.A. Brett, interview, London, December 2010.

44 Nekyon Adoko (MP), 'Parliamentary Debates' vol. 87, p. 9.

45 E.A. Brett, interview, London, December 2010.

46 Mahmood Mamdani, *Politics and Class Formation in Uganda*, p. 303.

47 William Kalema, interview, Kampala, December 2010.

48 Ibid.

49 'Uganda', *The Action Programme*, no. 46.

50 E.A. Brett, interview, London, December 2010.

51 The UDC was created in 1952 and used to spearhead the 'industrial and economic development of Uganda'. The UDC gained control of the largest of the former Asian businesses, including the bulk of both the Madhvani and the Mehta assets. It also gained control of the almost 100 British-owned subsidiaries that were nationalised in December 1972.

52 Jan Jelmert Jorgensen, *Uganda: A Modern History* (London: Croom Helm, 1981), p. 286.

53 E. A. Brett, interview, London, December 2010.

54 Jan Jelmert Jorgensen, *Uganda: A Modern History*, p. 290.

55 Nelson Kasfir, 'State, Magendo, and Class Formation in Uganda' (Commonwealth & Comparative Politics, 1983), p. 91.

56   'Uganda – Background to the Budget 1981–1982', 8.

57   H. Green, 'Magendo in the Political Economy of Uganda: Pathology, Parallel System, or Dominant Sub-mode of Production?', *Discussion Paper No 164*, Institute of Development Studies, University of Sussex, August 1981, p. 14.

58   E. A. Brett, interview, London, December 2010.

59   Nelson Kasfir, 'State, Magendo, and Class Formation in Uganda', p. 91.

60   Himbara, 'The Asian question'; V. Jamal, 'Asians in Uganda'; O'Brien, 'General Amin and the Uganda Asians' in *Expulsion of a Minority London* (Athlone Press, 1975); V. Jamal, 'Asians in Uganda 1880–1972: Inequality and Expulsion', in *Economic History Review*, p. 603.

61   E. A. Brett, interview, London, December 2010.

62   Himbara, 'The Asian question'; V. Jamal, 'Asians in Uganda', O'Brien; 'General Amin and the Uganda Asians' in *Expulsion of a Minority*.

63   V. Jamal, 'Asians in Uganda 1880–1972: Inequality and Expulsion' in *Economic History Review*, p. 603.

64   Since 1986, there has been a tremendous growth in indigenous businesses in Uganda, which has led the economy to grow six-fold between 1986 and 2010. By 2005, the 5,700 odd enterprises in 1972 had grown to over 89,503 registered enterprises according to the World Bank Indicators, 2011.

65   D. K. Mauzy, 'Malay Political Hegemony and "Coercive Consociationalism"', *The Politics of Conflict Regulation* (London: Routledge, 1997), p. 120.

66   Bank of Uganda, 2010.

67   http://data.worldbank.org.

68   Bank of Uganda, 2010.

CHAPTER THREE

1   Tonia Kandiero, 'Infrastructure Investment in Africa', African Development Bank, Development Research Brief, no. 12, August 2009, p. 1.
2   Ibid.
3   African Business Pages, 'Mombasa–Uganda Trade Route Problems'.

CHAPTER FOUR

1   World Trade Organisation Data 2011.
2   http://www.oecd.org/dataoecd/38/15/40279863.pdf.
3   Andrew Mold, 'Non-Tariff Barriers – Their Prevalence and Relevance for African Countries', Economic Commission for Africa, ATPC Work in Progress no. 25, 2005.
4   Kevin Watkins, Penny Fowler, *Rigged Rules and Double Standards: Trade, Globalisation, and the Fight Against Poverty* (Oxfam International, 2002).
5   World Bank, 'Defragmenting Africa: Deepening Regional Trade Integration in goods and services' (Washington D.C., 2012).
6   Ibid.
7   William Easterly, *The Elusive Quest for Growth* (MIT Press, 2002).
8   James Ferguson, *The Anti-Politics Machine: Development, Depoliticization, and Bureaucratic Power in Lesotho* (University of Minnesota Press, February 1994).
9   *Economist*, 19 August 1995.
10 Joseph E. Stiglitz and Andrew Charlton, *Fair-trade For All: How Trade can Promote Development* (Oxford University Press, 2006).
11 Dan Bolton, *Speciality Retailer* magazine.

12   World Trade Organisation figures.

13   US International Trade Commission.

CHAPTER FIVE

1   World Bank Group Financial Access Report, 2010.

2   Bank of Uganda Annual Report 2010/11.

3   Ibid.

4   Ibid.

5   Ibid.

6   Bank of Uganda Annual Supervision Report, December 2010, Issue No. 1.

7   Ha-Joon Chang, 'What is wrong with "Official History of Capitalism"' in: Edward Fullbrook, *A Guide To What's Wrong With Economics* (Anthem Press, 2004), p. 280.

8   World Trade Organisation data, 2011.

9   Ibid.

10   World Bank data, 2010.

11   World Trade Organisation data, 2011.

12   For further reading on the Iwakura Missions see: A. Cobbing, 'Life in Victorian London through the Eyes of Kume Kunitake, Chronicler of the Iwakura Mission'; A. Ohta, 'The Iwakura Mission in Britain: their observations on education and Victorian society'; O. Checkland, ' The Iwakura Mission, industries and exports'; Dr John Breen, 'Public statements and private thoughts: the Iwakura Embassy in London and the religious question', Discussion Paper, No. IS.98.349, March 1998, The Suntory Centre, Suntory and Toyota International Center for Economics and Related Disciplines, London School of Economics and Political Science.

CHAPTER SEVEN

1   K. Rothmyer, 'They Wanted Journalists to Say "Wow": How

NGOs Affect US Media Coverage of Africa', Joan Shorenstein Center on the Press, Politics and Public Policy Discussion Paper Series #D-61, January 2011.

2   Ibid.

3   L. A. Richey and S. Ponte, *Shopping Well to Save the World* (University of Minnesota Press, 2011).

4   Ibid.

5   Chinua Achebe, 'An Image of Africa: Racism in Conrad's *Heart of Darkness*', *Massachusetts Review*, 1977.

6   Calestous Juma, *The New Harvest: Agricultural Innovation in Africa*, p. 9.

7   World Trade Organisation time series data.

8   State Administration of Foreign Exchange, People's Republic of China and the People's Bank of China.

9   'A peek into Kenya's SACCO subsector', The Sacco Societies Regulatory Authority (SASRA), August 2011.

10   Ibid.

11   Chris Cramer, 'Confusion Reigns', paper presented at the Royal African Society, London, October 2010.

CONCLUSION

1   Leonard Sweet, *Summoned to Lead* (Zondervan, 2004).

2   Ibid.

Selected Bibliography

Abbink, Jon and Ineke van Kessel (eds), *Vanguard or Vandals: Youth, Politics and Conflict in Africa* (Leiden: Brill, 2005)

Abebe, Ermias, 'The Horn, the Cold War, and Documents from the Former East-Bloc: An Ethiopian view', *Cold War International History Project Bulletin* 8–9 (1996/1997): pp. 40–45

Abrahams, Ray, *Vigilant Citizens: Vigilantism and the State* (Polity, 1998)

Adam, C., W. Cavendish and P. S. Mistry, *Adjusting Privatisation: Case Studies from Seven Developing Countries* (London: James Currey, 1992)

Adam, Heribert et al., *Comrades in Business: Post Liberation Politics in South Africa* (International Books, 1998)

Addison, T. and L. Demery, 'The Alleviation of Poverty Under Structural Adjustment' (Washington DC: World Bank, 1987)

Adler, G. and E. Webster, 'Towards a Class Compromise in South Africa's "Double Transition": bargained liberalisation and the consolidation of democracy', *Politics and Society* 27 (1999)

Ake, Claude, *Social Science as Imperialism: The Theory of Political Development* (Ibadan University Press, 1979)

—— *Political Economy of Africa* (Longman, 1981)

—— *The Feasibility of Democracy in Africa* (Codesria, 2000)

Alexander, Jocelyn, JoAnn McGregor and Terence Ranger, *Violence and Memory: One Hundred Years in the 'Dark Forests' of Matabeleland* (Oxford, 2000).

Allen, Chris, 'Understanding African politics,' *Review of African*

Political Economy, Vol. 22, No. 65 (Sep, 1995): pp. 301–320; very helpful overview of the trajectories of African states (1995)

Amor, Meir, 'Violent Ethnocentrism: Revisiting the Economic Interpretation of the Expulsion of the Ugandan Asians', *Identity* 3, no. 1 (2003): pp. 53–66

Anderson, David M., *Eroding the Commons: The Politics of Ecology in Baringo, Kenya, 1890s–1963* (Oxford, 2002)

—— 'Vigilantes, Violence and the Politics of Public Order in Kenya', *African Affairs* (2002), vol. 101, issue 405: pp. 531–555; and subsequent response from Peter Kagwanja

—— 'Yours in Struggle for Majimbo: Nationalism and the Party Politics of Decolonization in Kenya, 1955–64', *Journal of Contemporary History*, Vol. 40, No. 3, (July 2005)

Andrew, Christopher and Vasili Mitrokhin, *The Mitrokhin Archive vol II – The KGB and the World* (London, 2005): pp. 423–70

Arrighi, G. and J. Saul, 'Socialism and Economic Development in Tropical Africa' in *Journal of Modern African Studies*, 6, 2 (1968)

Attwood, William, *The Reds and the Blacks* (Hutchinson, 1967)

Bagachwa, M. S. D. and F. Stewart, 'Rural Industries and Rural Linkages in Sub-Saharan Africa: A Survey', L. d'Agliano-QEH Development Studies Working Paper, No. 23 (Turin: Centro Studi Luca d'Agliano, 1990)

Balassa, Bela, 'Adjustment Policies and Development Strategies in Sub-Saharan Africa' in Moshe Syrquin et al. (eds), *Economic Structure and Performance* (New York: Academic Press, 1984)

Bangura, Yusuf et al. (eds), *Adjustment, Authoritarianism and Democracy* (Uppsala, 1992)

Bank of Uganda, *Quarterly Bulletin,* iii (1971)

Banugire, F. R., 'The Impact of the Economic Crisis on Fixed-income Earners' in: Weibe and Dodge (eds), 1987

——'Uneven and Unbalanced Development: Development Strategies and Conflict', in Rupesinghe (ed.), 1989

Baofo-Arthur, Kwame, 'Political Parties and Democratic Sustainability in Ghana', in *African Political Parties* edited by M. A. Mohamed Salih (London, 2003)

Barone, C. A., 'Dependency, Marxist Theory and Salvaging the Idea of Capitalism in South Korea', *Review of Radical Political Economy*, Vol. XV, No. I (1983)

Bates, Robert, *Markets and states in Tropical Africa* (London, 1981), seminal analysis of the way in which political systems create distortions in the economy

—— *Beyond the Miracle of the Market: the political economy of agrarian development in Kenya* (Cambridge University Press, 1989)

—— *When Things Fell Apart* (Cambridge, 2008)

Bayart, Jean-Francois, *The State in Africa: Politics of the Belly* (Harlow, 1993: 1st French edn, 1989)

Bayart, Jean-Francois, Stephen Ellis and Beatrice Hibou, *The Criminalization of the State in Africa* (James Currey, Oxford & Indiana University Press, 1999)

Bazaara, N., 'The Impact of Structural Adjustment on Food Production and Security in Masindi District: A case study of Mpumwe village' (Kampala: FEZ, 1992)

Beinart, William, *Twentieth-Century South Africa* (Oxford University Press, 2001)

Beinart, William and S. Dubow (eds), *Segregation and Apartheid in Twentieth-Century South Africa* (Routledge, 1995)

Benjamin, N. C., 'What Happens to Investment under Structural Adjustment: Results from a Simulation Model', *World Development* 20, 11 (1992): pp. 1335–44

Berman, B., D. Eyoh and W. Kymlicka (eds), *Ethnicity and Democracy in Africa* (Oxford, 2004): esp. Chaps 1, 3 and 15

Bernstein, Henry, 'Agricultural "Modernisation" and the Era of Structural Adjustment: observations on Sub-Saharan Africa' in *Journal of Peasant Studies*, Vol. 18, No. 1 (1990)

—— *The Food Question: profits versus people* (London: Earthscan, 1990)

Berry, Sara, 'Risk aversion and rural class formation in West Africa' in Bates, R. and M. F. Lofchie (eds), *Agricultural Development in Africa, Issues of Public Policy* (New York: Praeger, 1980)

—— *Fathers Work for their Sons: accumulation, mobility and class formation in an extended Yoruba community* (Berkeley and Los Angeles: University of California Press, 1985)

Bevan, D., P. Collier and J. W. Gunning (with A. Bigsten and P. Horsnell), *Peasants and Governments: An Economic Analysis* (Oxford: Clarendon Press, 1989)

Bibangambah, J., 'The Impact of Structural Adjustment Programmes on Agriculture in Uganda, with special reference to agricultural producers and farmers co-operative organisations 1981–1990' (Kampala: FEZ, 1992)

Bigsten, A. and S. Kayizzi-Mugerwa, 'Rural Sector Responses to Economic Crisis: A Study of Masaka District in Uganda' (Department of Economics, University of Gothenburg, Sweden, 1991)

Birmingham, David & Phyllis M. Martin (eds) *History of Central Africa Vol 2* (London & New York, 1983)

Bond, P., 'Neo-liberalism in Sub-Saharan Africa: From Structural Adjustment to NEPAD' in A. Saad-Filho and D. Johnston (eds), *Neoliberalism: A Critical Reader* (London: Zed Books, 2005): pp. 230–236

Boone, Catherine, *Political Topographies of the African State* (Cambridge, 2003)

Branch, Dan & Nic Cheeseman, 'The Politics of Control in Kenya: Understanding the bureaucratic-executive state, 1954–73', *Review of African Political Economy*, 33, 107 (2006)

Branch, Daniel and N. Cheeseman (forthcoming) 'Understanding the Lessons of the Kenya Crisis of 2008' (discusses Bates theory in *When Things Fell Apart*)

Branch, D., N. Cheeseman and L. Gardner (eds), *Our Turn To Eat: Kenyan Politics Since 1950* (Lit Verlag, Berlin 2010): Intro and Conclusion

Bratton, Michael, 'The Alternation Effect in Africa', *Journal of Democracy* 15, 4 (2004): pp. 147– 158

Bratton, Michael and Daniel Posner, 'A First Look at Second Elections in Africa with Illustrations from Zambia' in *State, Conflict and Democracy in Africa*, edited by R. Joseph (Boulder, 1999)

Bratton, Michael and Nic Van de Walle, 'Neo-patrimonial Regimes and Political Transitions in Africa', *World Politics*, 46, 4 (1994): pp. 453–489

—— *Democratic Experiments in Africa: regime transitions in comparative perspective* (Cambridge, 1997)

Brett, E. A., 'Problems of Cooperative Development in Uganda' in *Rural Cooperatives and Planned Change in Africa*, Vol. 4 (Apthorpe, R., ed.) (Geneva, 1970)

—— *Colonialism and Underdevelopment in East Africa: the Politics of Economic Change 1919– 1939* (London: Heinemann, 1973)

—— 'States, Markets and Private Power in the Developing World', *IDS Bulletin*, 17 (3) (1987)

Brown, Stephen, 'Authoritarian Leaders and Multiparty Elections in Africa: how foreign donors help to keep Kenya's Daniel arap Moi in power', *Third World Quarterly* 22, 5 (2001): pp. 725–39

Burch, D., *Overseas Aid and the Transfer of Technology* (Aldershot, UK, 1987)

Campbell, B. and J. Loxley, *Structural Adjustment in Africa* (Basingstoke: Macmillan, 1989)

Carter, Gwendolen (ed.), *African One-party States* (New York, 1964)

Chabal, Patrick and Jean-Pascal Deloz, *Africa Works: Disorder as Political Instrument* (Oxford, 1999)

Chang, Ha-Joon, *Kicking Away the Ladder: Development Strategy in Historical Perspective* (Anthem Press, 2002)

Chango Machyo, B., 'The World Bank, the IMF, and Deepening Misery in Uganda', The Fourth Mawazo Workshop (1985)

Checole, K., 'IMF, Conditionality and its Impact on Industrial Output and Technology in Africa' in *Mawazo*, Vol. 5, No. 3 (1984)

Cheeseman, Nic, 'Political Linkage and Political Space in the Era of Decolonisation' in *Africa Today* 53 (2) (2006)

Cheru, P., *The Silent Revolution in Africa: Debt, development and democracy* (London: Zed Books, 1989)

—— 'Structural Adjustment, Primary Resource Trade and Sustainable Development in Sub-Saharan Africa', *World Development* 20 (4) (1992): pp. 497–512

Chipungu, Samuel (ed.), *Guardians in Their Time: Experiences of Zambians Under Colonial Rule 1890–1964* (London & Basingstoke, 1992)

Clarkson, S., *The Soviet Theory of Development: India and the Third World in Marxist-Leninist Scholarship* (London: Macmillan, 1979)

Clayton, Anthony, *The Zanzibar Revolution and its Aftermath* (London, 1981)

Commander, S. (ed.), *Structural Adjustment and Agriculture: Theory and Practice in Africa and Latin America* (London: James Currey for the Overseas Development Institute, 1989)

Constantine, Stephen, *Making British Colonial Development Policy 1914–1940* (London, 1940)

Cooper, Frederick, *Africa since 1940: The Past of the Present* (New York: Cambridge University Press, 2002)

Cooper, Frederick and Randall Packard (eds), *International Development and the Social Sciences: Essays on the History and Politics of Knowledge* (Berkeley, 1997): Introduction and Chap. 2

Coquery-Vidrovitch, Catherine, *Africa – Endurance and Change South of the Sahara* (Berkeley, 1992), originally published as *Afrique noire: permanences et ruptures* (Paris, 1985)

Cornia, G. A., R. Jolly and F. Stewart (eds), *Adjustment with a Human Face: Protecting the Vulnerable and Promoting Growth* (Oxford: Clarendon Press 1987)

Coulson, Andrew, *Tanzania: a Political Economy* (Oxford, 1982)

—— 'Agricultural Policies in Tanzania 1946–76', in: Judith Heyer (ed.), *Rural Development in Tropical Africa* (Basingstoke, 1981)

Coupland, R., *The Exploitation of East Africa* (Faber & Faber, 1968)

Cowan, G. L., *Privatisation in the Developing World* (New York: Greenwood Press, 1990)

Cowen, Michael and Robert Shenton, *Doctrines of Development* (London, 1996): Chap. 6

Cowen, Michael, 'Commodity Production in Kenya's Central Province', in Judith Heyer et al., *Rural Development in Tropical Africa* (London, 1981)

Cowen, Michael and Liisa Laakso (eds), *Multi-party Elections in Africa* (Oxford & New York, 2002): Chap. 1

Crook, Richard, 'Patrimonialism, Administrative Effectiveness and Economic Development in Cote d'Ivoire', *African Affairs*, 88, 351 (1989)

Crowder, Michael, *West Africa Under Colonial Rule* (Harlow, 1968)

Cruise O'Brien, B. Donal, John Dunn and Richard Rathbone (eds), *Contemporary West African States* (Cambridge University Press, 1989)

Cuba: an African Odyssey, ARTE France, 2007

Daniel, John, Roger Southall and Morris Szeftel, *Voting for Democracy: watershed elections in contemporary anglophone Africa* (Aldershot, Hants, England; Brookfield, Vt.: Ashgate, 1998)

Decalo, Samuel, 'Military Coups and Military Regimes in Africa', JMAS, 11, 1 (1973)

—— 'Modalities of Civil-Military Stability in Africa', JMAS, 27, 4 (1989)

Delf, G., *Asians in East Africa* (London: Oxford University Press, 1962)

Dell, S., 'On Being Grandmotherly: The evolution of IMF conditionality', *Essays in International Finance*, No. 144 (Princeton, New Jersey, 1981)

Demery, L. and T. Addison, 'Stabilisation and Income Distribution in Developing Countries' in: *World Development*, Vol. 15, No. 12 (1987)

Department for International Development (UK) http://www.dfid.gov.uk/Pubs/files/fragilestates-paper.pdf

DeRoche, Andy, 'Non-alignment on the Racial Frontier: Zambia and the USA 1964–68', *Cold War History*, 7, ii (2007): pp. 227–50

Derry, T. K. and T. Jamin, *The Making of Modern Britain* (Plymouth Press, 1956)

Diamond, Larry, *Class, Ethnicity and Democracy in Nigeria: The Failure of the First Republic* (Syracuse University Press, 1988)

Dodge, C. P., 'Rehabilitation or Redefinition of Health Services' in Weibe and Dodge (eds) (1987)

Dodge, C. P. and P. D. Weibe, *Crisis in Uganda: The breakdown of health services* (Oxford, 1985)

Dunn, John (ed.), *West African States: Failure and Promise* (Cambridge University Press, 1978)

Dunn, Kevin C., 'A Survival Guide to Kinshasa: Lessons of the Father, Passed Down to the Son' in: John F. Clark, ed., *The African Stakes of the Congo War* (New York: Palgrave MacMillan, 2004)

East African Royal Commission 1953–1955, *Report* (O.H.M.S. Cmd 9475)

Easterly, William, *The Elusive Quest for Growth* (MIT Press, 2002)

Economist, 19 August 1995

Ehrlich, Cyril, *The Uganda Company Ltd: The First Fifty Years* (Kampala: The Uganda Company Ltd, 1953)

—— 'Cotton and the Uganda Company, 1903–1909', *Uganda Journal*, September 1957

Elbadawi, I., et al., 'World Bank, Adjustment Lending and Economic performance in sub-Saharan Africa', World Bank Policy Research Working Paper (Washington DC, 1992)

Engberg-Pedersen, P. et al., *Limits of Adjustment in Africa* (James Currey, 1996): Chaps. 1–3

Engels, F., *Socialism: Utopian and Scientific*, tran. Paul Lafargu, (Leipzig, 1880)

—— 'The housing question' in: *Marx and Engels, Collected Works*, Vol. 12 (1979)

Essential Action, 'Campaign Against the IMF, World Bank and Structural Adjustment', 2001, http://www.essentialaction.org/imf

European Research Office, 'The Home Rules of Origin: The case for relaxation ERO Brussels', 1994

Failed States Index http://www.foreignpolicy.com/story/cms.php?story id=3865

Fanon, Frantz, *The wretched of the earth* (New York: Grove Weidenfeld, 1969)

FCO 31/1375, Letter from BHC Kampala to FCO London, 6 August 1972

Ferguson J., *Global Shadows: Africa in the Neoliberal World Order* (Durham and London: Duke University Press, 2006)

Forrest, Tom, *Politics and Economic Development in Nigeria* (Boulder, 1995)

Freund, Bill, *The Making of Contemporary Africa: The Development of African Society since 1800* (Basingstoke, 1998): Chaps 5 and 6

Galbraith, John S., *Mackinnon and East Africa 1878–1895: a study in the New Imperialism* (Cambridge University Press, 1972)

Galli, R., 'Liberalisation is Not Enough: Structural adjustment and peasants in Guinea Bissau' in *Review of African Political Economy*, Winter, No. 49 (1990)

Gann, Lewis, *A history of Northern Rhodesia: early days to 1953* (London, 1964)

George, Edward, *The Cuban Intervention in Angola, 1965–91: From Che Guevara to Cuito Cuanavale* (London, 2005)

Ghai, D. and Y. Ghai (eds), *Portrait of a Minority* (Oxford University Press, 1970)

Ghai, D., (ed.), 'The crisis of the 1980s in Africa, Latin America and the Caribbean: Economic impact, social change and political implications', *Development and Change*, 21, issue 3 (July 1990): pp. 389–426

Gibbon, P., Y. Bangura and A. Ofstad, *Authoritarianism, Democracy, and Adjustment: the politics of economic reform in Africa* (Uppsala, 1992)

Gibbs, David N., 'The UN, International Peacekeeping and the Question of "Impartiality": revisiting the Congo operation of 1960', *Journal of Modern African Studies*, 38, iii (2000): pp. 359–82

Gleijeses, Piero, *Conflicting Missions: Havana, Washington and Africa 1959–76* (Chapel Hill & London, 2002)

—— 'Cuba and the independence of Namibia', *Cold War History*, 7, ii (2007): pp. 285–303

—— 'Havana's Policy in Africa; new evidence from the Cuban archives', *Cold War International History Project Bulletin*, Issues 8–9: pp. 5–8

—— 'Moscow's Proxy? Cuba and Africa 1975–1988', *Journal of Cold War Studies*, 8, ii (2006): pp. 3–51

Good, Charles M., 'Rural Markets and Trade in East Africa: A Study of the Function and Development of Exchange Institutions in Ankole, Uganda' Research Paper No. 128, University of Chicago Department of Geography (Chicago, 1970)

Government of Uganda, 'Background to the Budget, 1981–1982' (Entebbe: Government Printers, 1981)

Green, H., 'Magendo in the Political Economy of Uganda: Pathology, Parallel System, or Dominant Sub-mode of Production?' *Discussion Paper No. 164* (Institute of Development Studies, University of Sussex, August 1981)

Gregory, John Walter, *The Foundation of British East Africa* (London: H. Marshall & Son, 1901)

Gregory, R. G., *India and East Africa: A History of Race Relations within British East Africa, 1890–1939* (Oxford: Clarendon Press, 1971)

Guevara, 'Che' Ernesto, *The African Dream: The Diaries of the Revolutionary War in the Congo* (London, 2000)

Gulhati, Ravi, Swadesh Bose and Vimal Atukorala, 'Exchange Rate Policies in Africa: how valid is the skepticism?' in *Development and Change*, Vol. 17, No. 3 (1986)

Hailey, W. M., *An African Survey: A Study of Problems Arising in Africa South of the Sahara* (London: Oxford University Press, 1938)

Hanhimaki, Jussi M. and Odd Arne Westad, *The Cold War: A History in Documents and Eyewitness Accounts* (Oxford, 2003)

Hansen, H. B. and M. Twaddle (eds), *Uganda Now: Between decay and development* (London: James Currey, 1988)

—— *Changing Uganda: The dilemmas of structural adjustment and revolutionary change* (London: James Currey, 1992)

Harbeson, John, *The Military in African Politics* (New York, 1987)

—— *Nation-Building in Kenya: The Role of Land Reform* (Evanston, 1973)

Harris, D., 'From Warlord to Democratic President: How Charles Taylor won the 1997 Liberian elections', *JMAS*, 37, 3 (1999)

Harris, L., 'The Bretton Woods system and Africa' in Bade Onimode (ed.) (1989)

Harris, N., *The End of the Third World* (Penguin: London, 1986)

Harrison, Graham, 'Economic Faith, Social Project, and a Misreading of African Society: the Travails of Neoliberalism in Africa', *Third World Quarterly*, Vol. 26, No. 8 (2005): pp. 1303–1320

—— *The World Bank and Africa: the construction of governance states* (Routledge, 2004): Introduction

Harvey D., *A Brief History of Neoliberalism* (Oxford University Press, 2005)

Havinden, Michael and David Meredith, *Colonial Development: Britain and its Tropical Colonies, 1850–1960* (London, 1993)

Havnevik, K. J. (ed.), *The IMF and the World Bank in Africa: Conditionality, impact and alternatives* (Uppsala: Scandanavian Institute of African Studies, 1987)

Havnevik, Kjell, *Tanzania – the Limits to Development from Above* (Uppsala, 1993)

Helleiner, G. K., 'Stabilisation, Adjustment and the Poor' in *World Development*, Vol. 15, No. 12 (1987)

Henze, Paul B., 'Moscow, Mengistu, and the Horn: difficult choices for the Kremlin', *Cold War International History Project Bulletin*, Issues 8–9: pp. 45–47

Herbst, Jeffrey, 'The structural adjustment of politics in Africa', *World Development*, 18, 7 (1990)

—— 'Responding to State Failure in Africa', *International Security* 21 (3) (1996): pp. 120–144

—— *States and Power in Africa: Comparative Lessons in Authority and Control* (Princeton: Princeton University Press, 2000)

Herschberg, James G., 'Anatomy of a Third World Cold War Crisis: New East Bloc evidence on the Horn of Africa 1977–78 – introduction', *Cold War International History Project Bulletin*, Issues 8–9: pp. 38–40

Heyer, Judith, 'Agricultural Development in Kenya from the Colonial Period to 1975', in Judith Heyer et al., *Rural Development in Tropical Africa* (London, 1981)

Hill, M. F., *Permanent Way: The Story of the Kenya and Uganda Railway* (Nairobi: East African Literature Bureau, 1949)

Himbara, David, *Kenyan Capitalists, the State, and Development* (Nairobi: East African Educational Publishers, 1994)

—— 'The "Asian Question" in East Africa: the continuing controversy of the role of Indian Capitalists in accumulation and development in Kenya, Uganda and Tanzania', *African Studies*, 56:1 (1997): pp. 1–18

Hinds, Alister, 'Imperial Policy and Colonial Sterling Balances 1943–56', *Journal of Imperial & Commonwealth History*, 19, 1 (1991): pp. 24–44

Hogendorn, Jan S. and K. M. Scott, 'Very Large-scale Projects: the lessons of the East African Groundnut Scheme', in R. Rotberg (ed.), *Imperialism, Colonialism and Hunger* (Lexington, 1983): pp. 167–88

Hollingsworth, L., *The Asians of East Africa* (London, 1960)

Hopkins, Anthony G., *Economic History of West Africa* (London, 1973)

Huntington, Samuel, 'The clash of civilisations' in: *Foreign Affairs*, 27: 3 (1993): p. 34

Hyden, Goran, *African Politics in Comparative Perspective* (New York: Cambridge University Press, 2006)

—— 'Top-Down Democratisation in Tanzania', *Journal of Democracy* 10, 4 (1999): pp. 142–155

Iliffe, John, *The Modern History of Tanganyika* (Cambridge, 1975)

—— *The Emergence of African Capitalism* (London, 1983)

—— *Africans: The History of a Continent* (Cambridge, 1995)

Independent (Kampala, Uganda), 21 December 2010

Isuru, Shigeto, *Japanese Capitalism: reactive defeat and beyond* (Cambridge University Press, 1993)

Jackson, Robert and Carl Rosberg, *Personal Rule in Black Africa* (University of California Press, 1982)

Jalee, P., *How capitalism works* (New York: Monthly Review Press, 1977)

Jamal, V., 'Asians in Uganda, 1880–1972: Inequality and expulsion' in: *Economic History Review*, 19 (4) New Series, 29, no. 4 (November 1976): pp. 602–616

—— 'Structural Adjustment and Food Security in Uganda', WEP Research Working Paper (Geneva: ILO, 1985)

Jamal, V. and J. Weeks, 'The Vanishing Rural-Urban Gap in Sub-Saharan Africa' in *International Labour Review*, Vol. 127, No. 3 (1988)

Jennings, Michael, 'Development is Very Political in Tanzania: Oxfam and the Chunya Integrated Development Programme 1972–76' in Ondine Barrow & Michael Jennings (eds), *The Charitable Impulse: NGOs and Development in East and Northeast Africa* (Oxford, 2001): pp. 32–109

—— 'Almost an Oxfam in Itself: Oxfam, Ujamaa and development in Tanzania', *African Affairs* 101, 405 (2002): pp. 30–509

—— *Surrogates of the State: NGOs, Development and Ujamaa in Tanzania* (Bloomfield, 2007)

—— 'Building Better People: modernity and utopia in late colonial Tanganyika', *Journal of Eastern African Studies* 3, I (2009)

Jorgensen, Jan Jelmert, *Uganda: A Modern History* (London: Croom Helm, 1981)

Jung, C. and I. Shapiro, 'South Africa's Negotiated Transition: democracy, opposition and the new constitutional order', *Politics and Society*, 23, 3 (1995)

Kaberuka, Will, 'An index for Industrial Production for Uganda: 1966–1975', Unpublished M.Sc. dissertation, Makerere University, 1979

Kajubi, Senteza, 'Coffee and Prosperity in Buganda: Some Aspects of Economic and Social Change', *Uganda Journal* 29, No. 2 (1965)

Kanet, Roger E., 'African Youth: the Target of Soviet African Policy', *The Russian Review*, 27 (1968): pp. 75–161

—— 'Superpower Quest for Empire: the Cold War and Soviet support for wars of national liberation', *Cold War History*, 6, iii (2006): pp. 52–331

Kanyinga, Karuti, 'Ethnicity, Patronage and Class in a Local Arena: high and low politics in Kiambu, Kenya, 1982–1992' in Karuti Kanyinga, Peter Gibbon, A. S. Z. Kiondo and P. Tidemand (eds), *The New Local Level Politics in East Africa: studies on Uganda, Tanzania and Kenya* (Uppsala, 1994)

Kanyire, H., *Structural Adjustment and Agricultural Production/ Productivity: The case of smallholder subsistence and commercial farming* (Kampala: FEZ, 1992)

Kapuscinski, Ryszard, *The Emperor: Downfall of an Autocrat* (New York, 1989: 1st edn, 1978)

—— *Another Day of Life* (Penguin, 1987: 1st edn, 1976)

Kasfir, Nelson, 'State, Magendo, and Class Formation in Uganda', *Commonwealth & Comparative Politics*, 21:3 (1983), pp. 84–103

Killick, T., 'The IMF and Economic Management in Kenya', Overseas Development Institute Working Paper No.4 (London, 1981)

Kipkorir, Benjamin (ed.), *Biographical Essays on Imperialism and Collaboration in Colonial Kenya* (Nairobi, 1980)

Kirschke, Linda, 'Informal Repression, Zero-sum Politics and late third wave transitions', *JMAS*, 38 (2000): pp. 383–405

Knott, T. H. and G. J. Miller, *Reforming Bureaucracy: The Politics of Institutional Choice* (Englewood Cliffs, NJ: Prentice Hall, 1987): p. 255

Korner, P., *The IMF and the Debt Crisis* (Zed Books: London, 1987)

Kox, Henk, 'Export Constraints for sub-Saharan Africa (Series Research Memoranda, Free University of Amsterdam, 1990)

Kraxberger, Brennan, 'The Geography of Regime Survival: Abacha's Nigeria', *African Affairs*, Vol. 103 (2004): pp. 413–30

Kriger, Norma, 'ZANU(PF) Strategies in General Elections: 1980– 2000 – Discourse and Coercion', *African Affairs*, Vol. 104 (2005): pp. 1–34

Krugman, P. and L. Taylor, 'Contractionary Effects of Devaluation' in *Journal of International Economies*, 1978

Kwesi Aubynn, Anthony, 'Behind the Transparent Ballot Box: The Significance of the 1990s Elections in Ghana' in Michael Cowen and Liisa Laakso (eds), *Multi-Party Elections in Africa* (Oxford, 2002)

Kynoch, Gary, 'Crime, Conflict and Politics in Transition era South Africa', *African Affairs,* Vol. 104 (2005): pp. 493–514

Laakso, Liisa, 'When Elections are Just a Formality: Rural-Urban Dynamics in the Dominant-Party System of Zimbabwe' in

Michael Cowen and Liisa Laakso (eds), *Multi-Party Elections in Africa* (Oxford, 2002)

LA Times, 7 August 1972

LacLau, E., *Politics and Ideology in Marxist Theory* (London, 1977)

Lal, D., *The Poverty of Development Economics* (London, 1983)

Lall, S., 'Structural Adjustment and African Industry', *World Development*, 23 (12) 1995

Lambert, M., 'Violence and the War of Words: Ethnicity vs. Nationalism in the Casamance', *Africa*, 68, 4 (1998)

Lee, J. M. and M. Petter, *The Colonial Office, War and Development Policy* (London, 1982)

Lefebvre, Jeffrey A., *Arms for the Horn: US Security Policy in Ethiopia and Somalia 1953–1991* (Pittsburgh, 1991)

—— 'The United States, Ethiopia and the 1963 Somali-Soviet Arms Deal: containment and the balance of power dilemma in the Horn of Africa', *Journal of Modern African Studies*, 36, iv (1998): pp. 43–611

Lemarchand, René, 'Political Clientelism and Ethnicity in Tropical Africa: Competing Solidarities in Nation-Building', *American Political Science Review* 66 (February 1972): pp. 91–112.

Lewis, Peter, 'Economic Statism, Private Capital, and the Dilemmas of Accumulation in Nigeria', *World Development*, 22, 3 (1994)

Leys, Colin, *Under-development in Kenya: The Political Economy of Neo-colonialism* (London: Heinemann Educational Books, 1975)

—— 'Capital Accumulation, Class Formation and Dependency: the significance of the Kenyan case', *Socialist Register* (1978)

Lindberg, Staffan, 'It's Our Turn to Chop: Do Elections in Africa feed Neo-patrimonialism Rather than Counter-act it?', *Democratization* 10 (2) (2004): pp. 121–140

—— *Democracy and Elections in Africa* (Baltimore, 2006): Introduction and esp. Ch. 3

Lindbolm, C. E., *Politics and Markets: The world's political economic systems* (New York: Basic Books, 1977)

Lipton, M., *Why Poor People Stay Poor: A Study of urban bias in world development* (London, 1977)

Lodge, Tom, 'Political Corruption in South Africa', *African Affairs*, Vol. 98, No. 387 (1998): pp. 157–188

—— *Politics in South Africa from Mandela to Mbeki* (2002)

Lofchie, Michael *Zanzibar: Background to Revolution* (Princeton, 1965)

Lonsdale, John and Bruce Berman, 'Coping with the Contradictions: the Development of the Colonial State in Kenya', *Journal of African History* 20, iv (1979)

Low, D. A. and John Lonsdale, 'Towards the New Order', intro to Low & Smith (eds), *Oxford History of East Africa*, vol. iii (Oxford 1976), pp. 1–64

Lugard, Frederick D., *The Rise of our East African Empire: early efforts in Nyasaland and Uganda* (London: Cass, 1968)

M'Bokolo, Elikia, 'French Colonial Policy in Equatorial Africa, 1940s & 1950s', in Prosser Gifford and W. R. Louis (eds), *Transfer of Power in Africa* (New Haven, 1982): pp. 173–210

Mackintosh, M., 'Abstract Markets and Real Needs' in: Bernstein, H. et al. (ed.) 1990

MacQueen, Norrie, *The Decolonisation of Portuguese Africa: Metropolitan Revolution and the Dissolution of Empire* (London, 1997): Chaps 1 and 2

Madhvani, Manubhai, *Tide of Fortune: a Family Tale* (London: Manubhai Madhvani Bermuda Trusts, 2008)

Mamdani, Mahmood, *From Citizen to Refugee: Ugandan Asians come to Britain* (London: Francis Pinter, 1973)

—— *Politics and class formation in Uganda* (Monthly Review Press: New York, 1976)

—— 'Extreme but Not Exceptional: Towards an analysis of the agrarian question in Uganda' in *Journal of Peasant Studies*, Vol. 14, No. 2 (1987)

—— 'The Uganda Asian Expulsion: Twenty Years After', paper presented at workshop on *Ugandan Asians Twenty Years after the Expulsion* (Queen Elizabeth House, Oxford University, 1992)

—— *Citizen and Subject* (New Jersey: Princeton University Press, 1996)

—— *When victims become killers: colonialism, nativism, and the genocide in Rwanda* (New Jersey: Princeton University Press, 2001)

Mandel, E., *An introduction to Marxist Economic Theory* (Pathfinder Press: New York, 1970)

Mandela, Nelson, *Long Walk to Freedom: the autobiography of Nelson Mandela* (1994)

Mangat, J. S. A., *History of the Asians in East Africa c. 1886 to 1945* (Oxford: Oxford University Press, 1969)

Mapuri, Omer R., *The 1964 Revolution: Achievements and Prospects* (Dar es Salaam, 1996)

Marsden K. and Therese Belot, 'Private Enterprise in Africa: creating a better environment', World Bank Discussion Paper, No. 17 (Washington DC: World Bank 1987)

Masefield, G. B., *Agricultural change in Uganda, 1945–1960* (Palo Alto, California: Stanford University Press, 1965)

Mauzy, D. K., 'Malay Political Hegemony and "Coercive Consociation-alism"', *The Politics of Conflict Regulation* (London: Routledge, 1997)

Mazrui, Ali, *On Heroes and Uhuru-Worship* (EALB, 1967)

Mbembe, Achille, *On the Postcolony* (London & Berkeley, 2001): esp. Chap. 2

McGowan, Patrick J., 'African Military Coups d'etat, 1956–2001: frequency, trends and distribution', *Journal of Modern African Studies*, 41, 3 (2003): pp. 339–370

McHenry, Dean, *Tanzania's Ujamaa Villages; the implementation of a rural development strategy* (Berkeley, 1979)

McWilliam, Michael, 'The Managed Economy: agricultural change, development and finance in Kenya' in Low & Smith (eds), *Oxford History of East Africa*, vol. iii (Oxford 1976): pp. 251–89

Medard, Jean-Francois, 'The Underdeveloped State in Tropical Africa: political clientelism or neo-patrimonialism' in: Christopher Clapham (ed.), *Private Patronage and Public Power* (London, 1982)

Migdal, Joel S., *Strong Societies, Weak States: State-Society Relations & State Capabilities in the Third World* (Princeton: Princeton University Press, 1988)

Miller, C., *The Lunatic Railway* (New York: Macmillan, 1971)

Ministry of Planning and Economic Development, Uganda, 'Background to the Budget 1981–1982' (Entebbe: Government Printers, 1981)

Mistry, P., *African Debt: the case for relief for sub-Saharan Africa* (Oxford, 1988)

Mitchell, Peter, 'Economic Reform and Political Transition in Africa: the quest for a politics of development', *World Politics*, 49 (1), (1996), pp. 92–129

Mkandawire, T., 'The Road to Crisis, Adjustment and Deindustrialisation: The African case', *Africa Development*, Vol. XIII, No. 1, 1988

—— 'Crisis and adjustment in Sub-Saharan Africa' in Ghai, D. (ed), 1989

—— 'Maladjusted African Economies and Globalisation', *Africa Development*, 30, 1/2 (2005): pp. 1–33

Mohan, G. et al. (eds), *Structural Adjustment: Theory, Practice and Impacts* (Routledge, 1999)

Mohan, Giles and Tunde Zack Williams (eds), *The Politics of Transition in Africa: State, Democracy and Development* (Oxford, 2004)

Montiel, P., 'Empirical Analysis of High Inflation Episodes in Argentina, Brazil and Israel' (Washington DC: IMF, 1988)

Moore, D., 'Sail On, O Ship of State: Neo-liberalism, Globalisation and the Governance of Africa', in David Moore, *The World Bank: Development, Poverty and Hegemony* (Scottsville: University of KwaZulu-Natal Press, 2007): pp. 227–266

Mosley, P., J. Harrigan and J. Toye, *Aid and Power: The World Bank and Policy-based Lending*, Vols. 1 and 2 (London: Routledge 1991)

—— 'Contradictory Class Perspectives on the Question of Democracy: The case of Uganda', in A' Nyongo, P. A. (ed.), *Popular struggles for democracy in Africa* (London, 1987)

—— 'Uganda: Contradictions of the IMF Programme and Perspective' in *Development and Change* (21) 1990

Mosley, P. and J. Weeks, 'Adjustment in Africa', *Development Policy Review* 12(3), OP3345 Affairs, Vol. 104 (1994): pp. 449–468

Moyo, Dambis, *Dead Aid: why aid is not working and how there is another way for Africa* (London: Allen Lane, 2009)

Munene, J. C., *The Psychological Contract and Organisation Citizenship Behaviour: Why structural adjustment may negate its objectives* (Kampala: FEZ, 1992)

Mustapha, Abdul Raufu, 'Back to the Future: multi-ethnicity and the state in Africa' in L. Basta and J. Ibrahim (eds), *Federalism and Decentralization in Africa: The Multicultural Challenge* (1999)

—— 'The Nigeria Transition: Third Time Lucky or More of the Same?' *ROAPE*, 80 (1999)

Mwansasu, B. U. and Cranford Pratt, *Towards Socialism in Tanzania* (Toronto, 1979)

Mwenda, Andrew M. and Roger Tangri, 'Patronage Politics, Donor Reforms and Regime Consolidation in Uganda', *African Affairs* (2005)

Nabudere, D. W., *Imperialism and exploitation in East Africa* (London: Zed Press, 1981)

—— *Imperialism and Integration in East Africa* (Zed Press, 1982)

Nafziger, E.W., *Economic Development* (Cambridge: Cambridge University Press, 2006): pp. 677–690

New Vision, 12 April 2007 (Kampala, Uganda): Tenywa, Gerald, C. Businge and S. Candia

New Vision, May 2007 (Kampala, Uganda): Mamdani, Mahmood

Nekyon, Adoko, MP, *Parliamentary Debates*, Vol. 87: pp. 9–10

Nkumbi, S., *The Impact of Structural Adjustment Policies on Small Scale Industries* (Kampala: FEZ, 1992)

Nugent, Paul, *Big men, Small Boys and Politics in Ghana* (Pinter, 1995)

—— *Africa Since Independence* (Basingstoke: Palgrave, 2004)

Nyerere, Julius, *Freedom and Socialism: A Selection of Writings and Speeches 1965–67* (Dar es Salaam, 1968)

Nyong'o, Peter Anyang', 'Accelerated development and industrialisation in Africa' in *Mawazo*, Vol. 5, No. 4 (1984)

—— 'The One-Party State and Its Apologists', in P. Anyang' Nyong'o (ed.), *30 Years of Independence in Africa: The Lost Decades?* (1992)

O'Brien, Justin, 'General Amin and the Uganda Asians', *The Round Table*, 63, 249 (1973): pp. 91–104

Obote, Milton, *The Common Man's Charter* (Entebbe: Government Printer, 1970)

Odingo, R. S., *The Kenya Highlands: Land Use and Agricultural Development* (Nairobi, 1971)

Ogot, Bethwell Alan and W. R. Ochieng' (eds), *Decolonisation and Independence in Kenya, 1940–93* (London, 1995): esp Introduction and Chap. 2 (both by E. S. Atieno Odhiambo)

Okello, John, *Revolution in Zanzibar* (Nairobi, 1967)

Olukoshi, Adebayo, 'West Africa's Political Economy in the Next Millennium: Retrospect and Prospect', *Monograph Series 2/2001* (CODESRIA, 2001)

—— 'A Transition to Nowhere' in Michael Cowen and Liisa Laakso (eds), *Multi-Party Elections in Africa* (Oxford, 2002)

Ominde, S. H., *Land and Population Movements in Kenya* (London, 1968)

Onimode, B., *The Political Economy of the African Crisis* (London: Zed Books, 1988)

—— *The IMF, the World Bank, and the African debt*, Volumes 1 and 2 (London: Zed Books, 1989)

—— *A Future for Africa: Beyond the Politics of Adjustment* (London: Earthscan for the Institute for African Alternatives, 1993)

Onslow, Sue, 'A Question of Timing: South Africa and Rhodesia's unilateral declaration of independence 1964–65', *Cold War History* 5 (ii) (2005): pp. 129–59

Onyach-Olaa, Martin, 'Privatisation: Myths and Realities in the Ugandan Context', paper delivered at the Uganda-Economic Association Seminar, 1992

Ottaway, Marina, *Soviet and American Influence in the Horn of Africa* (New York, 1982)

Overseas Development Institute (ODI), http://www.odi.org.uk/odi-on/fragile-states/

Overseas Development Institute, Prospects for Developing Countries: Trade and Capital, 1994

Owusu F., 'Pragmatism and the Gradual Shift from Dependency to Neoliberalism: The World Bank, African Leaders and Development Policy in Africa', *World Development*, 31 (10) (2003): pp. 1655–1672

Oya, C., 'Sticks and Carrots for Farmers in Developing Countries: Agrarian Neoliberalism in Theory and Practice' in: A. Saad-Filho and D. Johnston (eds), *Neoliberalism: A Critical Reader* (London: Zed Books, 2005)

Oyugi, W. O., P. Wanyande and C. O. Mbai, *The Politics of Transition in Kenya: from KANU to NARC* (Nairobi, 2003)

Patel, Hasu H., 'General Amin and the Indian exodus from Uganda', *A Journal of Opinion*, Vol. 2, No. 4 (Winter, 1972): p. 12

Patman, Robert G., *The Soviet Union in the Horn of Africa: The Diplomacy of Intervention and Disengagement* (Cambridge, 1990)

Payer, C., *The debt trap: The IMF and the Third World* (New York, Monthly Review Press, 1974)

—— *The World Bank: A Critical Analysis* (New York: Monthly Review Press, 1982)

Pearce, R. D., *Turning Point in Africa: British Colonial Policy, 1938–48* (London, 1982)

Peterson, Don, *Revolution in Zanzibar: An American's Cold War Tale* (Boulder, 2002)

Posner, Daniel, *Institutions and ethnic politics in Africa* (Cambridge, 2005) Chaps 2 and 3; despite the title this is a discussion of the impact of democratisation on ethnic identities in Zambia

Rakner, Lise, *Political and Economic Liberalisation in Zambia 1991–2001* (Uppsala, 2003)

Ranger, Terence, 'The Invention of Tradition in Colonial Africa', in E. Hobsbawm & T. Ranger (eds), *The Invention of Tradition* (Cambridge, 1992)

—— 'The invention of tradition revisited: the case of colonial Africa' in T. Ranger & O. Vaughan (eds), *Legitimacy and the State in Twentieth Century Africa* (London, 1993)

Reno, William, *Warlord Politics and African States* (Lynne Rienner Publishers, 1998, 1999)

—— *Corruption and State Politics in Sierra Leone* (Cambridge University Press, 1995)

Riddell, R., *Manufacturing-Africa* (James Currey: London, 1990)

Rizzo, Matteo, 'What was Left of the Groundnut Scheme? Development disaster & the labour market, southern Tanganyika 1946–52', *Journal of Agrarian Change*, 6, ii (2006): pp. 205–38

Roberts, Andrew, *The Colonial Moment in Africa* (Cambridge, 1990), reproduced from *The Cambridge History of Africa*, Vol. 7

Rodney, Walter, *How Europe Underdeveloped Africa* (Dar es Salaam: Tanzania Publishing House, 1972)

Rudebeck, I., 'The Effects of Structural Adjustment in Kandjadja, Guinea Bissau' in *Review of African Political Economy*, Winter, No. 49 (1990)

Rupesinghe, K., *Conflict and Resolution in Uganda* (London, 1989)

Rwegasira, D., 'Exchange Rates and the Management of the External Sector in Sub-saharan Africa' in *Journal of Modern African Studies*, 22 (3), (1984)

Saad-Filho, A., 'From Washington to Post-Washington Consensus: Neoliberal Agendas for Economic Development' in A. Saad-Filho and D. Johnston (eds) *Neoliberalism: A Critical Reader* (London: Zed Books, 2005)

Sandbrook, R. and R. Cohen, *The Development of an African Working Class* (London, 1975)

Saul, J., 'The Unsteady State: Uganda, Obote and General Amin' in *Review of African Political Economy* (1976)

Saunders, Christopher and Sue Onslow, 'Southern Africa in the Cold War 1975–1990', *Cambridge History of the Cold War*, Vol. III (Cambridge, 2009)

Sawyerr, A., 'The Politics of Adjustment Policy' in: *African Journal of Political Economy*, Vol. 2, No. 4 (1989)

Scott, James, *Seeing Like a State: How Certain Schemes to Improve Human Condition Have Failed* (New Haven & London, 1998): Chapter on the Groundnut Scheme

Seekings J., 'From the Ballot Box to the Bookshelf: studies of the 1994 South African general election', *Journal of Contemporary African Studies* 15, 2 (1997)

Sender, John and Sheila Smith, *The Development of Capitalism in Africa* (Oxford University Press, 1990)

Sender, J., 'Re-assessing the Role of the World Bank in Sub-Saharan Africa', in J. Pincus and J. Winters (eds), *Reinventing the World Bank* (Cornell University Press, 2002)

Shubin, Vladimir, 'Unsung Heroes: the Soviet military and the liberation of southern Africa', *Cold War History*, 7, ii (2007): pp. 251–62

Simon, D., 'Neo-liberalism, Structural Adjustment and Poverty Reduction Strategies' in V. Desai and R. Potter (eds), *The Companion to Development Studies* (Arnold, 2002): pp. 86–92

Sklar, R. L., 'Developmental Democracy' in: *Comparative Studies in Society and History*, 29 (4) (1987)

Smith, Zeric, 'The impact of Political Liberalisation and Democratisation on Ethnic Conflict in Africa: an empirical test of common assumptions', *JMAS*, 38 (2000)

Speller, Ian, 'An African Cuba? Britain and the Zanzibar Revolution', *Journal of Imperial & Commonwealth History*, 35, ii (2007)

Spence, Jack, 'Southern Africa in the Cold War', *History Today*, February 1999: pp. 43–49

Sorrenson, M. P. K., *Land Reform in Kikuyu Country* (London, 1967)

Southall, R., 'The Centralisation and Fragmentation of South Africa's Party System', *African Affairs*, 97, 389 (1998)

Stein, H., 'Rethinking African Development', in: H-J. Chang (ed.), *Rethinking Development Economics* (London: Anthem Press, 2003)

Suri, Jeremi, 'The Cold War, Decolonisation, and Global Social Awakenings: historical Intersections', *Cold War History* 6 (iii) (2006): pp. 353–63

Szeftel, Morris, 'Political Graft and the Spoils System in Zambia –

the state as a resource in itself', *Review of African Political Economy*, 9, 24, (1982): pp. 4–21; very useful discussion of how to think about state-related corruption in Africa

—— 'Misunderstanding African Politics: corruption and the governance agenda', *Review of African Political Economy* 25, 76, (1998): pp. 221–240

—— 'Between governance and underdevelopment: Accumulation and Africa's catastrophic corruption', *Review of African Political Economy* 27, 84 (2000)

Tanzi, Vito, 'The Impact of Macroeconomic Policies on the Level of Taxation in Developing Countries', IMF working paper 88/95 (Washington DC, 1988)

Tareke, Gebru, 'The Ethiopian-Somalia War of 1977 Revisited', *International Journal of African Historical Studies*, 33, iii (2000): 635–67

Tarp, F., 'Stabilisation and Structural Adjustment: a macroeconomic framework for analysing the crisis in sub-Saharan Africa' (London and New York: Routledge 1993)

Taylor, L., 'IMF Conditionality: Incomplete theory, policy malpractice' in: Mayers, R. (ed.), *The Political Morality of the IMF* (1987)

—— *Varieties of Stabilisation Experience* (Oxford University Press, 1988)

Throup, D. and C. Hornsby, *Multi-party Politics in Kenya: the Kenyatta and Moi states and the triumph of the system in the 1992 election* (London, 1998)

Tickner, V., 'Structural Adjustment and Agricultural Pricing in Mozambique' in: *Review of African Political Economy*, March, No. 53 (1992)

Tilly, Charles, *Big Structures, Large Processes, Huge Comparisons* (New York: Russell Sage Foundation, 1984)

Tiruneh, Andargachew, *The Ethiopia Revolution 1974–1987: transformation from an aristocratic to a totalitarian autocracy* (Cambridge, 1993)

Trocaire, 'UNCTAD vii: Problems and perspectives', Trocaire North-South Issues, series ii (1987)

Turk, Danilo, 'How World Bank–IMF Policies Adversely Affect Human Rights' in: *Third World Resurgence*, No. 33 (1992)

Toye, J., *Dilemmas of Development* (Oxford, 1987)

—— 'Interest Group Politics and the Implementation of Adjustment Policies in Sub-Saharan Africa' in: *Journal of International Development* 4, 2 (1992)

Tumusiime-Mutebile, E., 'A Critique of Professor Mamdani's Uganda: contradictions of the IMF programme and perspective', Ministry of Planning and Economic Finance, Kampala, 1990

U.S. Department of State http://www.state.gov/s/crs/rls/rm/48620.htm

Uganda Manufactures Association, 'Manufacturers Directory', UMA 1994

—— 'Budget Recommendations', UMA 1995

UNCTC, 'Transnational Corporations and Non-fuel Primary Commodities in developing countries' (New York, 1987)

UNDP, World Bank, 'Adjustment in the 80s', (Washington, DC)

United Nations Economic Commission for Africa, 'African Alternative Framework to Structural Adjustment Programmes' (Addis Ababa, 1989)

Vail, Leroy (ed.), *Creation of Tribalism in Southern Africa* (London, 1989): Introduction

Van de Walle, N., *African Economies and the Politics of Permanent Crisis, 1979– 1999* (Cambridge, 2001)

—— 'Presidentialism and Clientelism in Africa's Emerging Party Systems', *Journal of Modern African Studies*, 41 (June 2003): p. 310

van Kessel, Ineke and Barbara Oomen, 'One Chief, One Vote: The Revival of Traditional Authorities in Post-Apartheid South Africa,' *African Affairs* 96 (1997), 385 (1997): pp. 561–586

Villalon, Leonardo and Peter VonDoepp, *The Fate of Africa's Democratic Experiments* (Indianapolis, 2005): esp. Chaps 1 and 12

von Freyhold, Michaela, *Ujamaa Villages in Tanzania: Analysis of a Social Experiment* (London, 1979)

Wangwe, S., 'Impact of the IMF/World Bank philosophy in Tanzania, in Havnevik, Kejell (1987).

Weibe, P. D. and C. P. Dodge, *Beyond Crisis: development issues in Uganda* (Kampala, 1987)

Westad, Odd Arne, 'Moscow and the Angolan crisis 1974–76: a new pattern of intervention', *Cold War International History Project Bulletin*, Issues 8–9: pp. 21–32

—— *The Global Cold War: Third World Interventions and the Making of Our Times* (Cambridge, 2007)

White H., 'Adjustment in Africa', *Development and Change*, Vol. 27, (1996): pp. 785–815

Williams, Gavin, 'Why Structural Adjustment is Necessary and Why it Doesn't Work', *ROAPE*, Vol. 21, no. 60 (1999)

Williams, Paul, 'State failure in Africa', http://www.gwu.edu/~elliott/faculty/williams07.pdf (2005)

Windrich, Elaine, *The Cold War Guerilla: Jonas Savimbi, the US Media, and the Angolan War* (New York, 1992)

Wood, A., *The Groundnut Affair* (London, 1950)

Wood, Geoffrey, 'Business and Politics and the Criminal State: Equatorial Guinea', *African Affairs*, Vol. 103 (2004): pp. 547–68

World Bank, 'Accelerated Development in Sub-Saharan Africa (The Berg Report)' (Washington DC: The World Bank, 1981)

—— 'Adjustment in Africa: reforms, results, and the road ahead' (Washington DC, 1994)

—— 'Can Africa claim the 21st Century?' (Washington DC, 2000)

—— 'Accelerated Development in Sub-Saharan Africa: An agenda for action' (Washington DC, 1981)

—— 'Report on Adjustment lending' (Washington DC, 1988)

—— 'Sub-Saharan Africa: From crisis to sustainable growth' (Washington DC, 1989)

—— 'Report on Adjustment Lending II: policies for the recovery of growth' (Washington DC, 1990)

—— 'World Development Report 1990 (New York: OUP, 1990)

—— 'Structural adjustment and the poor' (Washington DC, 1991)

—— 'Economic Performance and Effectiveness of Bank Supported Adjustment Programmes in Sub-Saharan Africa' (Washington DC, 1991)

—— 'Third Report on Adjustment Lending' (Washington DC, 1992)

—— 'Uganda: Growing out of Poverty' (Washington DC, 1993)

—— 'Adjusting Africa: Recovery, Reforms and the Road Ahead' (Washington DC 1994)

—— 'The East Asian Miracle', World Bank Policy Research Report (Washington DC, 1995)

Yates, Barbara, 'Structural Problems in Education in the Congo (Leopoldville)', *Comparative Education Review*, Vol. 7, No. 2 (Oct., 1963): pp. 152–162

Young, Crawford, *The African Colonial State in Comparative Perspective* (Yale University Press, 1997)

Zolberg, Aristide, *Creating Political Order: the party-states of West Africa* (Chicago, 1966)

Index

'Kony 2012' (video) 171
Korea, South 116, 117, 118, 147
Kroencke, Mark 157, 162
Kutesa, Hon Sam 88
Kyagalanyi Coffee Limited (KCL)
   129–30, 133, 181
Kyarumba sub-county, Uganda 72,
   79, 81, 181
Kyazze, Pastor Michael 105
Kyondo sub-county, Uganda 72

Lagos, Nigeria 59
Lamb, Harriet 183–4
LDH (La Doria) x, 99, 130, 144, 145,
   147, 150
Lear, John 91
Lencioni, Patrick xviii
Liberia 6
Limit X (gospel band) 104–5
Londis 144
Lord's Resistance Army (LRA)
   89
Los Angeles: West Angeles Church
   105–6
Lugard, Frederick, Baron 17
Lumumba, Patrice 7–8

Mabira forest, Uganda 32
McDonnell, Brendan 155
McFadyen, Ted 148
McGowan, Patrick J. 19
McGregor, Grant 145
Mackinnon, William 17, 35
Madhvani, Kalidas Haridas 41
Madhvani, Manubhai: *Tide of
   Fortune* 41, 42, 44
Madhvani, Muljibhai 41
Madhvani, Vithaldas Haridas 41

magendo (black market) economy
   50, 51
Mahango sub-county, Uganda 79,
   80, 181
Major, John 93
malaria xxvii
Malawi xx
Malaysia 52–4, 147
Mali 7, 9, 19
Maliba sub-county, Uganda 70, 127,
   197
Mamdani, Mahmood 15–16, 41, 43,
   173
Mandela, Nelson 25–6, 165
Maniraho, Tharcisse 81, 178
Mascarenhas Monteiro, António 25
Matte, Janet 71, 72, 73–5, 76, 81
Mauritania 12
Mauritius 22
Mauzy, D. K. 53
Maxwell, John xviii
Mazrui, Professor Ali 173, 174
Mbale, Uganda 64–5, 68
   Mount Elgon farmers 60, 65–9
Mbeki, Thabo, President of South
   Africa 25
Media Tenor 170
Meijer Supermarkets (USA) 104,
   162
Mellado, Him 157
micro-finance 82, 178–9
mines, copper 70
Mittal, Lakshmi 155
Mobutu Sese Seko, Marshall Joseph,
   President of Democratic
   Republic of Congo 7, 10
Mokili, Mohamed 179
Mombasa–Uganda railway 36–7